CHURCHES

IN CULTURAL

CAPTIVITY

CHURCHES IN CULTURAL CAPTIVITY

A HISTORY OF THE SOCIAL ATTITUDES
OF SOUTHERN BAPTISTS

•

JOHN LEE EIGHMY

WITH AN INTRODUCTION AND EPILOGUE
BY SAMUEL S. HILL, JR.

THE UNIVERSITY OF TENNESSEE PRESS
KNOXVILLE

On February 19, 1970, during a faculty-student basketball game at Oklahoma Baptist University in Shawnee, John Lee Eighmy suffered a fatal heart attack. One of the many tragic features of his unexpected death at the age of forty-two was the cessation of his work on this book. Begun in a general way when he was a graduate student in history at the University of Missouri, *Churches in Cultural Captivity* was an enterprise into which he poured a multitude of sacrificial hours, amidst heavy professional involvements in teaching and campus leadership. His colleagues marvel that this study came to fruition in view of his strenuous devotion to teaching and constant immersion in University affairs. In a memorial tribute, two of his closest colleague-friends described him as "close to being the indispensable man on the faculty."

The manuscript was more than 95 percent complete at the time of his death. The University of Tennessee Press requested that I undertake to finish the bibliographical details which Professor Eighmy himself was attending to during the last day of his life. In addition, the Epilogue is my composition, as are the brief bibliographical note and the introductory statements which follow here.

I am especially anxious to do justice to my responsibility in writing the Epilogue. The author of a monograph composed from findings in primary documents should be permitted to write his own epilogue, if he wishes one at all, by way of consolidating, interpreting, and projecting. Since John Eighmy was prevented from entertaining that option, and the Press editors deemed its inclusion desirable, the task falls to another, one who knew Eighmy's mind ever so slightly and whose familiarity with the primary materials is at best unsystematic. It is my earnest hope that I may not dishonor his labor and our memory of him by seeming to "put words in his mouth" or presuming to infer from data of which he did and I do not have command.

Those familiar with the literature based on research in the religious history of the South will know that other books, most importantly Rufus B. Spain's *At Ease in Zion: Social History of Southern Baptists, 1865–1900* (Vanderbilt University Press, 1967), both antedated this study and dealt with many of the same data and issues. Indeed, Eighmy acknowledges that he is heavily dependent upon Spain's research. But the two books are different, and Eighmy's is complementary. The reason is not merely that Spain's encompasses a brief period whereas Eighmy's is more comprehensive. Rather a longitudinal study of this kind accomplishes a distinctive set of objectives; it shows the reader what issues persist, how institutions respond to new social conditions, and that modifications and innovations occur with the passage of time. The wide sweep of Eighmy's book facilitates "knowing who we are and how we got that way." This objective in historical investigation reflects also Eighmy's interests as liberal educator and churchman. While never a propagandist or highly explicit advocate, he was also emphatically not a positivist. We have on the pages of this volume the careful practice of the historian's craft as data-gathering, organization of materials, and interpretation. I am told by John Eighmy's friends that he was a hopeful man, as expressed by active participation in efforts to bring about constructive change. The dynamic pace of this book accords with the author's own manner of living.

Another important aspect of the methods and goals of Eighmy's work is the fact that it lies closer to intellectual history than to social history. The primary sources consulted in this research were state newspapers, convention annuals, reports, and program projections, all produced by official denominational leadership. Therefore what we mainly learn here is what public figures and formal occasions produced in order to reflect and govern Baptist life. It is to be expected then that this work does not deal with how the rank-and-file perceived these pronouncements, what ordinary churchmen had to do with generating their creation in the first place, and how these official views actually functioned in the day-to-day life of individuals, communities, and congregations.

Thus, this is not popular history in the sense that letters and diaries of non-professionals or general social movements and currents make their way explicitly into the interpretations given. Consequently, Eighmy's study, because it focuses, is restricted and because it uses certain methods, is forced to omit others which might have illuminated the topic. As it happens in this case, his methods are unusually productive in view of the fact that Southern Baptist official policy mirrors popular opinion, since the denomination's leadership operation is remarkably responsive to the loudest voices from the largest choruses in the constituency. The study has yet to be undertaken which probes the subtle differences between what is preached-promoted by the professional leadership and what is perceived by the masses of members. I hypothesize that that is the deepest level of the real story of Southern Baptist life. But John Eighmy did not set out to tell that story, and no one else appears ready to undertake it at this time. When that goal is pursued, this book will serve as an invaluable resource.

Professor Eighmy's acknowledgments appear elsewhere. But I have some of my own to indicate here. First, I am indebted to the University of Tennessee Press for inviting me to live with this manuscript for a time and for working with me so constructively. I likely would not have had the invitation, however, without encouragement to the Press from my colleague, Professor Robert Moats Miller. Then I owe much to my dean, Raymond H. Dawson, of the College of Arts and Sciences, University of North Carolina, for provision of a semester to engage in various writing projects.

Finally, I have occasion to be grateful to Dean William E.

Neptune of Oklahoma Baptist University for sponsoring a two-day visit to that distant campus. There I had enjoyable and editorially profitable conversations with him, Professor Eighmy's dean, and with Mrs. Ruby Eighmy, who afforded me every courtesy and much insight into her late husband's life and career. Nor can I forget hours of interchange with several of John Eighmy's associates, especially Professors James Farthing, James Hurley, William Mitchell, and Jim E. Tanner. Whatever degree of sensitivity and judiciousness appears in my editorship is due largely to all of them.

SAMUEL S. HILL, JR.

Chapel Hill, N.C.
July 12, 1971

Wonilliam Faulkner once re-marked to some students that a character in one of his novels was a "bucolic, provincial, Southern Baptist." Asked to elaborate, he explained that the religion of a Southern Baptist was an "emotional condition that has nothing to do with God or politics or anything else."[1]

Many knowledgeable persons would probably agree, for scholars and journalists have long portrayed Southern Baptists as Bible-pounding hardshells who preach an anti-intellectual religion of damnation and moral prohibitions. The social contributions of Southern Baptists, if considered at all, are usually regarded as insignificant, irrelevant, or hopelessly reactionary.

Such easy categorizing, while understandable in part, cannot pass for social history; Southern Baptist life and thought have enough substance to merit careful study. The Southern Baptist Convention, since its founding in 1845, has come to occupy a distinctive place in the American culture. Southern Methodists, who came from an identical environment, moved up the social scale and eventually reunited with the Northern church. Southern Baptists, however, continued to reach the plain people and refused all overtures of reunion from the North. And unlike Southern Presbyterians, who remained within the former Confederacy, Baptists took their churches to every part of the nation.

1. Frederick L. Gwynn and Joseph L. Blotner, *Faulkner in the University* (Charlottesville, Va., 1959), pp. 173, 189.

Their phenomenal growth has recently made them the nation's largest Protestant body.

Southern Baptists, from their colonial beginnings, have responded to social issues more significantly than is generally recognized. Although their Anabaptist forebears set the Christian against the world and the frontier revivals prepared converts for the afterlife, the early Baptists were never aliens to temporal affairs. They readily joined the movement for the Revolution and battled for constitutional guarantees of civil liberty. The churches watched over their members and demanded temperance, marital fidelity, and generally good citizenship. Baptist ministers as much as other clergymen debated the morality of slavery until, in the end, that very issue united the churches in the South and separated them from their brethren in the North. A major denomination born of social controversy had thus come to terms with its environment.

Devotion to evangelical religion did not preclude an interest among Southern Baptists in the more secular issues of the nineteenth century. Churchmen felt obliged to address the problems of secession, war, and the status of the emancipated Negro. The decline of the rural South and the corresponding rise of urbanization, immigration, and labor agitation were matters of grave concern to them. For sixty years, Southern Baptists assumed the role of a cultural establishment by sanctifying a secular order devoted to states' rights, white supremacy, laissez faire economics, and property rights.

But that is only half their history. At the turn of the twentieth century the social-gospel movement awakened American Protestantism to the need for social criticism and reform. Contrary to what is almost universally assumed by scholars, the social gospel had a direct influence on Southern Baptists. It destroyed the uniformity of their nineteenth-century social thought and created two opposing interpretations of the church's earthly mission. One, holding to the evangelical tradition, limited the church's mission to individual reformation, a position that, in effect, usually upheld the values of the existing social order. The other, accepting the social-gospel doctrine of the corporate nature of evil, stressed the reformation of society and a concern for man's earthly welfare. During the next several decades the conflict between these two concepts became evident when Southern Baptists discussed their social responsibilities or tried to relate the Christian ethic to the problems of war, the economic order, or race relations. Not only did the social-gospel ideology survive, it also won increasing respect in the seminaries and among church leaders. By the middle of the century the Southern Baptists had created two full-time agencies devoted to social issues.

To establish that a progressive tradition existed does not mean that it controlled denominational attitudes. There remains the question of why Southern Baptist social views have continued to be more provincial and conservative than those of most other Protestant denominations. Generally, those denominations that have proved receptive to social Christianity began as European establishments with hierarchical forms of government and with traditions of public responsibility. Southern Baptists, on the other hand, came from the free-church tradition with its sectarian emphasis on democracy in church government and separation from society. In Baptist polity the ultimate authority resides in individual, autonomous congregations, whose support of denominational programs is voluntary. Congregations elect their own pastors, and large assemblies, the membership of which is also chosen by the churches, control convention agencies. Church leaders, possessing little independent authority, stress consensus and cooperation. Their work is largely the promotion of institutional goals: budgets, buildings, and conversion and enlistment of new members. Pragmatic considerations rule out involvement in controversial social issues that might undermine the broad base of support in the churches.

The analysis given above might be challenged on the basis of the record of the American Baptist Convention (Northern), which, despite local church democracy, has often supported the social positions of liberal Protestantism. A study by Paul M. Harrison concludes that, based on the number of persons participating in policy decisions, democracy really does not function in the American Convention. A similar examination of

Southern Baptists by Donald F. Trotter yielded the same conclusion.[2] However, disputing the oligarchic character of denominational decision-making is not the purpose here. Rather it is to argue that local sentiment greatly influences the expression of social opinion in the organized life of Southern Baptists. The effective operation of the democratic principle cannot be measured entirely by the amount of direct participation. Church leaders are restrained from supporting progressive social causes not so much by formal church directives as by the potential reaction of ordinarily complacent constituents, most of whom are lower- and middle-class whites, whose cooperation is essential to the denomination's organized activities.

But how can the difference in the social record of Northern and Southern Baptists be accounted for in view of the contention that democratic churches work against progressive social action? Part of the answer lies in regional and organizational differences, but that hardly solves the problem. It is necessary to find an additional condition, the coordinate of church democracy, in order to explain Southern Baptist conservatism. That coordinate is an aggressive program of evangelism. Southern Baptists have grown seven times faster than Northern Baptists since the 1845 schism, when memberships were about equal. While Northern Baptist leadership embraced liberal social causes and suffered division because of it, Southern Baptists directed their attention to expansive efforts. In the interest of a united evangelical outreach, social issues were neglected as divisive distractions. The simple gospel of personal evangelism found wide appeal precisely because it was unencumbered by the demands of social Christianity.

The restrictions that democracy and evangelism place on the church's prophetic voice have produced one important compensation. Southern Baptist declarations on public issues probably correspond much more closely than do social pronouncements

2. Paul M. Harrison, *Authority and Power in the Free Church Tradition, a Social Case Study of the American Baptist Convention* (Princeton, 1959), pp. 9, 13, 61, 111, 157–77; Donald F. Trotter, "A Study of Authority and Power in the Structure and Dynamics of the Southern Baptist Convention" (D.R.E. thesis, Southern Baptist Theological Seminary, 1962), pp. 133–62.

from the more socially active denominations. Social opinion qualified by consideration of a large constituency's tolerances should be examined in terms quite different from those applied to papal decrees or policy statements from the National Council of Churches. Churchmen and social historians who hope to understand the interrelationships of religion and culture would do well to consider Southern Baptist social thought not as a variant in Protestant behavior so much as a norm that approximates the social consciousness of most white, middle-class, church-going Americans.

JOHN LEE EIGHMY

Shawnee, Oklahoma
January 20, 1970

ACKNOWLEDGMENTS

Many persons and institutions contributed to this study, although it is possible here only to acknowledge some of the more substantial debts incurred. Former teachers Irvin G. Wyllie and Lewis E. Atherton first inspired a study that draws upon the specialties of both men—American intellectual history and the American South. Their guidance and encouragement were greater than either of them realized.

Numerous libraries entrusted valuable books and manuscripts to the postal service in compliance with loan requests. For the extensive use of library facilities, I am indebted to the staffs at Oklahoma Baptist University, Southern Baptist Theological Seminary, Southwestern Baptist Theological Seminary, the University of Missouri, the University of Oklahoma, and Vanderbilt University.

I must especially thank Miss Helen Conger, head librarian at the Dargan-Carver Library in Nashville, Tennessee, and Davis C. Woolley and Lynn E. May of the Southern Baptist Historical Commission for generous assistance and countless favors. Personnel associated with the Christian Life Commission and the Baptist Joint Committee on Public Affairs were helpful on repeated occasions.

Financial grants came at crucial stages in the research from Oklahoma Baptist University and from the Midwest Research Grants Program administered by the University of Wisconsin and the State Historical Society of Wisconsin.

Historians Lewis E. Atherton, Monroe Billington, Lynn E. May, and Robert A. Baker read portions of the manuscript at some stage in its preparation and offered valuable criticisms, suggestions, and corrections. Colleagues in other disciplines allowed this study to occupy more of their time than friendship would require. J. Don Reeves, Jim E. Tanner, William M. Baker, and especially William R. Mitchell shared the benefits of their insight and counsel. The last named read all of the finished work and saved the reader from many cumbersome passages.

Much help was also received through correspondence and interviews with Das Kelly Barnett, editor of *Christian Frontiers*; Henlee Barnette, professor of Christian ethics, Southern Baptist Theological Seminary; Henderson Barton, pastor in Nashville and son of Arthur J. Barton; Walter Pope Binns, vice-chairman of the Baptist Joint Committee on Public Affairs; Hugh A. Brimm, former executive secretary of the Social Service Commission; C. Emanuel Carlson, executive director of the Baptist Joint Committee on Public Affairs; W. Barry Garrett, associate director of the Baptist Joint Committee on Public Affairs; Acker C. Miller, executive secretary of the Christian Life Commission, 1953–59; Foy Dan Valentine, executive secretary of the Christian Life Commission; and Jesse B. Weatherspoon, former professor of Christian ethics at Southern Baptist Theological Seminary and former chairman of the Social Service Commission.

CONTENTS

CHURCHES

IN CULTURAL

CAPTIVITY

To MY WIFE, RUBY,

WHOSE PATIENCE AND AFFECTION

SUSTAINED A HUSBAND AND A FAMILY

I

BAPTISTS AND THE SLAVERY ISSUE

The Southern Baptist Convention was born in social crisis in 1845. For decades a national controversy over the institution of slavery had been building, and compromises on sectional differences had left unsettled the fundamental question dividing the country: should human servitude be allowed permanent status in a free society? This question ultimately overshadowed all other public issues. Religious institutions especially could not avoid involvement in a controversy of this magnitude because it was argued on grounds of morality and high principle. The North-South division of major national churches in the 1840's caused by the slavery dispute foretold the fate of the Union.

At the time of their separation, Southern Baptists defended slavery with a solidarity they had not always exhibited. As early as 1710 a South Carolina church had questioned the morality of cruelties permitted by the slave code. Churches of the Revolutionary War period often debated slavery, and many Baptists freed their slaves. A Georgia association petitioned the legislature to stop slave importations, and in North Carolina one church dismissed a member for trading in slaves. The Cedar Springs Church in South Carolina sought the advice of the district association about whether it was "agreeable to the gospel" to hold Negroes in slavery.[1]

1. William G. McLoughlin and Winthrop D. Jordan, "Baptists Face the Barbarities of Slavery in 1710," *The Journal of Southern History*, XXIX (Feb.–Nov.,

3

Virginia Baptists voiced considerable opposition to slavery prior to 1800. District associations declared slavery a violation of divine law, encouraged membership in abolition societies, and petitioned for emancipation legislation. In 1789 an antislavery resolution prepared by the prominent statesman John Leland and adopted by the state General Committee advised Baptists to "make use of every legal measure to extirpate this horrid evil from our land." However, opinion soon changed in Virginia, and local opposition to such pronouncements forced associational bodies to settle upon a policy of neutrality. When a proposed study of emancipation plans "excited considerable tumult" among the churches, the Ketocton Association reversed itself and declared emancipation to be an "improper subject of investigation." Likewise, objections to Leland's antislavery resolution caused the General Committee to drop the subject from future deliberations.[2]

When antislavery agitation arose among Baptists in Kentucky during the 1790's, most associations tried to avoid the divisive issue. For instance, the Salem Association refused to discuss an inquiry from a church regarding the lawfulness of holding slaves. An antislavery resolution adopted by the Elkhorn Association in 1789 met disapproval among member churches, whereupon the statement was recalled. In 1805 the Elkhorn Baptists announced: "This Association Judges it improper for ministers, churches, or Associations to meddle with emacipation [sic] from slavery or any other political subject and as such we advise ministers and Churches to have nothing to do therewith in their religious Capacities."[3]

Associations adopted a position of neutrality, hoping thereby

1963), 495–501; William W. Sweet, *Religion on the American Frontier, the Baptists, 1783–1830* (New York, 1931), p. 79; B. D. Ragsdale, *Story of Georgia Baptists* (Atlanta, n.d), III, 72; George W. Paschal, *History of North Carolina Baptists* (Raleigh, 1955), II, 237; Leah Townsend, *South Carolina Baptists, 1670–1805* (Florence, S. C., 1935), pp. 257–58.

2. Robert B. Semple, *A History of the Rise and Progress of the Baptists in Virginia* (Richmond, 1810), pp. 10, 79, 304; Garnett Ryland, *The Baptists of Virginia, 1699–1926* (Richmond, 1955), pp. 153–54, 304.

3. J. H. Spencer, *A History of Kentucky Baptists from 1769 to 1885* (n.p., 1886), I, 183–85.

to preserve unity among churches over which they had no authority. But this same lack of authority could not prevent ministers such as John Sutton, Joshua Carmen, Josiah Dodge, and William Hickman from pursuing their antislavery activities independently. Certain congregations withdrew from associations that refused to oppose slavery, and some emancipationist ministers divided churches. David Barrow, who had begun his antislavery career while living in Virginia, moved west in 1789 and soon became the leader of the cause. When Barrow split his own church, the North District Association publicly repudiated him for "preaching the doctrines of emancipation to the hurt and injury of the brotherhood."[4]

Unwelcome in the regular associations, Barrow and Carter Tarrant organized a separate fellowship in 1807 under the name Friends of Humanity, and twelve churches soon adopted the antislavery creed as a basis for membership. Although the Friends of Humanity spread antislavery principles to the North and East, the organization died out in Kentucky after 1820. Its dogmatic stand on a question many persons considered nonreligious proved impractical as a basis for church fellowship in an area where slavery was commonly practiced.[5]

A position of neutrality, adopted in Virginia and Kentucky around 1800 in the interest of unity, was soon rejected for the same reason by Baptists throughout the South. With the expansion of slavery, Southern attitudes moved toward a positive defense of the system, which Baptists were able to justify as quickly as other Southerners. David Benedict, a New Englander who toured the South in 1813, found a few Baptists still dissatisfied with the system; but the majority defended it as an inherited institution, supported—so they believed—by history and scripture, which had become an integral part of the Southern economy.[6] Richard Furman, the distinguished Charleston pas-

4. Sweet, *Religion on the American Frontier*, p. 83; David Benedict, *A General History of the Baptist Denomination in America* (Boston, 1813), II, 245–49.

5. Sweet, *Religion on the American Frontier*, pp. 83–88; Spencer, p. 186; Walter B. Posey, *The Baptist Church in the Lower Mississippi Valley, 1776–1845* (Lexington, 1957), p. 90; Benedict, II, 231, 246–48, 545.

6. Benedict, II, 206–13.

tor, offered the first formal apology for slavery by a Baptist. His remarks, addressed to the governor in behalf of the state Baptist convention, were occasioned by laws restricting the religious instruction of slaves as a precaution against further uprisings following an attempted revolt in 1822. Furman pleaded that masters were morally obligated to provide such training. Far from causing revolts, he reasoned, Christian teachings would make slaves more subservient since the Bible itself supported slavery.[7]

Baptists defended slavery through religious journals and at denominational gatherings by expounding on the fanaticism of abolitionism, the scriptural support of slavery, and the need for humane treatment and religious instruction of slaves. Churchmen complained mainly about religious neglect of the slaves because, in their rationale, justification of slavery ultimately rested on the opportunity the system provided for the African's salvation from heathenism.[8] To strengthen their case among the more practical-minded slaveholders, Baptist spokesmen were not above promising that religious teaching would make the slave "more honest, more industrious, and more obedient to his master."[9]

Although all Baptist periodicals in the South upheld the practice of slavery, a few editors hoped that it would not be a permanent institution.[10] William Sands and Henry Keeling of Virginia,

7. Richard Furman, *Exposition of the Baptists in Relation to the Colored Population of the United States in a Communication to the Governor of South Carolina* (Charleston, 1823), pp. 16–17; William S. Jenkins, in *Pro-Slavery Thought in the Old South* (Gloucester, Mass., 1960), p. 72, declared this document to be the "most significant pro-slavery statement in the early twenties."

8. See, for example, the *Proceedings of the Baptist State Convention of Texas, 1856* (Anderson, 1856), p. 15. Baptists opposed state laws against religious instruction for slaves. See Ragsdale, p. 79; Townsend, p. 255; *Minutes of the Virginia Baptists Anniversary, 1848* (Richmond, 1848), p. 7.

9. *Proceedings of the Baptist State Convention of North Carolina, 1847* (Raleigh, n.d.) p. 13. See also *Journal of the Proceedings of the Baptist State Convention in Alabama, 1844* (n.p.: n.d.), pp. 3, 13; *The Religious Herald* (Richmond), Jan. 20, 1832, p. 2; *The Christian Index* (Penfield, Ga.), Sept. 9, 1862, p. 2.

10. A thorough analysis of editorial opinion on slavery has been done by Roger H. Crook in "The Ethical Emphasis of the Editors of Baptist Journals Published in the Southeastern Region of the United States up to 1865" (Th.D. thesis, Southern Baptist Theological Seminary, 1947), pp. 139–227.

Jesse Mercer of Georgia, Thomas Meredith of North Carolina, and W. C. Buck of Kentucky all supported the American Colonization Society, founded to transplant free Negroes to Liberia. This project attracted attention far out of proportion to its accomplishments, probably because it promised removal of Negroes from association with whites. "Every man who looks on this subject rightly," wrote Jesse Mercer, "knows and feels, that if the black man is free, he ought to be in his own country—in the land of his fathers. Amalgamation and promiscuous intercourse are out of the question."[11]

In 1832, the year of the great slavery debate in the Virginia legislature, William Sands urged an end to slavery in that state. The antislavery views expressed by James Pendleton in the 1840's caused his removal as editor of a Tennessee paper in 1861 when the fact of his views was learned. W. C. Buck, editor of a Kentucky Baptist journal in the forties, favored emancipation because of the evils associated with the American system. He employed the curious argument that the servitude sanctioned in the Bible benefited the slave, whereas American slavery operated solely for the "luxury of the master." In North Carolina, Thomas Meredith likewise condemned American slavery as "an evil of great magnitude" that should be "banished from the earth" because it caused overwork, inadequate care, separation of families, and restrictions against religious training. Buck and Meredith probably retained their positions of prominence only because they regularly attacked Northern abolitionists and affirmed that the Bible supported the principle of slavery, if not the American practice.[12]

Most Baptist weekly periodicals ardently defended slavery. Perhaps the most systematic proslavery statement appeared in several denominational newspapers in 1844, when Richard Fuller, South Carolina minister and slaveowner, engaged in an extended debate over slavery with Francis Wayland, president

11. *The Christian Index* (Atlanta), June 15, 1837, pp. 372–73.
12. *The Religious Herald,* Jan. 20, 1832, p. 2; James M. Pendleton, *Reminiscences of a Long Life* (Louisville, 1891), pp. 92–94, 113; Crook, pp. 160, 170, 194–95; *Biblical Recorder* (Raleigh), Nov. 9, 1844.

of Brown University in Rhode Island. Fuller offered little originality in his arguments, but he presented a carefully reasoned
defense on moral and scriptural grounds. The clearly stated differences between these eminent divines, both regarded as mod-
erates in their sections, revealed that by the mid-forties slavery
had become an impassable barrier separating Baptists. The debate was published just as Southern Baptists were withdrawing
from the national mission societies, which had come under the
influence of the antislavery forces.[13]

The Baptist division was not unique, for Methodist and Presbyterian bodies underwent similar schisms. In one respect,
however, the experience of the Baptists differed: their loose
ecclesiastical structure made separation less difficult. In the
absence of a centralized authority, denominational agencies had
developed slowly and had remained powerless to compel individual church cooperation. The Baptist General Convention,
organized in 1814 to promote foreign missions, was the first
nationally oriented Baptist body; but, strictly speaking, it was
not an ecclesiastical body. Its membership consisted of mission
societies and churches that financed the organization, and its
functions were limited to soliciting funds and appointing
missionaries.[14]

The establishment of the General Convention, however restricted its activities, marked the emergence of Baptists as a
major religious group in America. In colonial days, the relatively
small number of Baptists was regarded as a radical sect because
they insisted on the individual's competency in spiritual matters
and demanded the complete separation of church and state.
These doctrines, along with their minority status, made the
Baptists natural enemies of the established churches and, in
some colonies, caused them considerable persecution. Whatever
the disadvantages they lived with, they made enormous gains in
membership during the revival movements. The Great Awakening, a wave of evangelical religion in the 1740's, multiplied

13. The debate was published as *Domestic Slavery Considered as a Scriptural
Institution* (New York, 1845).
14. Robert G. Torbet, *A History of the Baptists* (Philadelphia, 1950), pp.
261–71.

Baptists in all colonies, especially in the back country. By 1792 there were 891 Baptist churches, with 65,345 members. The Second Awakening, around 1800, doubled Baptist membership by 1812.[15]

The relationship between revival periods and Baptist growth was a natural one. The doctrine of salvation as a personal experience found an ideal setting in the highly emotional revival gatherings. As a consequence of their rejection of infant baptism in favor of baptism by immersion after a conversion experience, the Baptists came to rely upon the revival meetings for recruiting new members. Their emphasis on personal conversion also explains why they became champions of religious liberty. The doctrine of soul competency, or the priesthood of the believer, made salvation an experience between God and man entered into as an act of individual free will without benefit of an ecclesiastical intermediary. For Baptists the use of state authority to promote religion violated freedom of conscience. Consequently, they fought for the disestablishment of colonial churches and for church-state separation in state and national constitutions. Obviously, too, disestablishment immediately improved the Baptist position in competing for the unchurched.[16]

Their rapid growth, however, did create a strong, centralized denomination. The General Convention's attempt to undertake domestic missions and theological education failed after a decade. Mission work in the West received no organized national support until the founding of the American Baptist Home Mission Society in 1832. Both the General Convention and the Home Mission Society remained voluntary associations, and as such they were highly vulnerable to any divisive force within the denomination.

15. *Ibid.*, pp. 239–52; Sweet, *Religion on the American Frontier*, pp. 3–17. The figures used here came from William Cathcart, *The Baptist Encyclopedia* (Philadelphia, 1881), p. 1324.

16. William Cathcart in *The Baptists and the American Revolution* (Philadelphia, 1876), traces the Baptist resistance to restrictions on religious freedom, their support of the Revolution, and their efforts in behalf of the First Amendment to the national Constitution. See also Torbet, *A History of the Baptists*, pp. 252–61; Sweet, *Religion on the American Frontier*, pp. 12–17; William T. Thom, *The Struggle for Religious Freedom in Virginia: The Baptists* (Baltimore, 1900).

The earliest threat to the unity achieved through cooperative missionary endeavors arose over the alleged neglect of areas in the West and South by the newly created Home Mission Society.[17] A separate Western Baptist Convention, organized in 1833, promoted mission work in the West for about one decade. At the same time, Southerners accused the Home Mission Society of assigning most of its workers to the free states and territories while mission fields in the South were left destitute. As a result of such feelings a Southern Baptist Mission Society was established in 1839 and operated for a few years.

Most of the Home Mission Society's missionaries did in fact serve outside the South, but not because of any deliberate discrimination. Robert Baker's investigations show that while expenditures for work in Northern fields amounted to twice that for Southern areas, Northern churches contributed more than three times the amount supplied by the South. Expenditures in the slave areas actually exceeded receipts from Southern churches. In the face of Southern complaints, the Executive Board of the Home Mission Society detailed the desperate needs of the South and repeatedly appealed for applicants to work in the area; but the missionaries themselves, most of whom were Northerners, were unwilling to serve in slave territory. Thus, although Southern complaints were not altogether well founded,[18] they were widely believed in the South and signaled the beginning of the sectional distrust that culminated in complete separation in 1845.

The quarrel over missionary neglect probably would never

17. See, for example, *The Christian Index* (Atlanta), Mar. 15, 1844. William W. Barnes argued, unconvincingly in my judgment, that missionary neglect, not slavery, was the major cause for separation in "Why the Southern Baptist Convention Was Formed," *Review and Expositor*, XLI (Jan. 1944), 3, 12–17. Barnes, in *The Southern Baptist Convention, 1845–1953* (Nashville, 1954), pp. 12–18, 39, 61, gave more place to slavery but still stressed missionary neglect. Robert A. Baker, who like Barnes is a Southern Baptist, concluded that the charges of missionary neglect were unfounded in his *Relations between Northern and Southern Baptists* (n.p., 1948), pp. 35–37.

18. Robert A. Baker, *Relations between Baptists*, pp. 36–39. See also *The Seventh Report of the Executive Committee of the American Baptist Home Mission Society, 1839* (New York, 1839), pp. 12, 29, and subsequent annual reports for the years *1841*, p. 53, and *1842*, p. 13.

have led to separation if it had not been caught up in the slavery dispute. From the 1830's onward, abolitionists made slavery a divisive issue in all major denominations. They received important assistance from British clergymen who, having helped bring about abolition in British territories in 1833, immediately began pressuring American churches to join the movement. British Baptists were among the most active in this regard. In 1834 a group of London ministers urged the General Convention in the United States to support abolitionism.[19] The action of the British Baptists forced the officers of the General Convention to deal with the slavery question formally for the first time. In a reply to the demands of the British, the General Convention explained that the American federalist system prevented abolition by a simple act of Congress. The reply further noted that antislavery action by the General Convention would destroy denominational unity.[20] Undeterred, a British abolitionist delegation attended the 1835 General Convention in Richmond, Virginia. However, before addressing the assembly, the delegates were persuaded not to make an antislavery appeal.[21]

The General Convention's handling of the British ministers did not find favor in the North, where abolitionism had already gained a strong following.[22] In Massachusetts 130 ministers, led by C. S. Grosvenor of Salem, answered the London Baptist inquiry by pledging resistance to slavery. This action was the beginning of a movement that founded the Baptist Antislavery Convention in 1840. At its first meeting the abolition society drafted a statement to the Baptists of the nation making demands that, if carried out, would have excluded from national mission societies all persons who upheld slavery.[23] Southerners

19. Thomas F. Harwood, "British Evangelical Abolitionism and American Churches in the 1830's," *The Journal of Southern History*, XXVIII (Aug., 1962), 287–306.

20. Major portions of this reply are in William W. Barnes, *The Southern Baptist Convention, 1845–1953*, pp. 20–21.

21. Harwood, p. 290.

22. Robert A. Baker, *Relations between Baptists*, pp. 46–54, describes abolitionism among Baptists. For an invaluable collection of pertinent documents on the slavery controversy among Baptists, see A. T. Foss and E. Mathews, *Facts for Baptist Churches* (Utica, N.Y., 1850).

23. Foss and Mathews, pp. 45–48.

scorned this proposal as an outrageous example of irresponsible abolitionism. Churches, associations, and state conventions throughout the South expressed alarm that the abolitionists, by making opposition to slavery a test of fellowship, would disallow the neutrality of both the General Convention and the Home Mission Society, thereby destroying the very foundation of denominational cooperation.[24]

Southerners now feared that the mission societies would fall under the control of antislavery zealots. Even though more than half of the nation's 570,000 Baptists resided in the South in 1840,[25] Northerners exerted greater influence in the affairs of the national societies. Northern financial support for both the General Convention and the Home Mission Society was three times greater than Southern support;[26] and since contributions determined membership and voting, Northern churchmen had a decided advantage at the general meetings. In addition, Northern delegates attending the General Convention usually outnumbered their Southern counterparts by a margin of three or four to one. The imbalance was even greater for the Home Mission Society.[27] Southern participation was further discouraged by the fact that seven of the nine triennial meetings of the General Convention and all of the annual meetings of the Home Mission Society had been held in Northern cities. Moreover, Boston and New York were, respectively, the headquarters for these two groups, and the executive boards of each were composed of residents of these cities. Finally, in all the years prior to separation, the chief executive and nearly all the lesser officials of both societies had been Northerners.[28]

24. Robert A. Baker, *Relations between Baptists*, pp. 57–59.
25. This figure, which includes many slaves, comes from Cathcart, *The Baptist Encyclopedia*, p. 1324.
26. Robert A. Baker, *Relations between Baptists*, pp. 36–37, gives the figures for the Home Mission Society. Receipts by states for the General Convention were published in the *Baptist Missionary Magazine*, XXVI (July, 1846), 233–35.
27. Based on an analysis of those reported in attendance in the minutes of both organizations.
28. The president of the General Convention was a Southerner for about two-thirds of the time, but his duties were primarily confined to presiding at the triennial meetings. The convention also had a president of the Board of Managers, which office was held by Jesse Mercer of Georgia from 1830 to 1841. Ac-

In consideration of Southern fears, the mission executives tried not to display sympathy for abolitionism in their official capacities. However, it was common knowledge that many Northern Baptist ministers were abolitionists, some of whom were active in the mission societies.[29] Fearing that abolitionist influence might lead the societies to adopt antislavery policies, Southerners petitioned the executive boards demanding explicit dissociation from abolitionism.[30]

In November, 1840, the Board of Managers of the General Convention issued a lengthy policy statement pointing out that the convention sought the widest possible cooperation for the limited purpose of foreign-mission work. As for slavery, it was "wholly extrinsic and irrelevant" to the work of the convention. In reporting this action to the General Convention in 1841, the board declared that none of its officers were to use their positions to advance private views on slavery.[31] As further concessions, the abolitionist Elon Galusha was not reelected to the board, and William B. Johnson of South Carolina became the new president. The General Convention reiterated this position at its Philadelphia meeting in 1844, and despite the preponderance of Northern delegates in attendance the convention adopted a resolution disclaiming "all sanction, either expressed or implied, whether of slavery or of anti-slavery."[32]

Angered by the General Convention's concessions to the

---

cording to the minutes, Mercer attended the annual meetings of the board only once in eleven years. Although the actual reason for Mercer's absences is not known, it was probably because the distance involved was prohibitive.

29. Gilbert Hobbes Barnes, *The Antislavery Impulse, 1830–1844* (Gloucester, Mass., 1957), pp. 61, 64–65, 91, 175, 242; Robert A. Baker, *Relations between Baptists*, pp. 64–65.

30. Robert A. Baker, *Relations between Baptists*, pp. 59–60; Mary B. Putnam, *Baptists and Slavery, 1840–1845* (Ann Arbor, 1913), pp. 24–25. See the action of the Executive Committee of Georgia Baptists on this question in *Minutes of the Georgia Baptist Convention, 1841* (Penfield, 1841), p. 9.

31. *Minutes of Tenth Triennial Meeting of the Baptist General Convention, 1841* (Boston, 1841), app. A, pp. 80–81. The mission societies also tried to calm Southern fears by sending their agents to state conventions. See *Minutes of the State Convention of the Baptist Denomination in South Carolina, 1840* (n.p., n.d.), p. 3.

32. Foss and Mathews, pp. 75–76; *Baptist Missionary Magazine*, XXIV (July, 1844), 157. The South had only 80 of the 460 delegates present.

South, the abolitionists charged that the convention had compromised on a moral question. Between the 1841 and 1844 meetings the antislavery men created their own missionary organization under the auspices of the Baptist Antislavery Convention. They first sought only to bypass the General Convention in supporting missionaries but later organized a completely independent missionary agency, the Free Mission Society.[33]

The withdrawal of the abolitionist faction demonstrated the practical difficulties of neutrality when both sides were becoming intolerant of compromise. Although the noncommittal policy had been most consistently stated by the General Convention, its inadequacy appeared first in connection with the question of whether slaveholders had been chosen as missionaries by the Home Mission Society. The issue arose in 1844 after Northern editors expressed suspicion that some of the society's appointees owned slaves.[34] Secretary Benjamin Hill explained that his organization took no position on slavery but then reported, as a matter of information, that none of the appointees owned slaves.

Hill's reply put the Northern editors at ease, but it raised further questions in the South—specifically, could a slaveholder be appointed as a missionary? The editor of *The Christian Index*, in Georgia, challenged the secretary about the matter, warning that the denial of such an appointment would result in "rending the denomination asunder."[35] Hill's reply only reaffirmed the society's neutrality, which the Georgia editor considered an evasive answer. By this time several Northern papers were also demanding an unequivocal answer to the hypothetical question,[36] and the Home Mission Society found itself confronted with an issue it could not evade.

The matter of appointing a slaveholder dominated the annual meeting in April, 1844, where the principal debate featured abolitionist Nathaniel Colver and slaveholder Richard Fuller. After three days the society adopted a resolution offered by Fuller

33. Robert A. Baker, *Relations between Baptists*, pp. 67–68.
34. *Ibid.*, p. 76.
35. *The Christian Index* (Atlanta), Mar. 15, 1844; Mar. 29, 1844; Apr. 12, 1844.
36. Robert A. Baker, *Relations between Baptists*, p. 77.

reaffirming neutrality. The vote settled nothing, and the delegates knew it. At the closing session they named a committee to make plans for dissolving the agency if continued cooperation became impossible. Before the year ended, the society's Executive Committee was forced to make a decision about slavery when, as a test case, the Georgia Baptist Convention offered James E. Reeve for appointment as a missionary. The application noted specifically that Reeve owned slaves. No longer dealing with a hypothetical question, the Executive Committee could not avoid the issue. The seven-to-five vote against appointment proved decisive. When the society met in April, 1845, only a few Southerners attended. Thereafter, it became strictly a Northern organization.[37]

A few weeks after the Home Mission Society refused to appoint a slaveholder, a similar case was presented to the General Convention. The Alabama State Convention, in November, 1844, had demanded from the General Convention's executive board in Boston a "distinct, explicit avowal" that slaveholders qualified for foreign mission appointments. The board's reply completely reversed earlier policy by declaring: "One thing is certain, we can never be a party to any arrangement which would imply approbation of slavery."[38] The board further noted that if Southerners could not cooperate on these terms they should withdraw from the convention.

The decisions of the two mission boards at last made clear what Southerners had long feared: the national bodies had come under the influence of uncompromising abolitionists. Southerners, by demanding equal treatment from the national boards, had exercised a right they had under the constitutions and official policies of the societies. But whatever the validity of their

37. Foss and Mathews, pp. 88–93, 125; *Thirteenth Report of the American Baptist Home Mission Society, 1845* (New York, 1845), p. 7.
38. *Proceedings, Alabama, 1844*, pp. 3, 8; Putnam, p. 55; Foss and Mathews, pp. 104–106. The Board of Managers met in April, 1845, and supported the executive board's handling of the matter, but the managers declared that any decision on an actual application should be referred to the next triennial meeting of the convention. The action of the Board of Managers, however, did not matter because the call for organizing the Southern Baptist Convention had already been issued.

position, only a few of them expressed any hope for reversals of the decisions. Generally, they considered the rupture inevitable and welcomed the occasion to pursue a separate course.[39]

Attention promptly turned to the creation of a new regional organization; and in April, 1845, the Virginia Baptist Foreign Mission Society took the initiative by circulating a proposal for a new convention.[40] The following month, 293 delegates assembled in Augusta, Georgia, to establish the Southern Baptist Convention. The participants, many of whom had formerly helped to organize state Baptist conventions, understood the problems of establishing effective denominational organizations for democratic churches. Therefore, the constitution of the new body provided for a "general organization for Christian benevolence" to promote domestic and foreign missions and "other objects connected to the Redeemer's kingdom."[41] Thus, Southern Baptists abandoned the use of separate societies, each with a single type of work, in favor of one all-purpose convention that would have broad constitutional powers to conduct, through a system of subordinate boards, whatever work it chose to undertake. The delegates immediately appointed boards to supervise domestic and foreign missions, and several years later attempted to establish a publishing house and a theological school. However, these latter two projects did not achieve permanent status until after the Civil War.

In reality the convention's purposes exceeded its powers. Despite its centralized nature, the convention lacked indepen-

39. William B. Johnson of South Carolina was president of the General Convention, 1841–44. He advised his state convention against immediate separation in December, 1844. After the Board of Managers upheld the executive board's refusal to appoint a slaveholder, the South Carolina Convention met in special session in May, 1845, to appoint delegates to the meeting called to organize the Southern Convention. Johnson also shifted to the separationist position and became the first president of the Southern Convention. Some Southern Baptist editors cautioned against hasty separation. See Crook, pp. 162, 181–84, 188–89, 227; Raymond Hargus Taylor, "The Triennial Convention, 1814–1845: A Study in Baptist Co-operation and Conflict" (Th.D. thesis, Southern Baptist Theological Seminary, 1960), p. 153.

40. *Proceedings of the Baptist General Association of Virginia, 1845* (n.p., n.d.), pp. 26–28.

41. *Proceedings of the Southern Baptist Convention, 1845* (hereafter cited as *Proceedings, SBC* [Richmond, 1845]), p. 3.

dent ecclesiastical authority to fulfill its promise as a "general organization for Christian benevolence." The founders probably never intended that it sponsor much beyond missionary work. The constitution itself admitted the one great restriction on activities when it promised "fully to respect" the independence of local churches. The government of the convention fulfilled this promise. Although for some years individual contributors had voting power, the membership of the Southern Convention generally consisted of delegates from cooperating churches, an arrangement that was traditional in district associations and state conventions. The convention's direct ties to local churches must be given careful consideration in analyzing the social attitudes of Southern Baptists as expressed through their organized activities. The fact that both financial support and voting power came from independent and democratically governed churches exerted a powerful check on any activity that might not receive general support.

At the time of the founding of the Southern Convention, Baptists were already well organized within the states. In addition to the district associations, the oldest and smallest denominational units, there were ten state conventions; and by 1848 three additional conventions were organized in the Southwestern states. Each state was served by at least one Baptist periodical, and eight conventions supported educational institutions. Within their respective areas, the state and district bodies were autonomous and independent associations of churches. The Southern Convention as a denominational body, therefore, was superimposed upon the state and local bodies, with its membership composed of these same local churches. Although no formal ecclesiastical ties united the three organizational levels, they recognized an interdependence from the first, resulting in much practical cooperation and a strong sense of solidarity.

In view of Baptist emphasis on local church autonomy and the independence of state and district organizations, the creation of the Southern Convention, with its broad powers, was a major stride toward denominational centralization. Soon after its founding, however, a controversy engulfed the convention regarding its authority to act as the collective agent for the churches. The attack upon denominational bodies had begun when state conventions were first established, but in the 1850's the campaign centered on the Southern Convention itself. Under the leadership of James R. Graves, editor of the *Tennessee Baptist*, and James Pendleton, pastor-editor in Kentucky, the movement came to be known as "landmarkism," so called because Graves referred to his beliefs as the landmarks of Baptist orthodoxy. Basic to landmark theology was a peculiar form of "high church" doctrine that supposed that New Testament authority had been perpetuated historically through a succession of local congregations rather than by a succession of bishops, as in the episcopal tradition. The landmark Baptists argued that denominational agencies violated the authority of local churches, the only institutions divinely commissioned to conduct missionary work.[42]

Landmarkism seriously threatened the convention until the end of the century and left a permanent imprint on Southern Baptist life. An attempt to destroy the Foreign Mission Board in 1859 brought about a compromise by which churches holding landmark views could support missionaries directly. Meanwhile, landmarkism established itself firmly in many district associations, especially in the Western states, although its advocates failed to get control of any state convention. Landmarkism declined as an organized force within a decade after the death of Graves in 1892, but not before leaving many Southern Baptists with a strong suspicion of denominational power and a kind of frontier religious provincialism. The narrow legalism of landmark theology fostered doctrinal conservatism and denominational exclusivism. Many churches in the Western half of the convention, for example, followed the landmark doctrine of close

42. For an analysis of the landmark theology, see William W. Barnes, *The Southern Baptist Convention, 1845–1953*, pp. 98–119, and the same author's *The Southern Baptist Convention, A Study in the Development of Ecclesiology* (Fort Worth, 1934), pp. 11–12. Opposition to organized mission work went back to the early days of the General Convention when Daniel Parks, John Taylor, and Alexander Campbell split the Baptist ranks on this question. See Sweet, *Religion on the American Frontier*, chap. 5.

communion, which denied non-Baptist participation in the Lord's Supper ordinance for lack of proper baptism. This exclusivistic conception of the church provided doctrinal grounds for opposition to those forms of interdenominational cooperation featured by the social-gospel movement of the post-Civil War decades. Landmarkism also helps to explain why Southern Baptists opposed church union early in the twentieth century while Northern Baptists, little influenced by landmarkism, became strong supporters of the ecumenical movement.

The chief significance of the landmark agitation, however, is that it exposed the fundamental weakness of the denominational structure in providing leadership to interpret the church's responsibility to society. Since the Southern Convention depended upon the voluntary support of independent churches, its program, while constitutionally not restricted, was in fact confined to missions and related work which would receive undivided support. For the same reason, state conventions and Baptist journals generally would not advance social ideas that might prove divisive.

Local congregations alone enjoyed the ecclesiastical power to pursue an independent course, but they proved even less effective than denominational bodies in formulating a significant social message. The democratic organization of Southern Baptist churches made them highly sensitive to the opinions of their white lower- and middle-class members. Moreover, the typical church was largely given to a revivalistic program. Pastors showed great zeal for converting individuals and policing morality but assumed little responsibility for the larger problems of society.

By the middle of the nineteenth century, three major forces restricted Southern Baptist social thought and action: an ecclesiastical system of independent churches discouraged denominational activities other than mission work; revivalism kept the local churches preoccupied with the spiritual and moral welfare of individuals; and pressure of the social environment usually produced the silence, if not the sanction, of the local churches relative to the basic attitudes of the secular world. Thus, when these churches supported slavery, they were confirming on moral grounds a position that their region had already determined on secular grounds. In so doing, the churches forfeited their prophetic role within their culture. The study of Southern Baptist social attitudes, therefore, becomes largely an examination of how the prevailing secular values gained confirmation from a denomination that lacked institutional leadership capable of independent judgment and action.

II

WAR, FREEDMEN, AND RELIGIOUS RECONSTRUCTION

Wilbur J. Cash, in his perceptive study of the Southern mind, stated well the response of the churches to the Civil War when he observed that the pulpits of the South offered the "dark suggestion that the God of the Yankees was not God at all but the Antichrist loosed at last from the pit." The clergy viewed the war as "no mere secular contest but Armageddon, with the South standing in the role of the defender of the Ark, its people the Chosen People."[1] The performance of Baptists in the Confederacy substantiates the essential accuracy of this charge. Their allegiance to the Confederate cause made it entirely fitting that the initial meeting of the South Carolina Secession Convention should take place in the First Baptist Church of Columbia, where the delegates, before adjourning to Charleston for the formal act of separation, resolved that the state "should forthwith secede from the Federal Union."[2]

The attitudes of the Baptists throughout the South during the secession crisis closely corresponded to the position taken by their respective states. Denominational journals in the Deep South advocated secession even before their states voted to withdraw. The South Carolina Baptist newspaper, immediately following Lincoln's election, defended the right of secession and confidently anticipated such action by the state.[3] Likewise,

1. Wilbur J. Cash, *The Mind of the South* (New York, 1941), p. 80.
2. Ralph A. Wooster, *The Secession Conventions of the South* (Princeton, 1962), pp. 15, 21.
3. *Southern Baptist* (Charleston), Nov. 17, 1860.

the Alabama paper justified secession as the only practical course for the South after the victory of the "fanatical" Republican Party.[4] One month before Texas joined the Confederacy, the state's Baptist newspaper issued a vigorous secessionist editorial denouncing the "Black Republicans" as the enemy of both constitutional government and sound religion.[5]

Secession placed the states of the Upper South in the difficult position of choosing between the Union they wanted preserved and the rights of their sister states, which they believed to be jeopardized by federal power. Most Tennesseans wished only to stay out of the conflict, but neutrality ended in May, 1861, when the pro-Southern governor effected a military alliance with the Confederacy. During the months of indecision, editor James R. Graves, an experienced controversialist as leader of the landmark Baptist agitation, continually campaigned for secession. By June, when the voters ratified membership in the Confederacy, the *Tennessee Baptist* newspaper had taken the character of a partisan political journal.[6] Unlike Graves, the editors in Virginia and North Carolina exhibited great moderation. The Virginia newspaper called its readers to pray for a peaceful solution to the crisis. The editor maintained an "unbroken silence" on the "political question" of secession, arguing that the issue had no proper place in a religious paper.[7] In North Carolina, the last state to join the Confederacy, the Baptist paper cautioned against hasty action and, up to the time the state seceded, expressed hope for reconciliation of the sections.[8]

More than any other state, Kentucky tried to avoid committing itself to either side and did so until military action within the state forced support of the Union in September, 1861. Kentucky's desire for peace found expression in the Baptist newspaper, which offered the only strong pacifist appeal among

4. *South Western Baptist* (Tuskegee), Nov. 20, 1860.
5. *Texas Baptist* (Anderson), Jan. 3, 1860.
6. James G. Randall and David Donald, *The Civil War and Reconstruction*, 2d ed. (Boston, 1961), pp. 184–86. Graves was editor of the *Tennessee Baptist* (Nashville).
7. *The Religious Herald* (Richmond), Nov. 22, 1860; Dec. 6, 1860.
8. Crook, p. 252.

Southern Baptists. Editor Joseph Otis condemned the promotion of secession and war by denominational bodies, some of which, he complained, had been turned into mere "political gatherings." Otis deplored both the division of the country and a union forced upon seceding states. Unable to support the cause of either side, he condemned the actions of both. In June, 1861, Otis concluded a long pacifist editorial with the declaration: "SINK OR SWIM, LIVE OR DIE, SURVIVE OR PERISH, WE ARE OPPOSED TO THIS WAR."[9]

Three state conventions met during the interval between Lincoln's election and their state's decision on secession. Each adopted a position which coincided with the policy of its state. One week after the presidential election, the Alabama Convention declared that the Union had failed and that the only hope of justice for the South lay in a separate government, which the convention pledged itself to defend.[10] Florida Baptists, meeting before a single state had seceded, declared their "hearty approbation" of those determined to preserve the integrity of Southern states even if it meant the "disruption of all existing political ties."[11] The Kentucky ministers, assembled only a few days before the state legislature voted neutrality, petitioned their lawmakers to take all necessary steps to keep the state out of war.[12]

The Baptist conventions that met after secession gave unqualified support to the Southern cause. Special reports on the "state of the country" invariably blamed disunion on the fanatical disregard of Southern rights by Lincoln's party. These reports described the South's position in the most partisan terms. The Confederacy, acting only in defense of liberty and independence, was assured of divine help and ultimate triumph in a righteous cause.[13] After the war began, Baptist support became even more zealous. Shortly after Fort Sumter the delegates at

9. *Western Recorder* (Louisville), June 1, 1861; Randall and Donald, pp. 227–31.
10. *Minutes of the Alabama State Convention, 1860* (Tuskegee, 1860), pp. 11–12.
11. *Proceedings of the Baptist Convention of the State of Florida, 1860* (Monticello, Fla., 1860), p. 7.
12. *Minutes of the General Association of Baptists of Kentucky, 1861* (Lexington, 1861), pp. 27–28.
13. See, for example, *Minutes, Virginia, 1861*, pp. 15–16.

the Georgia Convention rose to their feet in approving a resolution declaring that the Baptists would not be "behind any class of our fellow citizens in maintaining independence of the South by any sacrifice of treasure or of blood."[14] The Southern Baptist Convention met in Savannah during the second month of the war. Its president, Richard Fuller, like many in his home state of Maryland, was strongly pro-Southern, even though the state remained in the Union. Fuller headed the committee reporting on the national crisis. The report, after detailing the offenses of the North, applauded the "noble course" of the Confederate government and declared that "every principle of religion, of patriotism, and of humanity calls upon us to pledge our fortunes and lives" in repelling the "savage barbarity" being inflicted upon the South.[15]

Dedication to Southern independence did not slacken during the war. The most common form of patriotic expression was the observance of special days of fasting and prayer set aside by Confederate officials. Many churches proudly donated bells to be cast into cannon. The Baptist journals generally bolstered morale and offered moral justification for a war against the Yankee invaders. Editors unsparingly praised Southerners for their nobility, courage, and innocence while portraying men of the North as barbarians interested only in satisfying their lusts, greed, and love of plunder. Pronouncements on the war expressed confidence and determination even in the face of defeat. The Southern Convention, after two years of fighting, declared: "While deploring the evils of war, and earnestly desiring peace, we have no thought of ever yielding."[16] Until the very end, Baptists remained confident of victory for the hallowed cause. Consequently, military reversals and ultimate defeat called for some kind of explanation. The Georgia Convention in 1864 saw the "hand of God" at work even in defeat, which came to chastise the Southern people for their sins.[17] Similarly, the Southern

14. *Minutes, Georgia, 1861*, p. 5.
15. *Proceedings, SBC, 1861* (Richmond, 1861), p. 64.
16. *Ibid.*, 1863, p. 54.
17. Ragsdale, III, 78.

Convention, after reaffirming the righteousness of the South's purpose, acknowledged that God had sent "terrible calamities" as calls to repentance.[18] By attributing defeat to the mysterious workings of an all-wise Providence, the Baptists could retain their belief in a personal deity without repudiating a single political conviction by which they had supported the Confederacy and without accepting any responsibility for the catastrophes of war. As the Virginia editor put it, the outcome of the war "shed no light" on the morality of slavery, secession, or war.[19]

If the Baptists could refuse to renounce the social doctrines on which the Confederacy had been founded, they could not ignore the new social realities brought about by defeat, the most important being the emancipation of the Negro. Baptists in particular were obliged to consider the implications of emancipation for the simple reason that, under slavery, Negroes had affiliated with Baptist churches more often than with those of any other denomination. Several reasons account for the success of Baptists as evangels of the black race. Their emphasis on personal conversion and congregational participation in church life offered special attractions to the enslaved. Belief in human equality in matters of the spirit allowed no racial barrier to confine the Baptist movement. Masters usually welcomed Baptist preaching, which stressed an otherworldly hope and personal morality, because such teaching did more to strengthen than to undermine the slave system. Those who preached to the slave population were fully conscious of such practical considerations. One minister, in an appeal for the support of work among the slaves, calculated that conversion would increase the value of slaves by more than 10 percent.[20]

Historians of the Negro church have emphasized the close parallel between the Christianization of the slaves and the periods of religious revival in which the Baptists played a leading role. The religious awakenings which spread the Baptist church among white settlers also reached the slave population. Preach-

18. *Proceedings, SBC, 1863*, p. 54.
19. Rufus B. Spain, *At Ease in Zion: Social History of Southern Baptists, 1865–1900* (Nashville, 1967), pp. 19–20.
20. *Minutes, Alabama, 1846*, p. 18.

ers, who labored without benefit of formal training, offered a fervent gospel, both simple and personal in its appeal, that attracted the unlettered regardless of race. The Baptist meetings gave to the penitent slave a joyous religion with a future hope as well as a momentary escape from a rigorous plantation life.[21]

Although Christianity spread itself among the blacks and whites at the same time and in much the same manner, it was never allowed to effect a social brotherhood of the races in any practical sense. On the contrary, the conduct of church life offers some of the earliest evidence of the white man's determination to keep the races separate in social relations. It has often been pointed out that slaves commonly worshiped with whites. Baptists seem to have gone further than other denominations in allowing Negroes to participate in church life. In matters of discipline, for example, Negroes sometimes exercised limited responsibility over their own members. But the presence of slaves in white congregations can easily obscure the more important fact that the churches, while respecting the Negro's spiritual equality, helped originate the pattern of racial segregation.[22] When slaves attended white churches they normally sat in special sections and never enjoyed an equal voice in church affairs. The instances of black ministers appearing before white con-

21. Carter G. Woodson, *The History of the Negro Church*, 2d ed. (Washington, D. C., 1945), p. 22; Workers of the Writers' Program, *The Negro in Virginia* (New York, 1940), pp. 99, 103. Methodist work among the slaves was on a more organized basis, but was otherwise very similar to the Baptist effort. See Donald G. Mathews, "The Methodist Mission to the Slaves, 1829–1844," *The Journal of American History*, LI (Mar., 1965), 615–31.

22. Numerous sources touch on the relationship of the races in religious activity. Especially useful are James Benson Sellers, *Slavery in Alabama* (University, Ala., 1950), pp. 299–300, 321; Orville W. Taylor, *Negro Slavery in Arkansas* (Durham, 1958), pp. 178–80; Workers of the Writers' Program, pp. 100–109, 143–47; Everett Dick, *The Dixie Frontier* (New York, 1948), pp. 96, 185, 188. See also Comer Vann Woodward's *The Strange Career of Jim Crow* (New York, 1955), p. 16, and Charles E. Wynes's supporting monograph *Race Relations in Virginia, 1870–1902* (Charlottesville, Va., 1961), pp. vii–viii, which argue that systematic social segregation did not develop until late in the nineteenth century. In view of the wide attention to Woodward's thesis, it should be emphasized that segregation was firmly established in Southern custom before the Civil War. See Kyle Haselden, *The Racial Problem in Christian Perspective* (New York, 1964), p. 29.

gregations were but curious variants which tell little about racial dynamics. In the main, the slave's religious needs were met in separate services featuring special instruction on the slave's duty by the master or a white minister. On many occasions, white Baptists made clear their preference for separation in religious activities. State conventions frequently discussed how best to give religious instruction to the blacks. The method most highly recommended called for separate meetings and, whenever possible, the use of separate quarters.[23]

To the whites, racial separation befitted the slave's subordinate status, but the practice sometimes actually elevated the position of the individual Negroes. A racially separated church was but one step away from a religious life conducted by the slaves themselves. The slave community engaged in a considerable amount of religious activity independent of whites. What has been called the "invisible institution"[24] under slavery went largely unrecorded, but it laid much of the groundwork for the rapid emergence of separate Negro churches after emancipation. Of course, all states had special slave codes that included prohibitions against the assembling of slaves unsupervised by whites; but these laws, often made more rigid by exaggerated fears of insurrections, were not strictly enforced.[25]

Whatever the actual restrictions, the Negro community produced some outstanding leaders and several all-Negro churches. George Leile, a freedman licensed in the Baptist ministry before the Revolution, preached to the people of his race on plan-

23. *Minutes of the Baptist State Convention of Texas, 1851* (Washington, Tex., 1851), p. 14; *1856*, p. 15; *1857*, p. 17. See also *Proceedings of the General Association of the Baptists of Tennessee, 1849* (Nashville, 1850), p. 37; *Minutes, Kentucky, 1860*, p. 24; *Minutes, Virginia, 1845*, p. 5; *1863*, pp. 76–77; *Proceedings of the Mississippi Baptist State Convention, 1850* (Jackson, 1850), pp. 22–23.

24. E. Franklin Frazier, in *The Negro in the United States* (New York, 1949), p. 343, credits this term to George F. Bragg, *History of the Afro-American Group of the Episcopal Church* (Baltimore, 1922), p. 39. See also Workers of the Writers' Program, p. 109.

25. Workers of the Writers' Program, pp. 143–47; Sellers, *Slavery in Alabama*, p. 294; J. A. Whitted, *A History of the Negro Baptists of North Carolina* (Raleigh, 1908), p. 10.

tations in South Carolina with great success and, for a time, ministered to the Silver Bluff Church near Augusta, the first all-Negro Baptist congregation in America. One of his converts was Andrew Bryan who, with his brother, conducted services for blacks in Georgia. After much abuse from whites, he gained permission from authorities to establish the First African Baptist Church in Savannah in 1788, which had 1,500 members by 1812. William Moses founded the African Baptist Church of Williamsburg in 1776. He was whipped subsequently for holding public meetings, but the church survived. His successor, Gowan Pamphlet, led the church into the Dover Association (white) in 1791. Black preachers Collin Teague and Lott Carey of Richmond were appointed missionaries to Africa by the Baptist General Convention in 1820. Some black ministers gained notoriety for their preaching skills. Best known was John Jasper, who organized a Negro church in Richmond where many whites came to hear his famous sermon, "The Sun Do Move." All-Negro Baptist churches operated in most of the principal cities of the South before the Civil War.[26]

The major responsibility for the spiritual care of the slaves, however, remained with the whites; and Baptists continually concerned themselves with the problem of Christianizing the black population. Reports on the matter were made at state conventions from their founding. The reports made the masters responsible for the slave's spiritual welfare, a position which very sensibly respected the owner's property rights while placing on him the major burden for religious care. Local churches were also admonished to minister to the bondsmen. Many white pastors, including such prominent figures as Basil Manly, James C. Furman, Richard Fuller, and Isaac Taylor Tichenor, held separate services for Negroes as a regular practice.[27] Most outstanding was the work of Robert Ryland, pastor of the African Baptist

---

26. Woodson, pp. 35–36, 97–104; Workers of the Writers' Program, pp. 100–104; *Baptist Home Missions in North America* (New York, 1883), pp. 387–90; Frazier, p. 346; Sellers, *Slavery in Alabama*, p. 300; Benedict, II, 189–94.

27. Francis Butler Simkins, *A History of the South*, 3d ed. (New York, 1963), p. 165. Walter L. Fleming, *Documentary History of Reconstruction* (New York, 1950), II, 247.

Church in Richmond and author of a special catechism for instructing the slaves.[28] Despite occasional white criticism, Ryland served the church for twenty-five years while he was president of Richmond College. Missionaries employed by state conventions often gave a portion of their services to slaves.[29] The Southern Convention instructed its newly created Home Mission Board to "take all prudent measures for the religious instruction of the colored population."[30] The agency annually reported on the subject and assigned a few of its appointees to work among the blacks.

The desire to evangelize the Negroes brought problems in church-state relations because of laws restricting the instruction of slaves. The Home Mission Board, in a typical reaction, acquiesced to legal restrictions by advising that all work with Negroes be conducted orally where laws prohibited instruction in reading.[31] State conventions, likewise, specified that instruction should always be oral and in the presence of whites to conform to the slave codes. The Virginia Convention in 1835 instructed its workers to "guard against even the most remote infraction of either the letter or the spirit of the laws of our state."[32] At other times, Southern Baptists were not so compliant about infringements on religious activities. As early as 1801, the Charleston Association petitioned the legislature to modify state laws restricting religious instruction.[33] The Virginia Convention of 1848 established a committee to petition the legislature to allow meetings of black congregations in the presence of whites.[34] Nathaniel Crawford, president of Mercer University, declared a Georgia law forbidding slaves to read to be an "outrage upon humanity

28. Woodson, pp. 140–45. Ryland's own account of the history of the church appeared in *The Religious Herald* (Richmond), July 1 and 8, 1880.
29. *Minutes, Virginia, 1835*, p. 3; *1850*, p. 6; *Minutes, Texas, 1852*, pp. 13, 15; Sellers, *Slavery in Alabama*, pp. 304–305; Orville W. Taylor, pp. 181–82.
30. *Proceedings, SBC, 1845*, p. 15. A very favorable account of Southern Baptist mission work among the blacks appears in Mary Emily Wright, *The Missionary Work of the Southern Baptist Convention* (Philadelphia, 1902), pp. 313–22.
31. *Proceedings, SBC, 1849*, p. 39.
32. *Minutes, Virginia, 1835*, p. 3.
33. *Baptist Home Missions*, p. 390.
34. *Minutes, Virginia, 1848*, p. 7.

... a disgrace to Christianity and the civilization of our people."[35] Even during the Civil War, Georgia Baptists had a hand in modifying a law denying licenses to black ministers.[36] These occasional challenges to the slave codes may be credited to the strong devotion of Baptists to religious freedom; but it must also be remembered that since the opportunity afforded by slavery to Christianize the Negro race had always been the principal grounds on which churchmen justified slavery, they were bound by conscience to oppose laws denying religion to the slave population.

In the post-Civil War period, white Baptists continued to acknowledge special obligations to the Negro, but systematic efforts to facilitate the freedmen's religious reconstruction were almost negligible. Southern Baptists were much less enthusiastic about helping the emancipated Negro develop religious leadership and organizations than they had been about evangelizing the Negro slave. They sometimes excused themselves for their inaction by holding the North entirely responsible for all the problems associated with emancipation. They also shared the general suspicion of most Southerners toward programs to uplift the Negro because such efforts were usually associated with carpetbaggers and Radical Republicanism.[37] But inaction was not altogether owing to lack of desire. The records of denominational meetings are filled with reports outlining the urgent needs of the blacks and appealing for aid. However, always overshadowing the plight of the freedman were the financial needs of the white churches and denominational agencies. The Home Mission Board receipts declined to their lowest point during Reconstruction, and the Sunday School Board discontinued operations for several years because of indebtedness.[38]

Perhaps an immediate show of generosity and initiative in

35. Ragsdale, III, 80.
36. [Samuel Boykin], *History of the Baptist Denomination in Georgia* (Atlanta, 1881), p. 264.
37. Alratheus Ambush Taylor, *The Negro in South Carolina during Reconstruction* (Washington, D. C., 1924), p. 117; Winfred Ernest Garrison, *The March of Faith, the Story of Religion in America since 1865* (New York, 1933), p. 21; *Proceedings, SBC, 1875*, pp. 73–75.
38. Victor I. Masters, ed., *The Home Mission Task* (Atlanta, 1912), pp. 20–26.

elevating the status of former slaves is too much to expect from the defeated South. Unfortunately, the settlement of the most important religious question raised by emancipation would not wait for more auspicious times. Would the black man, now a citizen, worship in the white man's church, where many blacks held membership, or carry on a separate church life, as many others had been doing? Southern Baptists issued formal declarations which carefully avoided either favoring or opposing separation, but the underlying sentiment always seemed to anticipate the eventual departure of black members. Shortly after the war, the Alabama Convention advised Negroes to retain their present relationship but affirmed "their right to withdraw from our churches and form organizations of their own."[39] The Virginia Convention that same year declared that since "it is most likely they will prefer" separation, "encouragements [should be] offered them to accomplish their object."[40]

More important in determining the racial division of Baptists than any announced church policy was the fact that blacks could remain in white churches only on the same basis of inequality that had prevailed under slavery, for Baptist democracy did not extend to black members after emancipation. The editor of the Virginia church newspaper expressed the feelings of white Baptists on this issue. He reasoned that if biracial churches continued they would afford opportunities for social equality which would inevitably lead to the "mongrelization of the noble Anglo-Saxon race."[41] Separation, therefore, fulfilled the strongest desires of each race. Blacks wanted to escape white control, and a segregated church offered an inoffensive way for them to express their freedom. Whites preferred separation because after emancipation a biracial church suggested equality. Moreover, withdrawal relieved whites of an inconsistency they were unprepared to correct, namely, denying blacks an equal voice in church affairs in violation of the doctrine of congregational government.

39. *Minutes, Alabama, 1865*, p. 10. Se also *Minutes, South Carolina, 1865–1866* (Greenville, 1866), p. 240.

40. *Minutes, Virginia, 1866*, p. 26.

41. Quoted in Spain, *At Ease in Zion*, p. 52; Workers of the Writers' Program, p. 249.

Religion thus became one area where emancipation could be expressed with the white man's encouragement. The church quickly became the central institution in the black community —for all, a haven in a discriminatory society; for many, the only opportunity to display their talents of leadership.[42]

Once the freedmen made clear their preference for separation, development of a completely segregated church came rapidly. White acquiescence turned to open encouragement. Baptist congregational policy facilitated the transition. Local white congregations ordained Negro leaders and helped organize new churches. Occasionally, when the whites moved to new quarters, the blacks inherited old church buildings. But most of the credit for the creation of a separate religious establishment must go to the Negroes themselves.[43] In most instances they supplied their own leadership and founded their own churches, and within a few years, most of them had withdrawn from the white churches. State organizations for Negro Baptists appeared in North Carolina in 1866 and in Alabama and Virginia in 1867. By 1882, Negro Baptists numbered 800,000, had convention organizations in every Southern state, and were publishing eight religious newspapers. In 1886 they established their first national body, the American National Baptist Convention.[44] In view of the freedmen's lack of preparation, the establishment of the Negro church stands as one of the most remarkable achievements of Reconstruction.

In the postwar decades, the most important source of help to Negro Baptists outside their race came from the Baptists of the North. The American Baptist Home Mission Society had abandoned its work in the slave states in 1845. During the war the society began working with Negroes in the Upper South. At the end of the war it received authority from federal officials to take

42. Benjamin E. Mays and Joseph W. Nicholson, *The Negro's Church* (New York, 1933), p. 6.
43. Alratheus A. Taylor, pp. 118–19; Charles Hays Rankin, "The Rise of Negro Baptist Churches in the South through the Reconstruction Period" (Th.M. thesis, New Orleans Baptist Theological Seminary, 1955), pp. 1, 52–60.
44. *Baptist Home Missions*, p. 421; B. F. Riley, *A History of the Baptists in the Southern States East of the Mississippi* (Philadelphia, 1898), p. 323.

over churches not served by "loyal ministers." Actually, the society did not make it a practice to take over churches, but it did
begin new work among the freedmen with the appointment of
sixty-five workers in 1865. By 1869 about one-third of the society's operations were in the South.[45]

The reentry of Northern Baptists into Southern fields caused
deep anxiety among whites in the South. The Virginia Convention in 1865 heard a lengthy report on the proposed work of the
Northern society among Negroes and strongly advised Virginia
churches not to cooperate. It was feared that Northern missionaries of the "radical party" would turn black people against the
whites by preaching "politics rather than religion" and "equal
suffrage rather than repentance."[46] At the first meeting of the
Southern Baptist Convention after the war, Isaac Taylor Tichenor, president of Alabama Polytechnic Institute and later head
of the convention's home-mission work, expressed this same distrust. Tichenor welcomed the labors of any "right-minded" missionary, but argued that, owing to the peculiar "character" of
the Negro people and the special "feeling" of whites, the work
should be conducted only by Southern men.[47]

Northern Baptists wanted to carry on the Negro work as a
joint project with Southern Baptists, but the race issue made
cooperation impossible. Representatives of the American Baptist
Home Mission Society proposed to the Southern Convention in
1868 the idea of cooperative support for Negro missions. The
Southern body received the delegation cordially and responded
by sending a committee of its most distinguished leaders to explore the offer at the next meeting of the Northern society.[48] The

45. William Wright Barnes, "Home Mission Board of the Southern Baptist
Convention," *Encyclopedia of Southern Baptists,* I (1958), 640; Robert A. Baker,
Relations between Baptists, p. 109.

46. *Minutes, Virginia, 1865,* pp. 11, 16–17.

47. *Proceedings, SBC, 1866,* p. 86. There was some hostility even to the idea
of educating the freedmen for religious purposes. A report to the South Carolina
Convention in 1868 opposed the establishment of a theological institute for
blacks for fear that they would be alienated from whites by the "arts of design-
ing and malignant men." See Alratheus Ambush Taylor, p. 117.

48. For the fullest account of the society's efforts at cooperation, see *Baptist
Home Missions,* pp. 423–33. The delegates from the Southern Convention were
J. B. Jeter, Richard Fuller, Basil Manly, John A. Broadus, and J. R. Graves. See

subsequent negotiations quickly revealed that basic disagreements over the social status of the freedmen would block any effective cooperation between the two bodies. In an opening statement, John A. Broadus, a member of the faculty of Southern Theological Seminary, explained that the Southern Convention wanted the right to approve all missionaries working with Negroes. A spokesman for the society objected to such a restriction as unacceptable to Northern churches which, presumably, would supply most of the money for the work. At this point in the discussion the officials of the society submitted a formal plan for the cooperative effort. The document stated specifically that the purpose of the program would be to "lift up the millions of freedmen to the exercise of all the rights and duties of citizenship and Christian brotherhood."[49] To the Southern delegation these words clearly meant social equality of the races, the despised doctrine of Radical Reconstruction. Basil Manly, speaking for the South, promptly rejected the proposal because of its implied "political" objectives. Thus ended the most serious effort to reunite Baptist denominational work after the war. Unless Southern Baptists could be assured that there would be no violation of their convictions in matters of race, cooperation with the North was out of the question.

This lack of cooperation did not deter the Home Mission Society from expanding its work in the South. It soon became clear that the fears of radicalism among missionaries were unwarranted, whereupon Southern leaders began to praise the work. Especially noteworthy was the approval of Jabez L. M. Curry, who would shortly achieve national prominence as general agent for the Slater and Peabody funds, the largest gifts to Negro education from Northern philanthropy. In a report to the Southern Convention in 1875, Curry even encouraged giving financial

also *Proceedings, SBC, 1868*, pp. 15, 17–20; *1870*, p. 36. For an account of these negotiations by a Southern Baptist, see Robert A. Baker, *Relations between Baptists*, pp. 104–107. Baker stresses disagreements over concepts of denominational administration and control, but he fails to recognize the underlying issue of race.

49. *Baptist Home Missions*, p. 427.

support to the Northern agency for its work with Negroes.[50] Having won the favor of their Southern brethren, the Northern missionaries moved quickly into every Southern state and actually obtained cooperative agreements with most of the state organizations for the joint sponsorship of work with the blacks. In 1882 the society had sixty-seven workers in the South, a figure three times the total force of the Southern Convention's Home Mission Board, and spent $85,000 in the region as compared to the total budget of $29,000 for the Southern board.[51]

The aggressive program of the Northern society raised questions about the continued operation of a separate Southern Convention. The denominational agencies in the South suffered steady financial decline in the postwar years, while the receipts of the Northern society rose sharply. Although the Southern Convention had in repeated actions expressed its determination to remain separate, the cooperation of state bodies with the Northern society kept alive the idea of reunion with Northern Baptists. The issue was finally disposed of at the 1879 convention. After a debate that went on for half a day, the delegates voted to maintain "fraternal" relations with Northern Baptists but to preserve separate organizations.[52] But the real test of continued separation rested with the struggling Home Mission Board of the Southern Convention, which had to bid against the Northern society for the allegiance of Southern churches. Instrumental in laying this issue before the churches was Edwin T. Winkler, pastor-editor in Alabama and author of a widely publicized appeal asking Southern Baptists to support their own mission board. He reviewed the recent spread of Northern agencies in the South, especially the Home Mission Society. "The facts prove beyond the possibility of questions," concluded Winkler, "that the Southern Baptist Convention is being sup-

50. *Proceedings, SBC, 1875,* pp. 72–73.
51. Robert A. Baker, *Relations between Baptists,* pp. 110–116, 171–73; *Baptist Home Missions,* p. 551; William Wright Barnes, *The Southern Baptist Convention, 1845–1953,* pp. 66–67.
52. *Proceedings, SBC, 1879,* pp. 14, 26. Earlier actions favoring separation are reported in *Proceedings, 1866,* p. 20; *1868,* p. 20; *1870,* p. 36; *1875,* p. 73.

planted in its own domain."[53] It was this very fear that led the convention that same year to take steps to revitalize the Home Mission Board by relocating it at Atlanta under a new executive secretary, Isaac T. Tichenor. Tichenor gave up the presidency of Alabama Polytechnic Institute and set out to consolidate Southern Baptists behind the work of the board. At that time less than half of the state conventions were cooperating with the board, but within five years, Tichenor had alliances with every state organization. After ten years the board's annual income reached $100,000, and the number of appointees had multiplied four times.[54] Tichenor's leadership at this critical period is generally credited with saving the Southern Convention from threatened disintegration.

Northern Baptists continued to sponsor mission work in the South even though they were losing official connections with state organizations. Their work touched all aspects of the church life of both races; but the most important phase was the educational work for the blacks, which had begun shortly after the war and increased steadily until it required a full-time superintendent in 1879. By 1882 the Home Mission Society had 78 teachers in a dozen schools. In all, the society had a hand in founding twenty-seven schools by 1894. In that year these schools enrolled nearly five thousand black students and employed 153 teachers at an annual cost to the society of about $100,000. Although much of this training was at the elementary and secondary levels, nine institutions became permanent Negro colleges.[55] Thus, in terms of expenditure and enrollment, Northern Baptist educational effort for Negroes exceeded that of any other denomination.

Southern Baptist work among the Negroes, while considerably

53. William Wright Barnes, *The Southern Baptist Convention, 1845–1953*, p. 76.

54. *Ibid.*, pp. 77–80; Robert A. Baker, *Relations between Baptists*, p. 155; Joe W. Burton, *Epochs of Home Missions* (Atlanta, 1945), pp. 74–76; William Wright Barnes, "Home Mission Board," p. 646.

55. Charles L. White, *A Century of Faith* (Philadelphia, 1932), pp. 104–106. *Baptist Home Missions*, pp. 438–66, has a description of each school. A comparison of denominational efforts appears in U. S. Department of the Interior, Bureau of Education, *Negro Education* (Washington, D. C., 1917), I, 307.

less than that of Northern agencies, was never altogether lack-ing.[56] The Southern effort suffered mainly from a lack of conti-nuity and coordination. Several state conventions reported work with Negroes occasionally, but no state had a continuous pro-gram. The Home Mission Board assigned missionaries to the blacks, but only for certain years. For brief periods the board held short-term institutes for Negro ministers and also assisted a considerable number of black ministers—eighty-six in 1890—but always on an irregular basis. A most promising program to unify all Negro missionary and educational work appeared in 1894. Known as the New Era Plan, it provided for the coordina-tion of Northern and Southern Baptist work with that of the Negro organizations. Hailed as the final answer for a mission program to the blacks, the announced plan received high praise all across the South. Its implementation, however, required forceful leadership and strong support from all parties, neither of which materialized. The plan went into full operation in only four states and employed no more than a dozen workers. After 1900 the promising cooperative effort quietly disappeared.[57]

The absence of systematic work among Negroes is all the more remarkable in view of the continuous attention given to racial problems in denominational circles. The urgent needs of the race were emphasized at almost every state and Southern convention and frequently occupied the columns of the Baptist press. The denomination, fully conscious of the social deprivations of the blacks, seemed incapable of constructive proposals which would effect any real change in their social position. Perhaps the real significance of the attention Southern Baptists gave to the race lies in their awareness of the problems confronting blacks and their chronic failure to contribute substantially toward improv-ing those conditions.

Still unexplained is why so much confessed concern and ad-mitted obligation produced so little practical effort. Of course,

56. Wright, p. 372; Rufus B. Spain, "Attitudes and Reactions of Southern Baptists to Certain Problems of Society, 1865–1900" (Ph.D. diss., Vanderbilt University, 1961), pp. 84, 93, 100, 105–106, 112–15.
57. Robert A. Baker, Relations between Baptists, pp. 190, 194–95; Charles L. White, p. 117; Proceedings, SBC, 1900, app. B, p. lxxii.

all denominational agencies were extremely hard pressed for funds, at least until the 1880's. Also the high proportion of Negroes who were already Baptists—frequently cited as reasons to help the blacks—probably lessened any sense of urgency among whites for supporting missions to the blacks. By 1890, Negro Baptists already equalled the number of white Baptists in the South, and the percentage of Baptists in the black population far exceeded that for the whites.[58]

As for the unwillingness of white Baptists to support any effective program to uplift blacks socially, the best answer seems to be that any such effort would have run against the mainstream of contemporary Southern policy. From the time of emancipation to the end of the century, Southern whites united to determine that the freedmen made equal under the Constitution would not enjoy equality in education, economic opportunity, social relations, or civil rights. The overwhelming evidence indicates that the highest expressions of conscience among Southern Baptists did not challenge their society's general pattern of discrimination. There were some notable exceptions, such as the defense of the Negro's voting rights by the Virginia Baptist newspaper and the Southern Convention in the late 1870's. On several occasions denominational bodies condemned racial violence and lynchings. But in the main, Southern Baptists, as often as other whites, endorsed the social practices and legal guarantees which assured white supremacy. They offered no measurable deterrent to the wave of anti-Negro legislation following the Populist movement of the 1890's. In fact, when states sought to disenfranchise Negroes through discriminatory voter requirements, all the Baptists newspapers in the South defended such legislation.[59]

Racial discrimination was the natural product of certain un-

58. Edwin Scott Gaustad, *Historical Atlas of Religion in America* (New York, 1962), pp. 148, 150; Riley, *A History of the Baptists*, pp. 322–23; William Wright Barnes, *The Southern Baptist Convention, 1845–1953*, app. A.

59. This paragraph is based in part on the findings of Spain, *At Ease in Zion*, pp. 69–93, 120–22, and Carl Dean English, "The Ethical Emphasis of the Editors of the Baptist Journals Published in the Southeastern Region of the United States, 1856–1915" (Th.D. thesis, Southern Baptist Theological Seminary, 1948), pp. 170–71.

disputed assumptions regarding the Negro's inferiority. Typical were the views of Edwin T. Winkler, Alabama editor and denominational official who was considered an authority on matters of race. Although he once addressed the American Baptist Home Mission Society on Negro education, Winkler remained unreconstructed on the Negro's social status. In 1874 a national journal reported his observations on Negro laborers in which he concluded that the freedmen were hopelessly indolent. Winkler saw no connection between lack of ambition and limited opportunity. Laziness was an incurable racial characteristic. He seriously proposed that the Negroes be sent to Mexico "where they may rest amid such conditions . . . as suits their constitution and their instincts. There they will feel at home, as they bask in the sun, and feast upon the spontaneous fruit of the tropics."[60] Southern Baptists literature abounds with reference to the myths about race so essential to white supremacy: the Negro's supposed preference for subordination, the divine sanctity of segregation, and miscegenation as the greatest evil associated with race and the certain consequence of social equality. These beliefs led Southern Baptists to defend separated churches in the interest of racial purity, to favor special education in trades on grounds of the race's inferiority, and to justify subjugation of blacks for the sake of social harmony. In short, they gave moral support to the whole Jim Crow system of discrimination that became part of Southern law at the close of the century.[61]

Southern Baptists revealed their commitment to racial inequality even when speaking of their religious mission to the Negro. In almost every instance, appeals to help the Negro were little more than calls for increased evangelism, which in itself entailed no threat to white supremacy. Moreover, the task of evangelism sometimes was presented as a means of upholding the existing racial system. One of the most revealing documents in this connection was the Home Mission Board report for 1891.

60. Charles H. Otken, *The Ills of the South* (New York, 1894), p. 257. Winkler was author of a catechism for slaves. He was president of the Home Mission Board for ten years. For his over-all conservative views, see Hugh C. Davis, "Edwin T. Winkler, Baptist Bayard," *Alabama Review*, Jan., 1965, pp. 33–44.
61. English, pp. 149–58; Spain, *At Ease in Zion*, pp. 69–96.

It was concerned with that critical problem in any biracial society: harmony between the races. According to the report, social peace could be maintained only if the Negro "understands and cheerfully accepts" a "subordinate place" in society. The board viewed its own work of evangelism as having a vital relationship to the achievement of this end. "We do not hesitate to affirm our confident belief that an expenditure . . . of fifty thousand dollars a year through the Home Mission Board . . . for the next ten years will settle this race question forever."[62] One can wonder about the seriousness of such a claim, but there is not a doubt about the attempt to make the gospel subservient to the demands of the secular order. This idea often appeared in discussions about race. At the close of the century, in a summary of its fifty-five year history, the board considered it necessary to emphasize that all its work with Negroes had been conducted with a "proper respect for the existing and ineradicable social conditions."[63] That Southern Baptists could represent as a legitimate gospel ministry a work which reinforced an admittedly discriminatory race policy shows that, on this issue, they were no less captives of their culture than they had been before the Civil War.

62. *Proceedings, SBC, 1891*, app. B, p. xxxvi.
63. *Ibid., 1900*, app. B, p. cxxvii.

III

BAPTIST BOURBONISM

The last days of Reconstruction marked the beginning of the New South, generally regarded as a time when the region turned from its rural past to economic diversification and industrial progress. The new leaders who overthrew the Reconstruction governments throughout the South were white business and professional men anxious to see their states promote industrial growth. Promising to end the extravagance and corruption associated with Radical Reconstruction, they established the one-party, "solid" South by uniting whites as Conservative Democrats. Posing as saviors of white society, they reduced educational and welfare services and earned the political label Bourbon because of their social conservatism. The New South's ruling oligarchy, representing the rising industrial class rather than the old planter aristocracy, managed the finances, railroad investments, and land holdings of the states, often to the enrichment of businesses in which they held interests.

Bourbon rule did almost nothing for the rural population, which had been suffering from a declining economy since the Civil War. Farmers' Alliance organizations in the West and South were trying to remedy a variety of national agricultural ills: low prices, high farm costs, inadequate credit, and excessive profits to middlemen. The agrarian revolt in the South, reaching small farmers of both races, fought for tax relief, public education, improved roads, dollar inflation, election reforms, business regulation, and an end to convict-leasing. The Southern Alliance, challenging the Bourbons for control of the Democratic party, managed to elect four governors and to win control of four state legislatures and two constitutional conventions in 1890. Thereafter the movement turned to the Populist party which tried, unsuccessfully, to unite white and black farmers and workers as an effective opposition party.

The agrarian revolt faltered when it assaulted the white solidarity effected by the Bourbon Democrats, even though the Bourbons themselves sometimes violated the principle of lily-white politics by using black votes against the Populists. The use of Negro votes by both sides revived white fears of "Negro domination." If whites divided, the blacks might gain political advantages that would undermine white supremacy. Southern whites sacrificed their differences in order to eliminate the black vote by enacting new voting requirements. Disfranchisement was the first step in creating the Jim Crow system that separated the races by law in public institutions and in privately owned restaurants, hotels, and transportation facilities.[1]

Although it was a major protest movement, the agrarian revolt made only a slight impression on Southern religion. The Baptist affiliation of Mississippi minister-educator Charles H. Otken, author of one of the best contemporary criticisms of the crop lien, and of layman Leonidas L. Polk, head of the Southern Alliance and a foremost Populist, had no apparent influence on church officialdom. Baptist conventions generally ignored agricultural problems altogether. A few Baptist editors endorsed the Farmers' Alliance and occasionally complained about railroad rates, speculation in farm goods, and credit costs; but taken all together, this sympathy for the farmers' cause was ironically negligible in view of the preponderance of rural churches in the denomination.[2]

1. Most useful for the period of Bourbon rule and Populism in the South are Comer Vann Woodward, *Origins of the New South, 1877–1913* (Baton Rouge, 1951), chaps. 1, 7, 9, 12; and Thomas D. Clark and Albert Kirwan, *The South Since Appomattox* (New York, 1967), chap. 3.
2. *Alabama Baptist* (Montgomery), March 1, 1888; *The Religious Herald* (Richmond), July 21, 1870; Oct. 16, 1884. I am much indebted to Spain's examination of convention minutes and periodicals in *At Ease in Zion*, pp. 127–35.

Baptist spokesmen, for the most part, expressed attitudes that were more Bourbon than Populist. Although country born, the denomination's leaders spent their mature years in the stronger town and city churches where they identified more with merchants, bankers, and professionals than with agrarian agitators. Preoccupied with church expansion and the strengthening of the denomination, most of them considered the ills of agriculture to be outside the realm of legitimate religious concern as revealed by their occasional attempts to address themselves to agrarian problems. These churchmen simply did not understand how agricultural conditions in an industrial society were determined by forces beyond the control of individual farmers. The clerical editors, many of whom privately owned their papers, treated farm problems in terms of the Puritan social ethic, which associated failure with some deficiency of character. Thus, the Georgia editor, after approving united action through farm organizations, concluded that the farmer's success depended "primarily on his own individual efforts, thrift and economy." A Tennessee journal advised farmers, suffering at the hands of monopolists and creditors, to trust God and economize. If the Baptist conscience was greatly disturbed by the crop lien, tenant, and sharecrop systems, the denomination's records fail to show it.[3]

On economic questions touching the industrial society, Southern Baptists were somewhat more outspoken. Their views differed little from those of conservative church leaders in the North who defended property rights against organized labor.[4] Most Southern Baptist editors accepted laissez faire economics without question and sided with employers in labor disputes. Successful businessmen turned philanthropists, such as Andrew Carnegie and John D. Rockefeller, were praised for their stewardship in furthering the "redemption of mankind."[5] Editors accepted uncritically the ideology of business success that made

3. *The Christian Index* (Atlanta), June 7, 1888, p. 13; *Baptist and Reflector* (Nashville), July 10, 1890, p. 8.
4. Henry F. May examined Northern clergymen's labor views in *Protestant Churches and Industrial America* (New York, 1949), pp. 91–106.
5. English, pp. 230–31.

material prosperity evidence of divine favor and poverty the just reward for imprudence. *The Religious Herald* defended inequality of wealth as the result of "natural and immutable laws" and advised the poor, lacking the virtues of industry, perseverance, and economy, not to envy the rich but to accept the state for which God had chosen them.[6]

In only a few instances did Baptist periodicals attack the evils of corporate wealth or complain about government favors to business. Among editors, J. W. Bailey of North Carolina was most critical of big business. He repeatedly supported improvements for workers and government regulation of the trusts. On one occasion, he went so far as to criticize a Baptist school in North Carolina for accepting "tainted money" from the Standard Oil Company.[7]

Bailey's editorials, however, were quite moderate compared to a series of articles on economic reform published in the Kentucky church journal in 1886.[8] Written by Arthur Yager, a political scientist at Georgetown College, a Baptist school in the state, they reflected the point of view of the newly formed American Economic Association, composed of liberal churchmen and professors who opposed laissez faire economics. Yager stoutly defended organized labor's use of the strike and boycott. Occasional acts of violence, he argued, should be overlooked in view of the justice of labor's goal to equalize its bargaining position against capital. Yager contended that the whole free-enterprise system was "fundamentally wrong" and must give way to a new form of cooperative industry before the interests of labor and the general public could be protected against the depredations of corporate wealth. He called for a "social revolution," ending in some form of state-controlled economy. Organized religion also received a share of criticism: "The morality of the church," he wrote, "is tainted by compromise with the

6. May 2, 1878, p. 2. See also Apr. 4, 1872, p. 2; and *The Christian Index* (Atlanta), July 19, 1883, p. 8.
7. English, pp. 238–41.
8. The five articles appeared on the front page of the *Western Recorder* (Louisville), Apr. 15, 29; May 6, 13, and 20, 1886.

existing order of things."[9] Yager's judgments, of course, were much too harsh to win support from his fellow Baptists, as evidenced by the writings of the Kentucky editor, who suggested in an antilabor editorial during the series that the proposed eight-hour day would only mean more time spent in riotous drinking and debasing amusements.[10]

Southern Baptist commentary on the labor question revealed mixed attitudes about union activity.[11] Usually they supported the goals but not the methods of organized labor. They upheld the right to organize, favored higher wages and shorter hours, advocated improved working conditions, and condemned child labor; however, when disputes led to strikes, picketing, and acts of violence, they turned against the unions. During the great labor disputes of the period, Baptist editors invariably blamed the unions for violating property rights. In their eyes, the disruption of social peace justified the use of troops against strikers. After the Pullman strike of 1894, the Georgia editor recommended the "bayonet and the bullet, promptly and fearlessly applied," as the proper way to handle labor violence.[12]

When Southern Baptists discussed labor problems, they displayed little comprehension of the great economic changes of their time. While they would allow workers the right to organize, they denied unions the power to equalize their bargaining position by collective action. The Baptists' failure to appreciate the complexity of labor problems was most apparent when they proposed sweeping moralisms as solutions to industrial disputes. The mission board in North Carolina, responding to labor discontent in the cotton mills in 1900, proposed that gospel

9. *Ibid.*, May 20, 1886, p. 1.
10. *Ibid.*, May 6, 1886, p. 41.
11. English, pp. 227–48, surveys the labor views of editors. See also Spain, *At Ease in Zion*, pp. 136–41.
12. *The Christian Index* (Atlanta), July 19, 1894, p. 4. The newspaper gave seven columns to denunciations of union activities and accused prolabor Governor John Peter Altgeld of being in "sympathy with the anarchists who would destroy our government." Antilabor editorials appeared on June 15, 1882, p. 8, and Nov. 23, 1882, p. 12. Similar views in other Baptist newspapers are cited in Spain, *At Ease in Zion*, pp. 136–41.

preaching was "the best remedy and surest preventative of the bloodshed, arson and war" that accompanied labor disputes. The Alabama Convention summed up the Christian message on the matter in two scriptural injunctions: employers were enjoined to "Do justly, love mercy and walk humbly with thy God," while workers were admonished to "Be content with your wages." The frequent references to "brotherhood" and the "golden rule" as remedies for economic conflict rested on the faulty assumption that evils in the industrial economy were caused by unregenerate men and not by imperfections in a system that left large concentrations of economic power free from government control and the demands of organized labor.[13]

The Baptists of the New South era echoed the praises of industrialization in the belief that it would save the region from economic backwardness, but at the same time they were apprehensive about losing their own cultural supremacy in an urbanized society. The problem that most concerned them was not one of slums, sweatshops, or child labor but the threat that foreign elements presented to their traditional religious and social values. Southern Baptists feared a mixed culture almost as much as they feared mixed races. Opposition to foreigners was cast in terms of preserving the purity of Southern culture from the unorthodox, the un-American, and the immoral. A report to the Southern Convention in 1890 warned that the "Rationalists and Socialists and Anarchists, and other heathens, who pollute by mere contact of association, are pouring into our Southland from materialistic Europe."[14] Southern Baptists were even more opposed to alien religious ideas, particularly Roman Catholicism. A Home Mission Board report on immigration lamented: "But the great misfortune of all of this is that these foreigners bring with them . . . their Romanism, and their want of morals. We

---

13. *The Religious Herald* (Richmond), June 2, 1887, p. 2, affirmed that "Christ has said all that is needful on this subject . . . the gospel and a pure Christianity present the remedy." *Baptist and Reflector* (Nashville), July 5, 1894, p. 1, on the occasion of the Pullman strike advised labor and management to "bear ye one another's burdens, and so fulfill the law of Christ." See also *Minutes, North Carolina, 1900* (Raleigh, 1900), p. 26; *Minutes, Alabama, 1886*, p. 12.

14. *Proceedings, SBC, 1890*, p. 16.

must evangelize them, or they will overwhelm us."[15] Although the Home Board responded to the presence of immigrants by increasing mission work in the cities, it clearly considered foreigners more of a menace than a missionary opportunity.

The problems thus far examined—the farm revolt, labor organization, and industrialization—were secular in nature. Among Southern Baptists, of course, private morality occupied a place of much greater importance than did secular issues, and they were certainly far more influential in determining standards of personal conduct than in shaping secular institutions. From their European beginnings, the Baptists had stressed the pietistic side of religion, which conformed easily to the individualism of the American revivals. The very success of the revivals created a problem of preserving the faith of converts who entered the churches with little religious preparation. To insure against impiety and unorthodoxy, local congregations relied on the practice of church discipline, by which erring members were subjected to public examination. Those guilty of sin or false doctrine were censured, suspended, or excluded from the fellowship, depending on the seriousness of their offense. Restoration could be effected, but only after an appropriate confession before the congregation.[16]

Although abandoned in more recent years, church discipline was a vital part of the life of nineteenth-century Baptists.[17] The most common causes for disciplinary action arose from participation in worldly amusements, such as drinking, gambling, card-playing, and dancing. Even the offenses of lying, cursing, and gossiping were subject to investigation. Churches sometimes exercised authority over cases of theft, assault, libel, civil disputes, and marital discord—matters usually under the jurisdiction of public agencies. By promoting a more upright and orderly com-

---

15. *Ibid.*, 1895, p. 38
16. A brief history of this practice together with a reproduction of the Discipline used by the Charleston Association in the eighteenth century appears in James Leo Garrett, *Baptist Church Discipline* (Nashville, 1962).

17. James Edward Humphrey, "Baptist Discipline in Kentucky, 1781–1860" (Th.D. thesis, Southern Baptist Theological Seminary, 1959), pp. 145–48, examined the state's five oldest congregations and found 1,636 discipline cases before 1860, of which more than half resulted in exclusion.

munity, Baptist churches became important civilizing agents, especially in frontier communities lacking well-established legal and educational institutions. Historians have long emphasized the individualism fostered by frontier religion, but the administration of Baptist discipline indicates that churches were also important in securing individual conformity to social norms.[18]

Not content with trying to order the lives of their own members, Baptists sought to control the morals of the whole community. Assuming that the morals of the good Christian should be those of the general citizenry, they considered it only proper to employ civil power to achieve this end. This use of secular power for moral ends, a practice that became increasingly apparent during the New South period when an industrialized society threatened traditional moral values, constituted a significant development in the social attitudes of Southern Baptists because it opened the way for greater denominational involvement in those social and political issues that would challenge American churches in the twentieth century.

The attempts to prevent the secularization of the Sabbath demonstrated the church's increasing reliance on the coercive power of the state. Church discipline against members who violated the Sabbath could not begin to determine community standards in an urban society. All major Protestant groups in the late nineteenth century reacted to the threat. Church-going Americans feared that immigrants would make the Sabbath a day of recreation and that industrialists would make it a day of work. As various organizations sought to unite church sentiment behind Sabbath legislation, Southern Baptists set aside their usual exclusive church policy to join the crusade. The Southern Convention and many state bodies supported the Sabbath or-

18. Posey, *The Baptist Church in the Lower Mississippi Valley*, pp. 38–53; Paschal, *History of North Carolina Baptists*, II, 216–36; W. Morgan Patterson, "Discipline in Baptist Churches and Culture on the Early Frontier," *Review and Expositor*, LXI (Winter, 1964), 538. The idea of churches as moral courts was first developed by William Warren Sweet. See his "The Churches as Moral Courts on the Frontier," *Church History*, II (Mar., 1933), 3–21. T. Scott Miyakawa's *Protestants and Pioneers, Individualism and Conformity on the American Frontier* (Chicago, 1964), develops the thesis that frontier religion fostered social conformity and organizations at the expense of individualism.

ganizations and favored numerous kinds of Sabbath legislation. Only a few leaders raised questions about the propriety of such action as a departure from reliance upon the individual's conscience in matters of religion. Most ministers readily accepted the advantages that civil power would offer in achieving a religious goal they believed to be beneficial to society as a whole. Thus, Southern Baptists adopted, almost unconsciously, one of the basic methods of an established church where their numbers could significantly influence public policy.[19]

Temperance reform offers an even better example of the use of civil authority for moral purposes. The temperance movement in America began with the limited objective of curtailing the excessive use of spiritous liquors. By the time of the founding of the American Temperance Union in 1833, the goal had changed from urging sobriety through moral suasion to demanding total abstinence and the legal suppression of the production and sale of all fermented and distilled beverages. The movement produced local-option laws in many areas and prohibition in thirteen Northern states by 1855. Since most of the state-wide dry laws were repealed or nullified by the courts within two decades, the prohibitionists launched a second drive in the 1880's that brought temporary success in a few Northern states.[20]

It has been customary for historians to treat temperance as one of the many social reforms that originated in the North during the second quarter of the nineteenth century. In the South, such movements as pacifism, feminism, collectivistic communities, not to mention abolitionism, made little headway; temperance, on the other hand, enjoyed wide support even though little legislation resulted. Southern Baptists, although never at the forefront of the national effort, supported the temperance cause from the beginning. Georgia Baptists, for example, provided many

19. The views of church people on proper Sabbath observation are treated in Francis P. Weisenburger, *Triumph of Faith: Contribution of the Church to American Life, 1865–1900* (Richmond, 1962), chap. 7. For Southern Baptist reactions, see English, pp. 65–116; *Proceedings, SBC, 1889*, p. 38; Spain, "Attitudes of Southern Baptists," pp. 323–26.

20. An excellent, brief account of prohibition is Clark Warburton, "Prohibition," *Encyclopedia of the Social Sciences*, XII (1935), 499–510.

leaders for the cause in that state, among them Adiel Sherwood, who founded the state's first temperance society in 1827. Plans for a state-wide organization received encouragement the next year at the Baptist convention, after which many of the delegates helped create the Georgia Temperance Society with Sherwood as secretary. Jesse Mercer, president of the state convention from 1822 to 1841, founded the first temperance journal in the South in 1834 and later promoted the cause as editor of the state Baptist journal.[21]

Baptists in other states similarly supported temperance from the 1830's onward. State conventions had temperance committees advocating total abstinence, promoting temperance societies, and offering memorials to legislatures.[22] Missionaries appointed by the Virginia Convention were instructed to work for temperance reform.[23] Every Baptist editor in the ante-bellum years supported the cause,[24] among them William Sands, the Virginia editor for three decades. Like many editors, he often wrote about the use of intoxicants by church members, concluding that total abstinence should be a condition for membership. He directed most of his attention to the manufacture and sale of alcohol. He considered the liquor business to be the nation's greatest social evil and the direct cause of most crime, pauperism, and broken homes. Sands urged his readers to work for the abolition of the liquor industry and voiced the thoughts of the majority of Baptists when he described such effort as a positive Christian duty and the highest form of patriotism and social service.[25]

21. Ragsdale, III, 83–87.

22. Paschal, *History of North Carolina Baptists*, II, 304, noted the existence of a state temperance committee as early as 1833. For some of the earliest and most significant reports to state Baptist conventions, see *Proceedings, Mississippi, 1838*, pp. 7–8; *1839*, p. 8; *1853*, p. 28; *Proceedings, Tennessee, 1839*, p. 16; *Minutes, Alabama, 1839*, pp. 8–9; *1842*, p. 7; *1845*, p. 17; *1846*, pp. 9–10; *Minutes of the Maryland Baptist Union Association, 1841* (Baltimore, 1841), p. 13; *Minutes, Georgia, 1842*, p. 12; *1844*, p. 15; *1846*, p. 16; *Minutes, Texas, 1854*, pp. 16–17; *1854*, p. 24.

23. *Minutes, Virginia, 1848*, p. 8. Reports in subsequent years indicated that the missionaries did promote temperance.

24. Crook, pp. 34–84.

25. *Ibid.*, pp. 34–41; *The Religious Herald* (Richmond), Mar. 1, 1833, p. 31; Mar. 8, 1833, p. 34; Dec. 15, 1835, p. 109; July 31, 1856, p. 2.

For Baptists, probably the greatest contribution to the temperance cause came from the local churches after they adopted a policy of total abstinence. Early nineteenth-century Baptists drank ardent spirits without censure, sometimes even at church gatherings. Although the frontier church allowed moderate "dram drinking," it had to wage constant war on drunkenness and related vices. A Baptist historian of the 1840's confessed that drunkenness was the "besetting sin" of many church members. Ante-bellum church records indicate that drinking accounted for more disciplinary action than any other cause. Investigations of misconduct often established a connection between drinking and other vices—infidelity, brawling, gambling, dancing, and profanity. Determined to control the morality of their members, the churches came to recognize the practical advantages of total abstinence, with the position gaining acceptance among temperance advocates in the 1830's.[26]

By mid-century the prevailing sentiment of Baptists condemned the liquor industry as inherently evil and insisted that total abstinence alone satisfied the Christian ideal.[27] The doctrinal statement widely used by churches in the 1850's specifically required members "to abstain from the sale and use of intoxicating drinks."[28] After the Civil War, when the national temperance movement was on the wane, Southern Baptists solidified their stand against alcoholic beverages,[29] and no less than ten state conventions between 1872 and 1894 admonished congregations to exclude members who used alcohol.[30] However, it is unlikely that denominational bodies in the free-church tradition would have taken such action had not leadership at the local level already reached a general consensus on the matter.

26. Posey, *The Baptist Church in the Lower Mississippi Valley*, pp. 42–43; Hosea Holcombe, *A History of the Rise and Progress of the Baptists in Alabama* (Philadelphia, 1840), p. 344; Humphrey, pp. 148–51.

27. Humphrey, pp. 152–54; Crook, pp. 83–84.

28. Raymond A. Parker, "Church Covenant," *Encyclopedia of Southern Baptists*, I (1958), 283.

29. Spain, *At Ease in Zion*, p. 177. Quite exceptional was a South Carolina editor's refusal to sign a prohibition memorial and his open admission that he occasionally used strong drink. See the *Baptist Courier* (Greenville, S. C.), Apr. 3, 1879, p. 2.

30. Spain, "Attitudes of Southern Baptists," pp. 272–73.

The Southern Baptist Convention reflected the denomination's commitment to total abstinence and legal prohibition when, for the first time, the delegates at the annual meeting in 1886 pledged to use their political and moral influence to destroy the liquor business. The next convention called upon Baptists to cooperate with other religious groups and with temperance organizations. After 1890, the convention supported prohibition at every annual meeting; and following the example of the state conventions, the Southern body in 1896 condemned church members who drank, sold liquor, or even visited a saloon.[31]

When Southern Baptists sanctioned the use of the state's coercive powers to control private morality, as they did in advocating temperance legislation, they were transgressing what they had often declared to be the boundary of proper church activity. The promotion of state-controlled morality would seem to be inharmonious with much of the Baptist tradition: freedom of conscience, church autonomy, and complete separation of church and state. Indeed, Southern Baptists often justified their lack of social activism by insisting that the church's rightful mission was to save individual souls, not society; and that genuine social progress could result only from individual, rather than collective, redemption.[32] It is significant that only rarely was this line of reasoning used to question denominational support of temperance laws in the nineteenth century.[33] The conviction that political action is inappropriate and ineffective as a means of fulfilling the church's mission was to remain an important part of Southern Baptist social attitudes. However, its use would be reserved to oppose involvement in social questions of a more con-

31. *Proceedings, SBC, 1886*, p. 33; *1887*, p. 30; *1896*, p. 45.

32. An excellent example of this attitude appeared in *The Religious Herald* (Richmond), Jan. 11, 1894, p. 1. The editor declared that the true mission of the church was "not to deal directly with communities, state and nation, but with the individual." The Christian's concern, he argued, was not "how to get ready to live down here, but live hereafter; to go to be with Jesus when we die." He conceded that Christ favored social reform, but "he waited for it as a necessary fruit of the blessed gospel received into men's hearts."

33. A resolution against "memorializing" the legislature for a temperance law appears in *Minutes, North Carolina, 1879*, p. 35. However, the convention memorialized the legislature the very next year. For similar opposition to political action, see *Minutes, Georgia, 1891*, p. 33; *Minutes, Alabama, 1893*, p. 55.

troversial nature, such as racial equality, labor relations, and social welfare; it would never seriously interfere with the denomination's participation in the temperance movement.

One possible exception to a record of invariable support of temperance was the Southern Baptist Convention's refusal to endorse the National Prohibition party even though prominent denominational figures headed the minor party in three elections. Green Clay Smith, the party's 1876 nominee, authored the first prohibition statement adopted by the Southern Convention; James B. Cranfill, vice-presidential candidate in 1892, served Texas Baptists as an editor and denominational officer; Joshua Levering, who led the Prohibition party in 1896, was three times president of the Southern Convention. All three men made repeated appearances in behalf of temperance before the Southern Convention, but they were so closely identified with their party that the convention considered it necessary specifically to dissociate itself from the partisan effort.[34]

The failure of the Prohibition party to win denominational endorsement can be explained on grounds other than opposition in principle to partisan politics. At no time did the party poll more than 2 percent of the national vote, failing even to gain solid backing from the nation's temperance forces. With so little promise of success, the party provided no real test of the willingness of Baptists to engage in corporate political action. Moreover, the leadership of the party was mostly Northern; and many of its goals, such as voting rights without regard to race or sex, liberal immigration, arbitration of international disputes, and direct election of the President, seemed quite radical by Southern standards.[35] Finally, the partisan approach to prohibition directly challenged Democratic solidarity in the South, and Southern Baptists were too much a part of their culture to depart from political orthodoxy.

Of course, Baptists were quite prepared to join a dry movement that would not threaten the solid South's one-party system,

34. "Prohibition Party," *The Cyclopaedia of Temperance and Prohibition* (1891), pp. 559–80; *Proceedings, SBC, 1887*, p. 30; *1894*, p. 35.
35. "Prohibition Party," pp. 563–69.

which was precisely the strategy of the Anti-Saloon League, founded in 1895. The league soon took command of the temperance forces and led the fight for national prohibition. Operating as a pressure group and campaigning for dry candidates regardless of party, the league scored quick results in establishing dry areas by local option, after which the organization worked for state-wide prohibition. The league's most spectacular gains were made in the South, which by 1913 had become a dry stronghold. An important reason for the league's success in the South was the solid commitment of the Baptists to prohibition prior to the league's operations in the region.[36]

When Southern Baptists joined the prohibition movement they were engaging in social reform activity to a degree not known since their struggles for religious freedom in the eighteenth century. The dry crusade thus serves as a useful dividing point in describing the development of the denomination's social attitudes. Half a century had passed since the founding of the Southern Baptist Convention, during which time the organization had retained much of its original character and social outlook. It remained a distinctly regional body, upholding social and theological tradition with a sense of special religious mission. In the post-Civil War years the denomination had concerned itself chiefly with internal matters: the survival of institutions and agencies, missionary expansion, and theological orthodoxy.[37] Although emancipation had removed the original issue dividing the Baptists, the Southern Convention held to its separate ways, consequently isolating itself from much of the social and theological ferment of the period. Religious readjustments necessitated by emancipation were made in accordance with deeply rooted regional beliefs. Specifically, the Baptists adopted racial separation in their churches as the most practical way to reconcile the Negro's freedom with white supremacy. For much the same reason, they later approved segregation as applied to social relations in general.

36. Herbert Asbury, *The Great Illusion, an Informal History of Prohibition* (Garden City, N. Y., 1950), pp. 99–100.

37. William Wright Barnes, *The Southern Baptist Convention, 1845–1953,* chaps. 5–9.

Southern Baptists were not well prepared to respond to the great social changes of the New South period. Their history and rural background had forged strong ties of loyalty to traditional cultural values. Facing a new industrial order, they failed to recognize the need for new ethical evaluations, expressing strong concern only over the loss of status they might suffer in an urbanized society. Numerically, at least, the New South did not alter the dominant position of the Baptists. At the end of the century, they enjoyed a growth rate exceeding that of not only all other churches but also the general population.[38] As the largest church group in all the former Confederate states except Louisiana, they bore a heavy responsibility for moral leadership. Their failure to measure up to this responsibility indicates that numerical superiority on the part of democratic churches preaching a voluntary faith does not assure moral initiative. Rather, churches successful in reaching the masses through an emphasis on the personal and spiritual side of religion tend to accept the values and institutions of their culture as divinely ordered.

If Southern Baptists may be indicted for the character of their response to the ills of the postwar South, they must also be credited with some evidence of improvement in social attitudes by the end of the century. Never again would this denomination be quite so uniformly conservative and slow to respond or so generally unenlightened and narrow in perspective. The development of a broader sense of social responsibility was associated most immediately with the prohibition movement. The dry crusade, to which Southern Baptists gave unqualified support, differed in important respects from their earlier attempts to combat the drink evil. Originating in the North, the Anti-Saloon League united church groups in aggressive political action. Moreover, the dry campaign was but one part of the much broader Progressive movement, which sought to correct many of the social ills that attended the industrial order. Prohibition

38. U. S. Department of Commerce and Labor, Bureau of the Census, *Religious Bodies: 1906* (Washington, D. C., 1910), I, 26, 40, 48, 55, 58. This report showed Baptists ahead in ten former Confederate states—Louisiana being the exception—plus Kentucky. They had more than half the church membership in Virginia, South Carolina, Georgia, Alabama, and Mississippi.

brought Southern Baptists into the arena of social action, where they soon became aware of issues other than temperance. Prohibition also helped to broaden the social concern of Southern Baptists because it had close ties to the social-gospel movement, that theological reorientation in American Protestantism which became the religious counterpart of progressivism.[39] The social-gospel movement challenged Protestant churches to support the social reforms of the progressive era. Thus, when Southern Baptists joined the dry crusade, they were beginning to affiliate with national movements of social protest while adopting the essential idea of the social gospel—direct church participation in social causes.

39. Aaron Ignatius Abell, *The Urban Impact on American Protestantism, 1865–1900* (Cambridge, Mass., 1943), 47; May, p. 126. The ideological connections between prohibition on the one hand and the social gospel and progressivism on the other have been convincingly demonstrated by James H. Timberlake, *Prohibition and the Progressive Movement, 1900–1920* (Cambridge, Mass., 1963), pp. 1–38. Timberlake argues that prohibition, like progressivism, was a middle-class movement concerned about the loss of the traditional American values of success, hard work, and thrift. Drunkenness was viewed as the destroyer of economic opportunity, political democracy, and an orderly society. Prohibitionists shared the optimistic hope of a better world that was characteristic of the social gospel and progressivism.

IV

THE SOCIAL GOSPEL MOVES SOUTH

During the years from Reconstruction to the end of the century, a generation of enterprising businessmen in industry, transportation, manufacturing, and finance built a new economic order in America and in the process created an enormous complex of social problems. While the economic lords of creation were accumulating vast fortunes by exploiting the nation's natural and human resources, millions of culturally unassimilated immigrants were crowding into unplanned cities to supply cheap labor for uncontrolled capital. Labor's unequal struggle for a larger share of the prosperity won little sympathy from public officials or the popular mind. Corporate wealth, on the other hand, was immune from public control while exercising decisive economic and political power over the nation. The economic injustices that could be attributed to industrialization presented a critical challenge to the nation's moral leadership, a challenge that was answered by the social-gospel movement. Essentially, the social gospel applied the ethics of Christianity to the unprecedented problems of an industrial society and thereby inspired American Protestantism's most productive movement for social reform.[1]

Churches of the Gilded Age initially reacted to industrialization either by openly defending the new order or by ignoring

1. The principal works on the social gospel are Charles Howard Hopkins, *The Rise of the Social Gospel in American Protestantism, 1865–1915* (New Haven, 1940); Abell, *The Urban Impact on American Protestantism*; and Henry F. May, *Protestant Churches and Industrial America*.

economic ills as irrelevant to religion. The more prestigious, old-line denominations followed the former course. Dependent on men of wealth, they disapproved of labor agitation and remained aloof from reform movements. The more influential urban churches were distinctly middle- and upper-class institutions presided over by well-educated clergy who made Calvinism conform to the success goals of their property-minded membership.[2]

Protestant acceptance of the existing order was reinforced by the revival tradition. Churches offering an otherworldly hope through personal conversion usually did not get involved in grave social issues.[3] Baptist political activity of the eighteenth century had been restricted to securing religious liberty. And although some pre-Civil War evangelists, notably Charles G. Finney, had supported humanitarian causes, most evangelists had confined their reform efforts to private morality and works of charity. Even so, it must not be supposed that religion directed toward the individual remained entirely neutral as the nation reexamined social policies and institutions. Evangelists from Dwight L. Moody onward, while devoting more attention to the neglected urban masses, found no fault with the industrial system; for revivals were often sponsored by employers who recognized the economic value of high morals among their workers. Thus, by presenting morality in terms of individual rather than social reform, revivalism functioned as a socially conservative force with the practical effect of upholding traditional values and institutions against basic social changes.[4]

Since neither the traditional churches of the socially dominant

2. Garrison, pp. 15–16, 147; Abell, pp. 3–5; Hopkins, *The Rise of the Social Gospel*, p. 16.

3. May, pp. 23–24.

4. Gilbert Hobbes Barnes, pp. 9–16; Charles C. Cole, Jr., *The Social Ideas of the Northern Evangelists, 1826–1860* (New York, 1954), pp. 15–16, 96–131, 204. Timothy L. Smith argues, in *Revivalism and Social Reform in Mid-Nineteenth Century* (Nashville, 1957), pp. 80–94, that the social gospel had its roots in the pre-Civil War revivals; but his evidence seems to substantiate the conclusions in this paragraph. The social conservatism of revivalists is a major theme in William G. McLoughlin, Jr., *Modern Revivalism: Charles Grandison Finney to Billy Graham* (New York, 1959), pp. 5–6, 56, 106–107, 116–17, 252–59, 276–80, 289, 294, 297–98, 306–26, 437–45, 478–82, 503–12, 526.

classes nor the revival-type religion of the masses offered an adequate answer to the problems of industrial America, Protestant thought had to undergo a thorough reorientation before ethical authority could be reasserted. Pioneers of the social-gospel movement took something of the revival zeal and something from the state-church notion of moral responsibility for public affairs and combined with them the prophetic element of social criticism. To alleviate the urban-centered problems of slums, crime, political corruption, and industrial strife, all of which they viewed as products of a fundamentally unjust social order to which churches had failed to apply ethical judgments, the clergy established weekday charitable, educational, and recreational programs. Further, they championed the cause of organized labor and advocated government control of corporate wealth.[5]

Many church agencies and organizations were founded to promote social Christianity. Some operated within denominational bounds while others reflected the trend toward union among Protestants to promote effective social action. The Evangelical Alliance, the Open and Institutional Church League, and the National Federation of Churches and Christian Workers prepared the way for the Federal Council of Churches of Christ in America, organized in 1908 to unite Protestants in the cause of social Christianity. The social creed adopted by the Federal Council of Churches, containing sections on education, health, prohibition, and the family, dealt mainly with improvements for the working class and advocated the "most equitable division of the products of industry that can ultimately be devised."[6]

Although the social gospel was not primarily concerned with questions of doctrine in the usual sense, its ideological roots were in the new liberal theology of the nineteenth century. Biblical scholarship had cast doubts on the literal accuracy of the Holy Writ by updating prophetic passages, showing multiple authorship of certain books, and explaining miracles on natural

5. Abell, pp. 27–28; Hopkins, *The Rise of the Social Gospel*, pp. 12, 24, 49.
6. Hopkins, *The Rise of the Social Gospel*, pp. 56–62, 280, 317; Abell, pp. 90–112, 192; Garrison, p. 165.

grounds. For many Protestants, such studies were undermining the foundations of their theology. At the same time, Congregational minister and writer Horace Bushnell was challenging the revival tradition of spontaneous conversion by showing that salvation could be a process of gradual development. The social-gospel preachers accepted the new theology. For them supernaturalism and otherworldliness too often had been a hindrance to social progress. They preferred the scientific, rational approach of higher criticism, which could be used to attack social conventions that helped perpetuate injustice. Thus, Bushnell's doctrine of Christian nurture heralded a need for a Christianized society that would ensure the proper environment for individual growth.[7]

Ministers from several denominations helped formulate the social gospel, but no group did more than Northern Baptists. Walter Rauschenbusch, professor of church history at Rochester Theological Seminary and one-time pastor in the slums of New York, is generally regarded as the greatest exponent of the new ideology.[8] He retained a strong pietistic faith but made social regeneration the principal task of corporate Christianity. Samuel Zane Batten, chairman of the Northern Baptist Convention's Social Service Commission, stated the essential message of the movement in *The Social Task of Christianity*.[9] Batten believed that the churches had become irrelevant to the industrial age because they had misconstrued or ignored the social intent of Christianity. The church, he argued, must not limit itself to individual evangelism; it must "seek the redemption of society." The crucial problem was no longer "how to make good individuals" but "how to make a good society." The new theology thus rejected Calvinism's pessimistic doctrine of depravity and the evangelical preoccupation with individual salvation. It stressed the goodness of man, the immanence of God, and an earthly view

7. Garrison, p. 88; Henry F. May, pp. 85–87; Hopkins, *The Rise of the Social Gospel*, p. 5.
8. Walter Rauschenbusch, *Christianity and the Social Crisis* (New York, 1909), and *A Theology for the Social Gospel* (New York, 1917). See also Shailer Mathews, *The Social Teachings of Jesus* (New York, 1897).
9. (New York, 1911), pp. 36–37, 42.

of redemption. Sin was interpreted in terms of social environment; salvation, in terms of social reform. Man became God's partner in the reconstruction of the social order.

Students of American religion have treated the social gospel almost exclusively as the Protestant response to the industrialization of the North, apparently in the belief that the South's rural nature, coupled with its conservatism, barred an acceptance of those religious ideas associated with social reform in the North.[10] It is true that the South's industrial development never equaled that of the North; but from the 1880's onward, substantial industrial growth in textiles, tobacco, wood products, and various minerals began to alter the fundamental character of the Southern economy.[11] Equally significantly, the South consciously adopted as its own the industrial standards of the North. The New South propagandists successfully promoted industrialization as a public and private venture, invited investments of local and outside capital, and generally preached the success goals of the business world. If there is a causal relationship between industrialization and social Christianity, one might expect South-

10. The works of Hopkins, Henry F. May, and Abell give no attention to Southern religion. Studies of twentieth-century Protestant social thought by Robert Moats Miller, *American Protestantism and Social Issues, 1919–1939* (Chapel Hill, 1958); and Paul A. Carter, *The Decline and Revival of the Social Gospel: Social and Political Liberalism in American Protestant Churches, 1920–1940* (Ithaca, 1954), likewise exclude Southern churches. Donald Meyer, *The Protestant Search for Political Realism, 1919–1941* (Berkeley, 1960), p. 45, says that Southern Methodists and Southern Presbyterians expressed no social concern until the 1930's, and that Southern Baptists were completely without social passion until 1941. The conclusions of these historians have the support of no less an authority than Comer Vann Woodward, who says that there were no important manifestations of liberal theology, the social gospel, or the ecumenical movement in Southern religion until 1913 (*Origins of the New South*, p. 450). It is my contention that much social thought in Southern religion which can be classified on the liberal side has been overlooked, and that exception must be taken to Woodward's too easy dismissal of social-gospel influence. My own conclusions were arrived at independently, but a few other studies briefly note evidence contrary to Woodward's observation. See Kenneth K. Bailey, *Southern White Protestantism in the Twentieth Century* (New York, 1964), pp. 40–43; Spain, *At Ease in Zion*, pp. 209–10; Virginius Dabney, *The Dry Messiah, The Life of Bishop Cannon* (New York, 1949), pp. 43, 168–70; and Hunter D. Farish, *The Circuit Rider Dismounts, A Social History of Southern Methodism* (Richmond, 1938), pp. 40–43.

11. Simkins, pp. 328–36; John Samuel Ezell, *The South Since 1865* (New York, 1963), chap. 8; Woodward, *Origins of the New South*, p. 17.

ern religion to have produced some form of social Christianity by the turn of the century.

Whatever the degree of industrial growth, a consideration of practical Christianity, particularly in the South, should not be confined to those reforms directed toward a business economy. The long-standing problems of illiteracy, farm tenancy, and racial injustice were in themselves sufficient cause for an aroused social conscience. It was, in fact, the recognition of these chronic problems, along with the problems arising from new Southern industry, that produced widespread social criticism resembling in many of its assumptions, methods, and objectives the ideology of the social gospel.[12]

The campaigns for social betterment drew heavily upon the South's religious resources, even though these crusades were usually conducted under the more secular banner of progressivism. Actually, progressivism and social Christianity were closely related, being the secular and religious aspects of one of the most productive reform eras in American life. Progressivism sought political reforms in the direction of greater democracy while attempting to destroy concentrated economic power in business hands.[13] The social gospel, which fully complemented Progressive aims, stressed humanitarian objectives such as slum

12. A considerable amount of social criticism by Southern liberals appeared in the late nineteenth and early twentieth centuries. George W. Cable's *The Silent South* (New York, 1885) earned the wrath of Southerners because he attacked racial discrimination. On his career as a reformer, see Arlin Turner's *George W. Cable, A Biography* (Durham, 1956), chaps. 14, 15, and 18. The succession of social criticism includes Walter Hines Page, *The Rebuilding of Old Commonwealths* (New York, 1902); Edgar Gardner Murphy, *Problems of the Present South* (New York, 1904); William Alexander MacCorkle, *Some Southern Questions Asked* (New York, 1908); Edwin A. Alderman, *The Growing South* (New York, 1908); Edwin Mims, *The Advancing South, Stories of Progress and Reaction* (New York, 1927); and Virginius Dabney, *Liberalism in the South* (Chapel Hill, 1932). Articles in *Sewanee Review* and *South Atlantic Quarterly* during the Progressive era offer abundant evidence of an aroused social conscience. See Alice Lucile Turner, *A Study of the Content of the Sewanee Review with Historical Introduction* (Nashville, 1931), pp. 64–107; and Dabney, *Liberalism in the South*, pp. 393–96.

13. Harold U. Faulkner, *The Quest for Social Justice 1898–1914* (New York, 1931), is one of the first thorough treatments of progressivism. Richard Hofstadter's *The Age of Reform: From Bryan to F.D.R.* (New York, 1955), the leading revisionist interpretation, stresses the reactionary elements in progressivism.

improvement, crime prevention, establishing the rights of labor, and ending child labor. The merger of the political-economic aims of progressivism with the humanitarian goals of the social gospel was especially characteristic of reform efforts in the South.

The South supplied its full share of leadership in the Progressive movement.[14] Some of the best-known features of progressivism—initiative, referendum, direct primary, and business regulation—won approval in southern states prior to their adoption in the North.[15] Nor was Southern progressivism limited to political reforms. Editors, educators, ministers, and other professionals pursued a broad range of causes with a humanitarian zeal that made the movement a counterpart to the social gospel in the North. Specialized organizations and publications campaigned for child-labor laws, better schools, and improved agriculture. Conferences and crusades mobilized public sentiment and pressured lawmakers in behalf of penal reform, public health, and prohibition. All of these causes found strong support in two highly regarded academic journals in the South: the *South Atlantic Quarterly* and the *Sewanee Review*, which were published by Trinity College (Methodist) and the University of the South (Episcopal), respectively.

In agriculture, Charles H. Otken, the Mississippi Baptist minister, combined Populist ardor with muckraker reporting to expose the evils of the crop lien and the one-crop system;[16] farm editor Clarence Poe preached a gospel of self-help through education, cooperation, and scientific farming;[17] Seaman A. Knapp,

14. Woodward, *Origins of the New South*, pp. 371–95, has valuable insights into Southern progressivism. Other studies establishing Southern progressivism in its rightful place are Arthur S. Link, "The Progressive Movement in the South, 1870–1914," *North Carolina Historical Review*, XXIII (Apr., 1946), 172–205; Anne Firor Scott, "Progressive Wind from the South, 1906–1913," *The Journal of Southern History*, XXIX (Feb., 1963), 53–70; and Herbert J. Doherty, Jr., "Voices of Protest from the New South, 1875–1910," *The Mississippi Valley Historical Review*, XLII (June, 1955), 45–66.

15. Woodward, *Origins of the New South*, pp. 371–74.

16. Otken, pp. 60, 72, 112, 130, 173.

17. Poe edited *The Progressive Farmer* (Birmingham, 1886–), formerly a Populist party sheet. He offered practical advice on how to implement better methods and urged farmers to operate on a businesslike basis. His ideas also appeared in *How Farmers Cooperate and Double Their Profits* (New York, 1915).

special agent for the Department of Agriculture in the South and adviser to the General Education Board on its program to improve farming methods, devised the demonstration method on farmer-owned fields to show the feasibility of scientific agriculture;[18] and Charles S. Barrett of the Farmers' Union worked for production controls and farm cooperatives.[19] In education, Progressive governors, ministers, and schoolmen, with the backing of Northern philanthropists, waged a campaign for better schools that doubled per capita tax support between 1900 and 1917.[20] New York merchant Robert Curtis Ogden financed the Conference for Education, at which ministers were as prominent as educators. Although at first devoted to promoting Christian education, the conference soon became a publicity agency for public school needs. The closely related General Education Board, a Rockefeller foundation, gave outright aid to Southern education which amounted to $129,209,167 by 1921.[21] Southern reformers also campaigned successfully against the convict-lease system and established effective public-health programs.[22]

The place that practical religion occupied in Southern progressivism was much in evidence in the movement against child labor. Before taking up that cause, Edgar Gardner Murphy, an Episcopal minister in Montgomery, Alabama, had worked for better education and racial justice. In 1900, Murphy and his fellow Montgomery ministers founded the Alabama Child Labor Committee, the first such organization in the nation; and once he had obtained legislation in that state, Murphy established the

18. Joseph Cannon Bailey, *Seaman A. Knapp, Schoolmaster of American Agriculture* (New York, 1945), pp. 133–74; The General Education Board, *The General Education Board, an Account of its Activities, 1902–1914* (New York, 1915), pp. 23–29.

19. Woodward, *Origins of the New South*, pp. 412–15.

20. *Ibid.*, p. 406.

21. Murphy, *Problems of the Present South*, pp. 205–31, is a firsthand account of the educational movement. Burton J. Hendrick, *The Training of an American, the Earlier Life and Letters of Walter Hines Page* (Boston, 1928), chap. 11, includes correspondence of another important figure in the movement. See also Raymond B. Fosdick, *Adventure in Giving, the Story of the General Education Board* (New York, 1962).

22. Jane Zimmerman, "The Penal Reform Movement in the South During the Progressive Era, 1890–1917," *The Journal of Southern History*, XVII (Nov., 1951), 462–92; Woodward, *Origins of the New South*, pp. 425–26.

National Child Labor Committee. The continuation of this work was placed in the hands of Alexander J. McKelway, a Presbyterian minister and editor who, after reading of Murphy's efforts, had used the columns of the *Presbyterian Standard* to support the adoption of a North Carolina child-labor law. Largely because of McKelway's leadership and the backing of the American Federation of Labor, every Southern state had an age-and-hour law by 1912.[23]

Perhaps the best example of the scope and character of Southern progressivism was the Southern Sociological Congress, founded in 1912. At the invitation of the reform governor of Tennessee, Ben Hooper, some seven hundred ministers, educators, social workers, and heads of health, penal, and welfare institutions assembled in Nashville for a four-day meeting, featuring sessions on child welfare, courts and prisons, public health, organized charities, racial problems, and the social mission of the church.[24] Charles Hillman Brough, a sociologist from the University of Arkansas, became president of the congress in 1916, the year of his election as a Progressive governor in Arkansas. Meeting annually until 1919, the organization sought to unite public officials and professionals in a broad program of social reform in which the South's "better citizens" would effect improvements along moderate lines.[25]

Besides revealing a vital progressivism, the Sociological Congress showed the prominent place of religion in Southern reform and more particularly the unmistakable influence of the social gospel.[26] More than one-fourth of the organization's officers and

23. Elizabeth H. Davidson, *Child Labor Legislation in the Southern Textile States* (Chapel Hill, 1939), pp. 27–41, 85, 122–26; Herbert J. Doherty, Jr., "Alexander J. McKelway: Preacher to Progressives," *The Journal of Southern History*, XXIV (May, 1958), 177–90.

24. James E. McCullough, ed., *The Call of the New South, Addresses Delivered at the Southern Sociological Congress, Nashville, Tennessee, May 7 to 10, 1912* (Nashville, 1912), pp. 7, 14 (hereafter cited as *The Call of the New South*).

25. *Ibid.*, pp. 16–20; Alexander J. McKelway, "Remarks of the Acting President," in *The South Mobilizing for Social Service, Addresses Delivered at the Southern Sociological Congress, Atlanta, Georgia, April 25–29, 1913*, edited by James E. McCullough (Nashville, 1913), p. 14 (hereafter cited as *The South Mobilizing for Social Service*).

26. For examples, see Wilbur F. Crafts, "The Potential Resources of the

participants were ministers, many noted for their interests in social betterment. John E. White, an Atlanta Baptist pastor and vice-president of the congress, had earned distinction as a dry crusader, an advocate of better race relations, and a promoter of mission work among the mountain people. Alexander McKelway of the National Child Labor Committee was chairman of the Committee on Child Welfare and presided over the second conference. The forceful general secretary for the congress, James E. McCullough, was a Methodist minister, principal of a training school for social workers, and an enthusiastic advocate of the institutional church. John A. Rice, whose Fort Worth church offered an institutional program, headed the Committee on the Church and Social Service. Brough himself was a lay preacher, and later became president of a Baptist girls' school.

The founding sessions of the Sociological Congress were significant occasions, for the nation's leading social-gospel ministers had been invited to address the gathering. Samuel Zane Batten lectured on the church's duty to Christianize society.[27] Walter Rauschenbusch discussed the recently adopted social creed of the Federal Council of Churches.[28] Charles S. MacFarland, executive secretary for the Federal Council, addressed the congress on four occasions, pleading for church unity in social reconstruction.[29] Graham Taylor, seminary professor and

South for Leadership in Social Service," in *The Call of the New South*, pp. 311–22; William P. Thirkield, "A Cathedral of Cooperation," in *The South Mobilizing for Social Service*, pp. 476–82; John A. Rice, "Report of the Committee on the Church and Social Service," in *The South Mobilizing for Social Service*, pp. 489–503; James E. McCullough, Introduction to *Battling for Social Betterment, Southern Sociological Congress, Memphis, Tennessee, May 6 to 10, 1914* (Nashville, 1914), p. 3 (hereafter cited as *Battling for Social Betterment*); "A Creed for a Crusade," in *The New Chivalry–Health, Southern Sociological Congress, Houston, Texas, May 8–11, 1915*, edited by James E. McCullough (Nashville, 1915), p. 11 (hereafter cited as *The New Chivalry–Health*).

27. Batten, "The Church and Social Service," in *The Call of the New South*, pp. 275–92; Batten, "Social Service and the Church," in *The South Mobilizing for Social Service*, pp. 512–33.

28. Rauschenbusch, "The Social Program of the Church," in *The South Mobilizing for Social Service*, pp. 504–11.

29. MacFarland, "The Church and Modern Industry," in *The Call of the New South*, pp. 292–307; MacFarland, "The Preparation of the Church for Social Service," in *Battling for Social Betterment*, pp. 98–108.

founder of a Chicago settlement house, spoke on the professional training of social workers.[30]

The presence of the nation's foremost social gospelers and ecumenists helped establish the congress as a kind of rallying point for social Christianity. Men of the South viewed the task of the organization as the promotion of "civic righteousness." They challenged their churches to develop a "social ministry" and frequently employed religious appeals in behalf of reform programs.[31] McCullough, in commenting on the "moral earnestness" of the participants, reported, "Every word breathed of prayer and social justice."[32]

The most striking parallel to the social gospel was the social program adopted by the congress. This statement of purpose sounded very much like the social creed of the Federal Council of Churches, but because of its attention to sectional problems, the social program may be rightly considered as a distinctly Southern version of the social gospel. It addressed the region's special ills—the convict-lease system, racial injustice, and educational backwardness. On the other hand, the declaration, except in its opposition to child labor, did not deal with labor problems at all, the issue of primary concern to the social gospelers in the more industrialized North. The remaining objectives were improved juvenile courts and reformatories, better care of defectives, uniform marriage laws, and the suppression of alcoholism and prostitution. The statement concluded with an appeal for the "closest cooperation between the church and all the social agencies" to obtain these goals.[33]

The Southern Sociological Congress effectively expressed the common hopes of a large number of socially concerned leaders who believed that the churches were essential and natural allies in any movement for social betterment. The churches themselves

30. Taylor, "Qualifications of Social Workers," in *The Call of the New South*, pp. 340–52.
31. G. W. Dyer, "Southern Problems that Challenge Our Thought," in *The Call of the New South*, pp. 25–33.
32. McCullough, Introductory Note to *The Call of the New South*, p. 7.
33. *Ibid.*, p. 9.

were quite aware of the current emphasis on social religion in America, and reactions to the new ideology ranged from extreme skepticism and qualified approval to enthusiastic endorsement. Opponents argued that social reconstruction was based on the faulty theological principle of "regeneration through environment," a radical doctrine that could lead the church away from its primary mission of individual conversion. Although not uncommon, objections to the new gospel were seldom unequivocal. Many critics admitted that the church had been too narrow, too individualistic, and too irrelevant to social ills. They would endorse the declared objectives of social Christianity but then argue that those ends could best be achieved as the natural fruit of individual regeneration.[34]

Evidence of a fundamental ambivalence toward religious progressivism may be found in the records of leading church groups in the South. The Presbyterians, probably the most thoroughly grounded in conservative theology, managed to accommodate some elements of the New Thought. For example, after refusing to participate in any of the preliminary sessions on church federation, the denomination became one of the founding members of the Federal Council of Churches.[35] Presbyterians exhibited mixed feelings about the social gospel. An address on the church's social mission, delivered on the occasion of its fiftieth anniversary, in 1911, opened with a pointed attack on theological errors in the social gospel but ended by praising

34. For Presbyterian criticism of the social gospel see Walter L. Lingle, "The Teaching of Jesus and Modern Social Problems," *Union Seminary Magazine*, XXVII (Apr., 1916), 205; and his review of Rauschenbusch's *A Theology for the Social Gospel*, in *Union Seminary Magazine*, XXIX (Apr., 1918), 274. See also A. D. P. Gilmour's reviews of three social-gospel books in *Union Seminary Magazine*, XXI (Oct.–Nov., 1909), 157–58; and J. P. Hawerton's "The Church and Social Reform," *Union Seminary Magazine*, XXV (Oct.–Nov., 1913), 30–34. Methodist objections were voiced by John T. Tigert in "Regeneration through Environment," *Methodist Review*, LI (Sept.–Oct., 1902), 913–15; and Frank M. Thomas in "Is the Methodist Episcopal Church Reaping?" *Methodist Review*, LXVIII, No. 3. (July, 1919), 548–50.

35. *Minutes of the General Assembly of the Presbyterian Church in the United States, 1904* (Richmond, 1904), p. 41. Opposition to the social-service program of the Federal Council appeared in *Minutes of the Presbyterian Church, 1913*, p. 17.

efforts for social betterment and finding fault with the church for not actively leading such movements.[36] Although the theologians of the church found more heresy than truth in the new theology, they reflected favorably on the increased attention to applied Christianity, especially in the institutional-type church.[37] Presbyterians paid their highest respects to social religion when the 1913 General Assembly, after devoting a session to social-gospel themes, joined other Calvinist bodies in drawing up a statement on Christian faith and social service.[38]

The Methodists were much more receptive to the Protestant social awakening. A 1900 editorial in the *Methodist Review*, the principal theological journal of the church, foresaw that twentieth-century religion would feature more interdenominational cooperation in order to bring about "the social, industrial and moral improvement of the masses."[39] Comment in that quarterly more often than not favored the new theology,[40] and book reviewers praised a score of social-gospel titles. From the North, Walter Rauschenbusch, Shailer Mathews, Charles Stelzle, and Washington Gladden, all prominent social gospelers, sent essays to the journal;[41] and many articles by Southern authors dealt with the rights of labor, improved conditions for Negroes, the evils of corporate wealth, and the institutional church.

36. Egbert Watson Smith, "The Mission of the Southern Presbyterian Church," *Semi-Centennial Memorial Addresses Delivered before the General Assembly of 1911*, pp. 41–56.

37. Dewitt M. Bencham, "Methods of City Evangelization," *Union Seminary Magazine*, XV (Dec., 1903–Jan., 1904), 105–18. The most unequivocal endorsement of the social gospel was Home Mission Board Secretary Charles L. Thompson's "The Institutional Church," *Union Seminary Magazine*, XV (Feb.–Mar., 1904), 233–37.

38. *Minutes of the Presbyterian Church, 1913*, pp. 11, 66. The full statement appeared in *Minutes of the Presbyterian Church, 1914*, pp. 161–63.

39. J. W. Hawley, "The Twentieth Century Protestant Outlook," *Methodist Review*, XLIX (Mar.–Apr., 1900), 316, 318.

40. See, for example, Wilbur F. Tillett, "Some Currents of Contemporaneous Theological Thought," *Methodist Review*, L (July–Aug., 1901), 560–75; J. T. Curry, "What is Higher Criticism?" *Methodist Review*, LIV (Jan., 1905), 472–78; Marion T. Plyer, "The Inevitable in the Southern Pulpit," *Methodist Review*, LII (Apr., 1903), 291–300.

41. The respective articles may be found in LIX (Apr., 1910), 223–29; LVI (Jan., 1907), 32–51; LVI (July, 1907), 457–67; LXII (Oct., 1913), 682–98.

In particular, Southern Methodists distinguished themselves as ecumenical leaders. They invited Elias B. Sanford, leader of the movement for church federation, to their 1902 General Conference to propose establishing the Federal Council of Churches and promptly approved the plan, the first such action by a church body. Then they sent fifty delegates to the Inter-Church Conference on Federation, including three bishops, one of whom, Bishop E. R. Hendrix, was a principal founder of the Federal Council; served on the preliminary National Conference on Federation in 1900; was chairman of the Business Committee, which drafted the federation plan in 1905; and was elected the first president of the Federal Council.[42]

Methodists endorsed the social gospel with the same enthusiasm that marked their ecumenism. The General Conference approved the social creed in 1914 and made the statement an official part of the church's *Book of Discipline*. This same conference expanded the church's temperance committee into a Commission on Temperance and Social Service in order to embrace the larger aims of the social gospel. Bishop James Cannon, famous dry crusader, headed the new commission and thereafter identified himself with various social causes, especially the labor movement. In the 1920's the commission became a budgeted agency with a broad social-gospel program.[43]

Southern Baptists experienced the influence of social Christianity even though they were among the few church groups refusing affiliation with the Federal Council of Churches. As compared to the Presbyterians and Methodists of the South, the Baptists had greater difficulty accepting the social-gospel ideology because their religious individualism, theological conserva-

42. Elias B. Sanford, *Origin and History of the Federal Council* (Hartford, 1916), pp. 359–67; Elias B. Sanford, *Church Federation, Inter-Church Conference on Federation* (New York, 1906), pp. 283, 287, 475, 611, 656. See the strong endorsement of the Federal Council in "Bishops' Address," *Journal of the General Conference of the Methodist Episcopal Church, South, 1910, p. 40.

43. *Journal of the Methodist Episcopal Church, 1914*, pp. 84, 249–50; *1926*, p. 382; *The Doctrine and Discipline of the Methodist Episcopal Church, South, 1914* (Nashville, 1914), pp. 373–74; Dabney, *The Dry Messiah*, pp. 162, 167–69. Cannon had a hand in the Interchurch Commission's inquiry into the great steel strike of 1919.

tism, decentralized authority, and denominational isolationism, taken together, formed greater barriers to cooperative social action by churches. The presence of such formidable barriers makes even more remarkable the evidence of social-gospel influence in Southern Baptist life.

V

THE SOCIAL GOSPEL COMPROMISED

The Southern Baptist Convention did not give important recognition to the challenge of an urban society until late in the nineteenth century when the Home Mission Board began voicing alarm about the threat to traditional Southern culture from immigration and industrialization. Although one special report complained about the "conditions of ignorance, congested population, overwork [and] child labor," it was the religious character of immigrants that most disturbed Southern Baptists.[1] Few of the uprooted were evangelicals; in fact, most of those who professed any faith were Roman Catholics. Expressing supreme confidence that evangelism could save the South from alien evils, the Home Board made annual appeals for more missions in the cities and established a department for work among the immigrants in 1899 that employed a staff of eighty-two by 1920.[2]

For some years the board remained optimistic even though efforts to convert foreigners were never equal to the incoming tide. By 1914, however, the board no longer viewed the immigrant as a promising opportunity for evangelism. Aliens were described as "ambitious dignitaries of the hierarchy" who intended to "Romanize America."[3] The board denounced unrestricted immigration as a threat to the nation's political and religious institutions and argued in its 1919 report that only

1. *Annual of the Southern Baptist Convention, 1902* (hereafter cited as *Annual, SBC* [Nashville, 1902]), pp. 18–19.
2. *Ibid.*, 1899, pp. 34–35; 1920, p. 403.
3. *Ibid.*, 1914, p. 308.

papists, exploiters of labor, and the steamship companies favored an open policy, whereas the "patriotic Americans have all along wanted immigration limited."[4]

Whatever its immediate effectiveness, the attempt to convert immigrants expressed the basic commitment of Southern Baptists to denominational expansion through personal evangelism. A convention-sponsored study in 1900 on goals for the twentieth century charted the path to future growth through closer coordination of local, state, and regional work in a unified program of enlistment and enlargement.[5] In 1907 the Home Mission Board launched a new department of evangelism that in the coming decades would give centralized leadership to a systematic program of mass and personal membership recruitment, carried to the churches through the state and district associations.[6] Perennial evangelism in every church became the keynote in Southern Baptist life. The results were remarkable. In the next half-century the denomination became the largest non-Roman body in America (almost eleven and one-half million members by 1969), with organized conventions in twenty-eight states and "pioneer" mission work in all fifty states.[7]

4. *Ibid., 1919,* p. 429.

5. *Ibid., 1900,* pp. 19–22.

6. See a summary of its work to 1914, *Annual, SBC, 1914,* p. 298; appraisals of the department's role in the denomination appear in Roland Q. Leavell, "Evangelism," *Encyclopedia of Southern Baptists,* I, 412, 416; and C. E. Autrey, "Home Mission Program of Evangelism," *Encyclopedia of Southern Baptists,* I (1958), 419–24.

7. Constant H. Jacquet, Jr., ed., *Yearbook of American Churches, 1971* (New York, 1971), pp. 67–68; *Annual, SBC, 1970,* pp. 107, 109. See also Bureau of Research and Survey, National Council of Churches, *Churches and Church Membership in the United States* (New York, 1957). Table 8 shows Southern Baptists to be the largest Protestant body in the eleven former Confederate states plus New Mexico, Oklahoma, Missouri, and Kentucky. These fifteen states, with the Baptist percentage of total Protestant membership, are Mississippi, 61.8 percent; Alabama, 60.6 percent; Georgia, 59.9 percent; Louisiana, 58.5 percent; Kentucky, 53.4 percent, South Carolina, 52.5 percent; Tennessee, 52.1 percent; Texas, 51.5 percent; North Carolina, 49.2 percent, Arkansas, 47.5 percent; Oklahoma, 46.2 percent; Florida, 44.8 percent; New Mexico, 44.1 percent; Virginia, 32.7 percent; and Missouri, 30.9 percent.

The membership statistics used by the National Council were compiled from the reports of the churches themselves. There is no reason to suspect that Southern Baptist figures are any less reliable than those of any other groups. Like other denominations, they include many persons with only a nominal relationship to the church; but, unlike many, they do not include infants. Among the major Protes-

Because of the emphasis on evangelism, the main thrust in Southern Baptist life ran counter to contemporary trends in Protestantism—liberal theology, ecumenism, and the social gospel. Opposition to liberal theology began in the nineteenth century when many denominations were dealing with charges of heresy within their ranks.[8] Defenders of Baptist orthodoxy forced the resignations of two professors at Southern Baptist Theological Seminary in Louisville, Kentucky: Crawford H. Toy and William H. Whitsitt. After ten years at the seminary, Toy, a German-trained Old Testament scholar who accepted the new critical approach to Biblical studies, was dismissed by the board of trustees in 1879 because his views denied the inerrancy of the Bible.[9]

Some years after Toy's dismissal, a much larger controversy involved William Whitsitt, professor of church history since 1872 and seminary president from 1895 to 1899. While a student in German universities, Whitsitt had learned the scientific method of interpreting historical evidence, which he applied to Anabaptist beginnings, particularly to the practice of baptism by immersion. The facts of history, Whitsitt concluded, indicated that Baptist forebears had not always practiced immersion. His findings completely undermined the widely held landmark doctrine claiming for Baptist churches a unique title to New Testament origins by reason of an uninterrupted succession of immersionists since apostolic times. After Whitsitt published his views in *A Question of Baptist History* (1896), the editor of Kentucky's *Western Recorder* attacked Whitsitt's views and demanded his removal. Other editors and local associations joined the agitation. When the trustees supported Whitsitt, the attackers moved against the seminary itself. Five state conventions threatened to withdraw their support of the seminary, and at the

---

tant churches, Southern Baptists have made the greatest numerical gains over the last century. From 345,951 in 1845, their numbers increased almost five times by 1900 (1,657,996). In the twentieth century, membership doubled in the first two decades and doubled again in the next three decades. In 1970 the membership was 11,487,708.

8. Garrison, pp. 94–99.
9. Kenneth K. Bailey, pp. 11–12.

1898 Southern Convention there was talk of severing relations with the school. At this point, Whitsitt, acting in the interest of denominational harmony, volunteered his resignation.[10]

Whitsitt's removal did not represent a complete victory for landmark theology, which exalted the authority of local churches to the point that effective denominational programs would be impossible. To the contrary, denominational trends were moving in quite the opposite direction, toward greater leadership from convention agencies that were continually expanding their programs. Actually, opposition to Whitsitt arose as much from fears of liberalism and so-called German rationalism as from belief in landmarkism; and in the end, denominational unity was prized above all other considerations. As for the question of Baptist origins, Whitsitt's views eventually gained general acceptance.[11]

The real significance of the Whitsitt controversy, along with the earlier removal of Crawford Toy, was that it exposed the extreme anxiety of Southern Baptists over their identity as a separate religious body. For some, landmarkism had validated claims to distinctiveness. However, the problem of legitimacy troubled Southern Baptists whether or not they accepted the succession doctrine because in truth they owed their separate existence, not to a theological position, but to the slavery controversy. The passing of time had made continued separation difficult to justify until the Toy-Whitsitt episodes called attention to the new theology, which had found adherents among churchmen of the North, including some Baptists. When Southern Baptists became aware of modernism, they began staking out doctrinal boundaries distinguishing them from other groups. Defending Biblical orthodoxy against the new theology and its frequent companions, ecumenism and the social gospel, gave them a new *raison d'être* at a time when landmarkism had lost its standing as a creditable and practical position. Now, more clearly than ever, Southern Baptists could explain their existence

---

10. *Ibid.*, pp. 12–16; William Wright Barnes, *The Southern Baptist Convention, 1845–1953*, pp. 136–38.

11. W. Morgan Patterson, "The Development of the Baptist Successionist Formula," *Foundations*, V (Oct., 1962), 344.

in comprehensive theological terms. They came to think of themselves as possessing at least three distinctive traits: loyalty to Biblical authority, separation from compromising ecumenism, and reliance on personal experience for conversion. In the security of these beliefs, they found the necessary authority to launch an aggressive program of expansion.

Among the many Southern Baptists who helped formulate this new sense of identity was Edgar Y. Mullins, who succeeded Whitsitt as president at Southern Seminary. He believed it necessary to reinterpret Baptist principles in the light of the many advances in scientific, sociological, and religious thought. In a series of lectures delivered at several Baptist conventions early in the century, Mullins argued that the Baptists, far from being otherworldly sectarians, had contributed much to the nation's secular institutions. The doctrines of soul liberty, democratic church government, and church-state separation, he claimed, had "furnished the spiritual analogues of our entire political system."[12] Sensitive to the spirit of progressivism in the nation, Mullins tried to show that Baptist beliefs were conducive to material and social progress. Although Mullins credited much social advancement to the Baptists, he found their greatest genius in the principle of soul liberty. The Baptists were the "only adequate interpreters of the Reformation,"[13] he insisted, because they alone had denied the state authority over matters of conscience. Their historic attention to the worth of the individual was not without contemporary significance in secular and religious affairs. Baptist ideals avoided the great heresies of the age: socialism, which would force equality on unequal men, and "socialized religion," which would seek progress through unregenerate men.[14]

The Mullins lectures, delivered in the South but published by a Northern Baptist agency, said nothing about regional differences. However, others in the denomination were soon arguing

12. Edgar Y. Mullins, *Axioms of Religion, a New Interpretation of the Baptist Faith* (Philadelphia, 1908), p. 270.
13. *Ibid.*, p. 258.
14. *Ibid.*, pp. 17, 201–209, 306.

that Southern Baptists had a peculiar destiny in the nation, among them, Victor I. Masters, head of the publicity department of the Home Mission Board from 1909 to 1921.[15] In this capacity, he wrote several small volumes that both reflected and influenced denominational thinking. Designed for use in church study classes, the books appealed for denominational loyalty and support by arguing that Southern Baptists had a peculiar mission in America. Masters developed his notion of divine purpose on the basis of two ideas: the superiority of the Anglo-Saxon race as represented by Southern whites and the perpetuation of what he called the "Anglo-Saxon evangelical faith" in Southern religion.[16] The first idea came from the nineteenth-century racial myth claiming superiority for Northern Europeans and their descendants. The American South more than the North or West had preserved its "Anglo-Saxon blood" by denying social equality to the Negro and by avoiding the corruption of the "ignorant and superstitious" immigrants, those "mud-sills of the monarchial State and a still more . . . monarchial Church."[17] He saw the absence of aliens as providential. The disguised blessings of poverty and a Negro population had made the South unattractive to undesirable immigrants, who settled in industrial centers where they destroyed the superior virtues that Puritan New England had given the North.[18]

More serious than the loss of racial superiority was the North's repudiation of evangelical religion. Masters reasoned that colonial revivals had rediscovered the New Testament method of evangelism, unknown to the Roman or Reformation churches.[19] The North lost its once vital evangelical faith because of the twin misfortunes of Romanism and rationalism—Romanism coming by way of the immigrant emissaries of the hierarchy and

15. See Victor I. Masters, *The Home Mission Task*, containing chapters on the mission of Southern Baptists to America by thirteen denominational leaders. See especially pp. 54–59, 65, 73, 84, 91–93, 134–39, 195, 294–95, 305–307.

16. Victor I. Masters, *The Call of the South* (Atlanta, 1918), pp. 208–209.

17. Victor I. Masters, *Baptist Home Missions* (Atlanta, 1914), p. 124.

18. Masters, *Call of the South*, p. 32. See also William T. Hatcher, "Housekeeping for Our Neighbor," in Victor I. Masters, ed., *The Home Mission Task*, pp. 91–92.

19. Victor I. Masters, *Making America Christian* (Atlanta, 1921), pp. 148–49.

rationalism developing from modern theology, which Masters traced to German scientific scholarship.[20] The South, on the other hand, having escaped alien peoples and ideas, retained its faith in Biblical doctrines and supernatural religion. For Masters, the mission of Southern evangelicals was plain: "We can meet and thwart this religio-political power by bringing the immigrant to Christ and by closing the doors against an unrestricted immigration."[21] Accordingly, Southern Baptists in particular had an "unmatched opportunity to serve the nation and the world by standing firm for the doctrines of the Bible."[22]

Masters's concept of regional Baptist orthodoxy demanded the complete rejection of ecumenism, and he used his position to establish a solid resistance to all interchurch overtures. When Southern Baptists dealt with this question, their primary concern was the preservation of their doctrinal identity and denominational independence. Thus, in 1909 a committee examined the relationship of the Home Mission Board to the ecumenical Home Mission Council and decided against making any restrictive commitments regarding mission work. And while the Southern Convention sent a representative to the World Conference on Faith and Order in 1911, their only purpose in doing so was to keep the convention informed. Southern Baptists published their first major policy statement on ecumenism in the 1914 Pronouncement on Christian Union and Denominational Efficiency, which advised against all interdenominational connections because true union required agreement on New Testament principles.[23] The document specifically objected to the lack of agreement among the participating churches on the nature of salvation, the administration of ordinances, and church-state relations—issues on which Southern Baptists could not compromise for the sake of outward unity.

Judging from statements made in 1914 and subsequent years, it is clear that Southern Baptists spurned church unity because

20. *Ibid.*, pp. 118, 143; Masters, *Call of the South*, p. 28.
21. Masters, *Baptist Home Missions*, pp. 130–31.
22. Masters, *Call of the South*, p. 26.
23. *Annual, SBC, 1914*, pp. 73–78.

of an overriding fear of organic union. Above all else they opposed the creation of a super Protestant church, the suspected goal of the ecumenists. On purely practical grounds, Southern Baptists realized that interchurch activity, whether aimed at mergers or mere cooperation, could only weaken their efforts to expand; and countless sermons, resolutions, and committee reports warned congregations against "entangling alliances" that would rob the churches of their "autonomy" and would silence their "distinctive witness" to the world.[24]

In view of the decisive rejection of ecumenism and theological liberalism, one would expect a similar reaction to social Christianity for allegedly having sent the church on a false mission of social reform to the neglect of personal evangelism. There is, indeed, ample evidence of this very criticism from as early as the 1880's.[25] Moreover, the attacks on the social gospel persisted in the twentieth century.[26] But to ascribe to the denomination an unqualified rejection of all elements of religious liberalism makes the mistake of assuming that the social gospel was inseparably bound to ecumenism and the new theology. At the very time Southern Baptists were turning away from church unity and modernism in theology, they were conceding much to the validity of social Christianity's appeal for the practical application of the Christian ethic. The social gospel managed to achieve a permanent place in Southern Baptist thought and in the organized life of the denomination even though in later years it would become a source of tension and outright controversy.

The first major contacts between Southern Baptists and social

---

24. William Roscoe Estep, Jr., "A Historical Study of the Ecumenical Movement" (Th.D. thesis, Southwestern Baptist Theological Seminary, 1951), pp. 153–61, deals with Southern Baptist reaction to ecumenism. The appendix of this work contains accounts of the action taken on the issue by the Southern Baptist Convention in 1909, 1912, 1914, 1916, 1919, 1940, and 1949. See also William Wright Barnes, *The Southern Baptist Convention, 1845–1953*, pp. 271–87; Mullins, *Axioms of Religion*, pp. 223–26, 232; Robert G. Torbet, "Baptists and the Ecumenical Movement," *Chronicle*, XXVIII (Apr., 1955), p. 95.

25. *The Christian Index* (Atlanta), June 28, 1888, p. 6; *The Religious Herald* (Richmond), Jan. 11, 1894, p. 1.

26. Masters was one of the most persistent critics of the social gospel. See his *Call of the South*, pp. 27, 162–63. Mullins offered perhaps the best answer to the social gospel in *Axioms of Religion*, pp. 17, 204–10.

Christianity came by way of the movement for prohibition, one aim of the social gospel to which Southern Baptists were already committed.[27] Although they were, in some respects, separate movements, social Christianity and prohibition had much in common and were often interrelated.[28] Both causes called Protestants to cooperative efforts and sought reform through political action. Liberal churchmen included prohibition in their program of social regeneration. Prohibition appeared in the social creed of the Federal Council of Churches and the social program of the Southern Sociological Congress. Thus, when Southern Baptists joined other denominations in the dry crusade, they were adopting the basic strategy and one of the specific goals of the social gospel.

The alliance with prohibition forces took on an official character through the action of various state conventions. The North Carolina Baptist Convention led in the formation of the league in 1901, and in the following year, Arkansas Baptists authorized a committee to aid in the work. In 1904 the Alabama Convention initiated plans for a state Anti-Saloon League, its principal promoters including the convention's executive secretary and the editor of the Baptist journal in the state. Other state conventions worked closely with the league by naming representatives to state organizations, promoting the league at church meetings, and supplying financial assistance. During these years every state convention participated in the dry movement through a standing committee on temperance.[29]

27. It should be noted that expressions of practical religion occurred that had no particular relationship to the social gospel. Between 1870 and 1900, state conventions established eleven institutions for the care of children; nine additional orphanages were founded by 1920. The first Southern Baptist hospital was established in St. Louis in 1884, and between 1903 and 1925, seventeen hospitals became affiliated with state conventions. The Southern Baptist Convention also sponsored humanitarian programs. In 1900 the Home Mission Board created a department for work with mountain people that supported forty-seven schools. A ministry to the urban poor began in 1912 when the Women's Missionary Union began operating "good-will centers" that mixed social welfare with evangelistic work. The number of centers grew to fifty under the sponsorship of local and state groups and the Home Mission Board.

28. Abell, p. 47; Henry F. May, p. 126.

29. Daniel Jay Whitener, *Prohibition in North Carolina, 1715–1945* (Chapel Hill, 1945), p. 134; *Proceedings of the Arkansas Baptist State Convention, 1902*

The Southern Baptist Convention joined the prohibition movement in 1908 by establishing a permanent committee on temperance. The circumstances behind this action reveal the close ties between the social-gospel ideology and prohibition. For some years the convention had expressed concern over mob violence and lawlessness in the South. A 1907 resolution concerning these problems proposed a special mass meeting on "civic righteousness" in conjunction with the next convention. Out of this special meeting came a statement urging Southern Baptists to "redeem society" by working for the abolition of "every wrong, public and private, political and social." In language characteristic of the social gospel, the delegates were challenged to become "aggressive builders of the new order" in preparation for the consummation of the kingdom. Immediately following the adoption of the statement, the convention created a Standing Committee on Temperance commissioned to join other denominations in the prohibition campaign.[30]

Since it operated without funds, the Temperance Committee's official duties consisted mostly of preparing annual reports on the progress of prohibition. However, the lack of finances did not prevent Chairman Arthur J. Barton from playing a leading role in the dry movement. In 1911 he presided over the national conference that framed legislation giving dry states protection against interstate liquor traffic; in 1915 he was chairman of the committee that drafted the national prohibition amendment. Barton also attended the International Conference Against Alcoholism in Italy as a representative of the United States government; and while he was superintendent of the Anti-Saloon League in Texas from 1915 to 1918, the state was voted dry. Barton kept the Southern Baptist Convention closely allied to the prohibition forces by means of reports and resolutions from the Temperance Committee, and in 1913 he led the convention

---

(n.p., 1902), p. 32; *Annual, Alabama, 1904*, pp. 24–27. James Benson Sellers, *The Prohibition Movement in Alabama, 1702–1943* (Chapel Hill, 1943), p. 102; *Minutes, Georgia, 1908*, p. 27; *Proceedings, Texas, 1908*, p. 94; *Minutes of the Missouri Baptist General Association, 1911* (n.p., 1911), p. 70; *Proceedings, Mississippi, 1903*, p. 39.

30. *Annual, SBC, 1908*, pp. 35–36; *1906*, p. 23; *1907*, p. 31.

to be the first church body to endorse the Anti-Saloon League's plan for national prohibition.[31]

Once Southern Baptists became deeply involved in the prohibition cause, they had little difficulty expanding their social concern to include other problems in society. The temperance committees, for example, that had been established in every state convention as well as the Southern Baptist Convention during the first decade of the twentieth century were all, within a decade or so, changed to social service committees, or commissions, to deal with a broader range of social issues. The creation of these social service committees followed a contemporary trend in American Protestantism. Church agencies established between 1900 and 1910 to carry out social-gospel programs included the Department of Church and Labor (Presbyterian Church, U.S.A.), the Joint Committee on Social Service (Protestant Episcopal), the Labor Committee (Congregational), the Federation for Social Service (Methodist Episcopal), and the Social Service Commission (Northern Baptist).[32] Southern Baptists took similar action after Samuel Zane Batten, chairman of the Northern Baptist commission, offered a resolution at the Baptist World Alliance in 1911 calling on all affiliated groups to set up social-action committees.[33] Southern Baptist leaders immediately began to implement the proposal. Within four years the Southern Convention and the state conventions in Georgia, North Carolina, South Carolina, Virginia, and Texas had created permanent committees along the lines suggested by Batten. The conventions even named their committees after the Northern Baptist agency which Batten headed.

The affirmative response to the Batten proposal may be credited in large measure to E. C. Dargan, who, as president of the Southern Baptist Convention from 1911 to 1913, had a direct hand in establishing a social-service commission in the Southern

31. *Ibid.*, *1913*, pp. 74–75; *1914*, pp. 33–34; *1915*, pp. 79–80; Henderson Barton, "Arthur James Barton," *Encyclopedia of Southern Baptists*, I, 146.

32. Hopkins, *The Rise of the Social Gospel*, pp. 280–95.

33. *The Baptist World Alliance, Second Congress, 1911* (Philadelphia, 1911), pp. 333–34.

Convention and in at least two state conventions.[34] Dargan's contribution to the cause of social Christianity antedated his years as convention president. During a brief period when he taught at Southern Baptist Theological Seminary, Dargan introduced a course in Christian sociology. His views on the role of the church in society were published in *Society, Kingdom, and Church* (1907). Although the book dealt with the church's responsibility for social improvement, Dargan's conservative theology prevented his full endorsement of the social gospel. He rejected the earthly nature of the kingdom of God and offered some reservations about secular reforms because they omitted individual conversion; but he insisted that the church had broad social responsibilities and should support secular reforms, without sacrificing the priority of man's spiritual needs.[35]

After leaving the seminary, Dargan took a pastorate in Georgia, where he led the state convention to establish a Social Service Commission in 1911. He was chairman of this commission until 1917. In his annual reports, Dargan gave prominence to questions of personal morality, especially temperance; but he also introduced many problems of a more strictly social nature: race relations, criminal-law reform, political corruption, and unjust labor conditions. Predictably, Dargan had great difficulty in formulating an effective program for denominational action beyond the local level. He suggested that the church could attack various social ills through a program of education, moral influence, and direct political action; and he argued quite logically that the methods used in the prohibition struggle should be applied to other social evils. In practice, however, he failed to propose comparable direct action in other areas. As much as he wanted Southern Baptists involved in social betterment, the nonauthoritarian nature of denominational bodies seemed to preclude convention-led social action. Thus, he proposed that the state convention call attention to various problems but leave

34. *Minutes, Virginia, 1911,* pp. 74, 91; *Minutes, Georgia, 1911,* p. 15.
35. Edwin C. Dargan, *Society, Kingdom, and Church* (Philadelphia, 1907), pp. 15, 19–20.

direct action to local churches and individuals.[36] The difficulty Dargan faced in finding an effective place for corporate action became a fundamental problem for Southern Baptists as they attempted to implement the social-gospel ethic within their decentralized church polity.

The Baptist World Alliance proposal came before the Southern Baptist Convention during Dargan's term as convention president. John Newton Prestridge, who as editor of *The Baptist Argus* had promoted the organizing of the alliance, introduced the recommendation to the convention in 1913.[37] He noted the victories being won for prohibition and then argued that churches should now broaden their attack to include other social evils. Batten, as author of the resolution passed by the alliance, was also on hand to press for favorable action. The resolution passed with little discussion and no opposition. In appointing the seven-man Social Service Commission, President Dargan made a fortunate choice in asking William Louis Poteat, president of Wake Forest College in North Carolina, to be chairman. Among Southern Baptists, he stood out as a layman possessing both learning and personal piety. Poteat advocated a liberal social philosophy fully in accord with the Progressive age that had produced the social gospel. On one occasion he had addressed the Southern Sociological Congress on the social task of the church, and in matters of faith, he similarly stood for an enlightened religion. Trained as a biologist at the University of Berlin, Poteat defended evolution as compatible with Christian faith, a belief that would make him the center of controversy in the 1920's. One of the earliest and foremost advocates of social Christianity, he was destined to play a key role in introducing the new ideas to the denomination.[38]

Poteat set forth his commitment to social Christianity in the Social Service Commission's first report to the Southern Con-

36. *Minutes, Georgia, 1913*, pp. 100–104.
37. *Annual, SBC, 1913*, pp. 75–76.
38. William Louis Poteat, "The Social Task of the Modern Church," in *The South Mobilizing for Social Service*, pp. 534–40; Dabney, pp. 300–301; Mims, *The Advancing South*, p. 15.

vention.[39] In it he described the kingdom of God as the "organic expression of the will of God in human relations, an all-embracing social ideal to be realized in the reign of righteousness in the earthly life of man." He defined the church as a social institution responsible for the solution of social problems and further declared that the church must insist that the state be "humane, democratic under the Christian law of fraternity and justice and that its legislation suppress unrighteous practices, restrain evil men and give life its opportunity." Regarding the economic order, Poteat called on the church to "check private greed and compose class antagonisms. It must erect Christian standards in the market place, and insist that the labor of women and children be regulated. . . . that the industrial system provide the minimum of necessary working hours with the maximum of wholesome life conditions, and that the workers have a fair share of the prosperity which they produced."

In suggesting means for achieving social regeneration, Poteat took into account the sentiments of his convention audience. He conceded that individual conversion was the first duty of the church, and he also recognized that the denomination was not yet prepared to undertake a social service ministry. Instead of calling for a broad convention-directed program of action, he challenged the local churches to support welfare legislation, to stir up public opinion against social evils, and to minister to the poor, the sick, and the defective. If Poteat relied upon means unequal to the goal of social salvation, the fault lay in the convention's democratic nature, which gave it little freedom to assume an unaccustomed responsibility for social ills.

Acceptance of Poteat's report did not mean that the convention fully endorsed the social gospel. In fact, it is doubtful whether many of those present understood the report's ideological origins and implications, for Southern Baptists certainly did not live up to its high challenge in the years that followed. The commission itself was seriously handicapped as a social-action agency, in that its duties were unspecified beyond an annual

39. *Annual, SBC, 1914*, pp. 36–38.

report on social problems, and for some years it operated without funds. The commission suffered further when it lost the leadership of Poteat, after a constitutional revision took committee appointments from the president and assigned them to a nominating committee[40] that combined the Social Service Commission and the older Committee on Temperance. Arthur J. Barton, who had been head of the Temperance Committee since 1910, was appointed chairman of the combined agencies. Why Barton was chosen rather than Poteat is a matter for speculation. Something could be said for Barton's committee seniority and his temperance work. Probably the nominating committee preferred him because he was a minister and professed a more conventional theology. One thing is certain, the man who would almost single-handedly chart the course of the commission for a quarter of a century lacked the broad social sympathies, the intellectual depth, and the liberal spirit of William Poteat. Barton's more conservative treatment of the issues soon made him the accredited spokesman for the convention on all social questions.

The Social Service Commission, even with its shortcomings, marked a growing feeling among Southern Baptists that serious attention must be given to their social responsibilities. Within two years after the creation of the commission, four state conventions established committees with similar functions. Poteat figures prominently in the founding of a Social Service Commission in North Carolina, where he addressed the 1912 state convention on social regeneration. A committee organized the following year to study the relationship between the state convention and social-welfare movements declared that the convention should take an interest in all reform issues, even to the point of cooperating with nonsectarian organizations such as the North Carolina Conference for Social Service and the Southern Sociological Congress. As a result of this study, the convention established its Social Service Commission. The reforms described by the commission as "the minimum which should exist in a

40. *Ibid.*, p. 95.

Christian state" included better health, education and housing; improved economic conditions; care for dependent children; recreational facilities; and remedial care for criminals.[41]

South Carolina Baptists appointed a Committee on Social Service and Public Morals in 1914. Although its annual reports, for the first few years, resembled those from other state committees, in 1920 the committee showed some originality in urging local churches to supervise benevolent activities in their communities. Church committees were encouraged to conduct studies of social problems and to provide for the social life of young people. The 1920 report also favored interdenominational efforts to solve community problems, particularly in regard to labor and race relations.[42]

From the reports of the early state committees, it is clear that the social gospel gave Southern Baptists the greatest difficulty at the point of defining the actual role of the church in bringing about social reform. The Texas Social Service Committee developed lines of thought on this matter that were almost contradictory. Its report simultaneously backed social-reform movements while claiming that evangelism alone could cure social evils. In 1915 the committee expressed concern about public health, political corruption, criminal punishment, farm tenancy, and labor conditions. To solve these problems, the committee called upon the churches to "return to the apostolic whole gospel, the gospel that gets 'the hell out of the life that now is' as the assurance that it will save from the "hell of which [sic] is to come.' "[43] Ultimately, the report promised that by "applying the Bible" the church could abolish everything from labor disputes to Sunday baseball. Subsequent reports compounded the ambiguity. One described the church as a humanitarian institution that had inspired social reform, social welfare organizations, and state welfare programs, while another cautioned that concern for social betterment must not displace evangelism since "social

41. *Annual, North Carolina, 1912*, pp. 73–75; *1913*, p. 85; *1914*, pp. 90–91; *1918*, pp. 90–91.
42. *Minutes, South Carolina, 1914*, pp. 102–108; *1920*, pp. 169–74.
43. *Annual, Texas, 1915*, pp. 26–28.

regeneration" could be achieved only by the "replacing of bad men by good men."[44] The essential problem exhibited here was the inability to appreciate the corporate nature of evil, coupled with the assumption that all social evil could somehow be cured if the church attended to its business of winning souls.

The Virginia Social Service Commission also examined the crucial problem of how the church should fulfill its social mission. At first this commission seemed in full accord with the social gospel, for it sponsored the most active social-service program in the denomination, including the publication of literature and the holding of annual conferences featuring such leaders as William Poteat, farm editor Clarence Poe, and sociologist Charles S. Gardner.[45] On the other hand, the Virginia Social Service Commission offered some of the most pointed criticisms of the social gospel's methodology because it involved the church in political and economic questions. Commission Chairman Armistead R. Long expressed misgivings about the recent interests of Southern Baptists in the social gospel and noted with concern that Poteat's 1914 statement at the Southern Convention could be traced directly to the social creed of the Federal Council of Churches. Long approved the goals of the social gospelers, but he objected to the use of direct action by the church. Such action, he argued, violated church-state separation by making the church authoritative through its use of the state's coercive powers. As an alternative to political action, he suggested that the church promote the kingdom of God indirectly through organizations and institutions that it inspired but did not control. Long's proposal would have restricted the practical impact of the social gospel without denying the social implications of Christianity; it would also have made the social gospel less political and more compatible with Southern Baptist beliefs about the nature of the church.[46]

The efforts of social-action committees were not the only at-

44. *Ibid., 1916,* pp. 27–29; *1918,* p. 31.
45. *Minutes, Virginia, 1913,* p. 62; *1915,* p. 103; *1916,* pp. 97–98.
46. *Ibid., 1914,* pp. 109–13.

tempts to interpret the social gospel within the context of Southern Baptist traditions. In these same years the convention's two theological schools responded to the challenge of social Christianity by introducing courses in sociology. Dargan had begun offering his course at Southern Baptist Theological Seminary after learning about the establishment of a department of sociology by Graham Taylor at Chicago Theological Seminary in 1894.[47] After Dargan resigned in 1907, the seminary created a full professorship in Christian sociology. The new post went to Charles S. Gardner, who held the position until 1929.[48] Gardner's formal training offered little promise of his contributions in this field. He had attended denominational colleges and Southern Seminary, but he held no graduate degrees. Largely a self-taught sociologist, he developed an interest in applied Christianity from reading the works of major social-gospel writers.[49]

Gardner helped spread the new ideas among Southern Baptists by incorporating the social gospel into his courses. For a text he wrote *The Ethics of Jesus and Social Progress*, which attempted to harmonize the goals of sociology with the Christian ethic, and he took special pains to show that the social gospel need not subvert Southern Baptist theology.[50] Thus, he defined the kingdom of God as the spiritual subjection of the individual to the will of God. But this relationship, he insisted, should lead toward the transformation of society. The church had a duty beyond individual reformation to work for a social order that conformed to Christian ideals. This social ideal required the state to do more than preserve order and protect property; it must

47. Edwin C. Dargan, "The Teaching of Sociology in the Seminary," *Seminary Magazine* (Mar., 1900), pp. 298–99.

48. For Gardner's contribution see F. M. Powell, "The Southern Baptist Theological Seminary Completes 75 Years of Struggle and Achievement," *Review and Expositor*, XXXI (July, 1934), 346; William Wright Barnes, "The Theological Curriculum of Tomorrow in the Light of the Past," *Review and Expositor*, XLIV (Apr., 1947), 153.

49. Earl R. Whaley, "The Ethical Contribution of Charles S. Gardner" (Th.M. thesis, Southern Baptist Theological Seminary, 1953), p. 15. Whaley specifically mentions the influence of Walter Rauschenbusch, George Herron, Shailer Mathews, Washington Gladden, and E. A. Ross.

50. (New York, 1914), pp. 7, 19.

regulate wealth, provide welfare services, and abolish conditions that produce crime and poverty.[51]

Like most social-gospel writers, Gardner saw capitalism as the main hindrance to social reconstruction. "The economic organization," he argued, "has resisted as yet more successfully than any other of the essential social functions the application of the principles of the kingdom."[52] Gardner blamed unregulated capitalism for slums, poverty, political corruption, and crime and declared that the competitive system was contrary to the Christian principles of love, service, and cooperation. He condemned social Darwinism because it lent justification to prosperity gained at the expense of the public good. Likewise, Gardner rejected classical economics because it used the fiction of natural law to support an antisocial economic system. Having made the economic system the chief offender in the unjust social order, he advocated its reorganization in order to realize the Christian society. He spoke only in general terms at this point, but the influence of Progressive thinkers was unmistakable when he discussed the concentration of private wealth, the socialization of industry, and public-welfare programs.[53]

For all his social-gospel enthusiasm, Gardner never lost sight of his Baptist heritage. He did not believe, for example, that the Christian society could be achieved by changing the social order alone; he made individual regeneration basic to the reformed society by insisting that the salvation experience must carry over into the whole life of man.[54] Here, of course, Gardner came close to the position of the social gospel's critics, who admonished the church to change the world by changing individuals. Gardner did not deal with the problems posed by making the regenerate society dependent upon regenerate men. Could the church do nothing for social reform until all men were redeemed? and what certainty was there that these redeemed men would work

51. *Ibid.*, pp. 75, 78–80, 349–50.
52. *Ibid.*, p. 110.
53. *Ibid.*, pp. 111–12, 193–96, 228, 244–48, 259–66, 269–76.
54. *Ibid.*, pp. 200, 202, 272–74.

for social justice? His failure to treat these questions points up the central problem Southern Baptists faced in trying to find a place for social Christianity without modifying the status assigned to personal evangelism.

Gardner's book, even with its failings, made an important contribution to the social attitudes of the denomination. It was the only full-length treatment of social Christianity by a Southern Baptist. Despite the author's borrowings from earlier writers, he showed originality in trying to reconcile personal and social religion. Most important, he demonstrated that one could adopt liberal social thought without accepting a liberal theology. He placed man's earthly relationships under the jurisdiction of the Christian ethic without sacrificing the spiritual and personal elements in religion, a point of crucial importance to his fellow Baptists.

By the end of the Progressive era, the social-gospel ideology had made definite inroads into the life and thought of Southern Baptists. Their seminaries offered courses on the social aspects of Christianity. After the adoption of prohibition, the social-service committees gave greater attention to the problems in the economic order, issues of war and peace, race relations, and other social questions. Within fifteen years, every state convention had a standing social-service committee, the annual reports of which afforded an opportunity for a cross section of leaders to express views on the church's responsibility for a wide range of social issues.

The considerable evidence of social-gospel influence does not mean that liberal social thought gained control of Southern Baptist life. The most that can be said is that the social-gospel ideology brought an end to the intellectual solidarity of the nineteenth century, when Baptist churches in the South functioned as cultural establishments in their uncritical support of the prevailing order. The teachings of social Christianity divided Southern Baptist thinking regarding the church's responsibility to society. The more conservative evangelical view claimed that personal religion fulfilled the church's social duty. On the other side, the social-gospel tradition called for collective action against evils that were social in nature. The coexistence of these two views in denominational life produced varied and sometimes contradictory responses to the social issues of the twentieth century.

VI

THE "NOBLE GESTURE"

The Social Service Commission of the Southern Baptist Convention concentrated almost exclusively on the dry campaign until after ratification of the Eighteenth Amendment in 1920, after which more attention was devoted to social questions such as world peace, race relations, and the economic order.[1] The treatment of these issues in the period between the two world wars provided for the first time a comprehensive record of the denomination's social attitudes. During these years the agency functioned with only minor changes in its operations and under the continuous leadership of one chairman: Arthur J. Barton, whose death in 1942, followed by the appointment of a full-time executive for the commission in 1947, marked the end of an era in the history of the agency.

The commission's treatment of social issues reflected the dichotomy in Southern Baptist attitudes about the church's social mission. The commission acknowledged its ties to the social gospel, and indeed, the whole operation of the agency assumed that the church's redemptive mission extended to all areas of society. On the other hand, the commission insisted that social redemption could never be realized without individual redemption, a position that, hopefully, would dispel the fears of

---

1. One indication of the new emphasis was the dropping of the word "temperance" from the official title of the commission in 1920. See *Annual, SBC, 1920,* p. 128.

those who saw social Christianity as antithetical to personal evangelism.[2]

Although the commission expressed an allegiance to both traditions, Barton somewhat misstated the case when he claimed that the agency had "always kept the two in balance." The annual reports show clearly that individualism in religion exerted a much stronger influence. Great emphasis was placed on matters of personal morality, such as temperance, gambling, and Sabbath-keeping. Here the commission set forth the Christian position in specific detail and called on the church to impose its standards on society. By contrast, social questions, such as peace, race, and labor, usually received very general and noncommittal treatments with no appeal for direct action. The agency operated on a philosophy that subordinated social reform to individual reform. As Barton said, the "salvation of society must be approached through the salvation of the individual."[3]

The commission offered a modified version of social Christianity partly because as a denominational agency it depended on the good will of the constituency. Since local churches cooperated on a voluntary basis, the need for consensus made unlikely a strong policy on any issue that might threaten unity. Other factors also limited the commission's operations; for instance, insufficient financial backing precluded a program of education and social action of much consequence. Furthermore, the Southern Convention had authorized no specific activity beyond making annual reports, and the full commission met only once or twice each year, mainly to approve a report prepared by the chairman. The membership, which grew from ten to more than twenty, served only one-year terms until the adoption of a rotation plan with three-year terms was adopted in 1934. In selecting the members of the commission the convention's nominating committee took care to have each state represented, a

2. *Ibid.*, 1922, p. 96; 1923, p. 101; 1936, pp. 25–26; 1922, p. 96; *Western Recorder* (Louisville), May 16, 1935, p. 1; Charles Price Johnson, "Southern Baptists and the Social Gospel Movement," (Th. D. thesis, Southwestern Baptist Theological Seminary, 1948), pp. 71–75. For the general reaction against the social gospel in Protestantism, see Paul A. Carter, pp. 48, 60, 110–21.

3. *Biblical Recorder* (Raleigh), Oct. 24, 1934, p. 1.

policy that did not always provide the best qualified persons or make meetings convenient. Most members were prominent ministers. Although their appointment was probably essential to sustain the convention's confidence, they contributed little toward making the agency an effective force for social Christianity.

And although the membership also included a few laymen and educators well qualified to deal with public issues, they exerted only minor influence. William Poteat sat on the commission during the twenties and thirties, and Charles S. Gardner served two three-year terms. Jesse B. Weatherspoon, Gardner's successor at Southern Seminary, joined the commission in 1930, became its chairman upon Barton's death, and then led the move that gave the agency a full-time executive. W. W. Gaines, an Atlanta lawyer and chairman of Georgia's Social Service Committee, voiced strong liberal views on labor and the New Deal during his fourteen years on the commission. United States Senator Hugo Black served one term before he achieved national prominence as a New Deal supporter and as President Roosevelt's first Supreme Court appointment. These men brought to the work a broad social vision, but their liberal social philosophy did not dominate the commission. Moreover, there is no evidence to suggest that they made any special effort either to change the commission's cautious policies or to effect a more aggressive program of action.[4]

Because the commission had no salaried workers and the individual members assumed little responsibility, the work of the agency depended largely on the initiative of the chairman. Barton's chairmanship took on added significance because it extended over a twenty-eight-year period. A forceful personality

4. See Poteat's *The Way of Victory* (Chapel Hill, 1929) and his address, "The Program of Jesus," *The Religious Herald* (Richmond), Nov. 28, 1935, pp. 3–5, 17. Gardner's articles, "The Problem of Democracy from the Psychological Point of View," *Review and Expositor*, XXIX (July, 1932), 305–46; "The Relation of the Individual to Society," *Review and Expositor*, XXVI (Jan., 1929), 3–26; and his text, *The Ethics of Jesus and Social Progress* (New York, 1914). Weatherspoon's maiden address at the seminary was published as "The Ethical Note in Preaching," *Review and Expositor*, XXVII (Oct., 1930), 391–406. Gaines headed the Georgia committee in 1925 and from 1929 to 1934. His views will be examined more fully in the next chapter.

in the center of convention affairs, Barton easily took command of the agency, and under his firm hand it gained an established place in denominational life. The position brought him little real power; yet diligent attention to the assignment assured him considerable recognition. Always a loyal denominational man, he became the authority entrusted with sensitive issues that were unfamiliar to many Baptists. With a single exception, he prepared every commission report; and, in addition, he carried on an extensive correspondence, wrote numerous articles, prepared news releases, delivered addresses all across the convention, participated in conferences outside the denomination, and represented the convention before congressional committees.[5] Barton's work was remarkable in one other respect: he performed these services without compensation in addition to his regular duties as a pastor and denominational executive.[6]

His lack of seminary training did not prevent Barton from holding a variety of important appointments. He spent more than half of his career as pastor in five states. Between churches, he held eight denominational posts, including executive positions with the home and foreign mission boards and three state conventions. During much of this time, Barton was also an active participant in the temperance movement. Prior to World War I he headed the Anti-Saloon League in Texas, and he was a leader in the campaign for national prohibition. During the prohibition era, he was chairman of the National Executive Committee of the Anti-Saloon League and president of the National Conference of Organizations Supporting the Eighteenth Amendment.

Barton's life-long association with the temperance cause illustrates a basic problem Southern Baptists had in carrying out the practical demands of the social gospel.[7] Barton accepted readily the idea that the church should address itself to all social issues, yet he never proposed the broad program of action envisioned by social-gospel adherents. Indeed, sometimes he took

5. Barton described his activities in *Annual, SBC, 1933*, p. 115.
6. His principal churches were in Alexandria, La. (1918–24), and Wilmington, N.C. (1930–42). He was executive-secretary for the state conventions in Arkansas, Texas, and Missouri.
7. *Annual, SBC, 1922*, p. 96; *1923*, p. 101; *1936*, p. 25.

pains to dissociate the commission from a supposed overemphasis on social action: "Southern Baptists stand unalterably opposed to any interpretation of the Gospel that would substitute social service for the Gospel, or that would make as our first objective in preaching the Gospel the transformation of the social order."[8]

Barton interpreted the social gospel in a way that left no doubt about his evangelical loyalty. To him, the "social implications" of Christianity were realized as the natural result of personal evangelism.[9] By making social religion the product of personal religion, Barton missed one of the main contributions of the social gospel, the idea that the Christian message addressed only to individuals does not ensure justice in social relations.[10] Barton's version of social Christianity, while satisfying most Southern Baptists who did not want their churches embroiled in social controversy, involved him in a glaring inconsistency in the treatment of issues related to personal morals as compared to social issues. He did not hesitate to engage in interdenominational cooperation and political pressure to preserve the Sabbath, to eliminate obscenity, and, above all, to abolish the liquor traffic; but he called for no such direct action in dealing with racial or economical ills.

Barton further separated the commission from social Christianity by his own social conservatism. Although his reports incorporated some progressive ideas, he assumed that all necessary improvements could be effected without disrupting the existing order. With considerable exaggeration he boasted that the commission had taken "advanced positions on all the great social problems affecting human society and government."[11] Barton imagined himself as a social progressive who had not forsaken a sound evangelical faith. Actually, his social views were never

8. *Western Recorder* (Louisville), May 16, 1935, p. 1.
9. *Biblical Recorder* (Raleigh), Oct. 24, 1934, p. 1.
10. Hopkins, *The Rise of the Social Gospel*, p. 16; Henry F. May, pp. 110–11, 126–27, 164, 170; Paul A. Carter, pp. 4–9; Samuel Zane Batten, *The Social Task of Christianity*, p. 151; Henry Clay Vedder, *The Gospel of Jesus and the Problem of Democracy* (New York, 1914), preface.
11. *Annual, SBC, 1933*, p. 116.

much ahead of the constituency on any issue, and in no instance were his reports opposed because they contained liberal ideas. Never offering strong criticisms of denominational attitudes, the reports reflected prevailing sentiment more often than they supplied enlightened leadership. The commission did not even represent the most progressive thought in the convention; some state Baptist journals and social-service committees were decidedly more friendly to the New Deal and more liberal on economic questions generally.[12]

The commission's long and detailed reports—sometimes running to fifteen thousand words—were presented to the Southern Baptist Convention in annual session. Adopted in conjunction with a major address on some phase of social morality, the reports furnished information on a variety of issues along with a few recommendations. Their content, for purposes of further analysis, may be classified under the general headings of war and peace, race relations, the economic order, and personal morality, with the last category including such diverse topics as temperance, Sabbath desecration, gambling, obscene literature, motion pictures, and divorce.

Southern Baptists issued statements on war and peace for some years before the Social Service Commission discussed the topics. The Southern Convention endorsed The Hague proposal of 1899, establishing a Court of International Arbitration, and President William Howard Taft's 1911 offer to arbitrate Anglo-American disputes. When war broke out in Europe in 1914, the state conventions of North Carolina and Georgia issued strong peace statements, the latter going so far as to denounce all wars as evil. However, Baptists, like most Americans, ultimately gave unqualified support to United States participation in the war. The Georgia Convention, reversing its previous opposition, now declared the war as a struggle to preserve those "eternal principles of freedom and brotherhood" for which "Baptists have

12. Patrick Henry Hill, "Ethical Emphases of the Baptist Editors in the Southeastern Region of the United States, 1915–1940" (Th.D. thesis, Southern Baptist Theological Seminary, 1949), pp. 163–68, 174, 208–209, 215–16, 218, 282–83. The state committees will be discussed in the next chapter.

always . . . stood." The Southern Convention president at the 1919 meeting likewise called the war a battle for Baptist principles, and editors of Baptist journals agreed that patriotic support of the war was nothing less than a Christian obligation.[13]

After World War I the Social Service Commission discussed the peace issue in almost every report and on one occasion participated in an interdenominational peace conference.[14] Enthusiastic endorsements were given to various international peace efforts with one major exception, the League of Nations. Approval of the league was withheld even though the 1920 convention in Washington, D.C., featured a celebrated address on the capitol steps by George W. Truett, pastor of the First Baptist Church in Dallas, Texas, urging ratification of the charter. Not until 1937, in the face of an international arms buildup, did the commission indicate a somewhat belated faith in the league as an instrument of peace. In contrast to its coolness toward the league, the commission approved wholeheartedly less controversial peace moves. It urged the calling of the Washington Peace Conference of 1921–22, which produced a disarmament agreement among the naval powers in the Pacific; it praised the Pact of Paris of 1928, in which fifteen nations renounced war; it endorsed the arms limitations worked out at the London Naval Conference in 1930; and it acclaimed the Pan-American Peace Conference of 1936 that brought pledges of noninterference by American states. The commission directed its strongest peace activity against congressional isolationists who blocked United States membership in the Permanent Court of International Justice. In nearly every report from 1924 to 1936, the commission urged membership in the World Court and finally carried its appeal directly to the Senate Foreign Relations Committee.[15]

While showing some real concern for world peace, Southern

13. *Annual, SBC, 1895*, p. 58; *1911*, p. 23; *1919*, p. 17; *Annual, North Carolina, 1914*, p. 91; *Minutes, Georgia, 1914*, pp. 28–29; *1915*, p. 43; *1917*, p. 44; Patrick H. Hill, pp. 248–72, 276–77.

14. *Annual, SBC, 1926*, p. 110. The meeting was called the National Study Conference on the Church and World Peace.

15. *Annual, SBC, 1937*, p. 73; *1921*, p. 84; *1930*, pp. 67–70; *1929*, p. 92; *1937*, pp. 73–74; *1936*, pp. 24, 34–35.

Baptists had little sympathy for pacifism at a time when antiwar sentiment reached a new high among Protestants.[16] The commission did succeed in having a resolution passed that accorded conscientious objectors the "right of their convictions" and provided for their registration at convention headquarters in order to certify their status before the government.[17] Unfortunately, during World War II the convention took no responsibility for the handful of Southern Baptist pacifists being supervised by non-Baptist peace organizations; and when the Executive Committee of the convention refused even to make a reimbursement for this service, Southern Baptists passed up a rare opportunity to give practical expression to their historic stand for freedom of conscience.[18]

For Southern Baptists, as for other Americans, world events rather than a priori abstractions determined attitudes regarding war. During the thirties, the Social Service Commission annually opposed war and arms expenditures, but when war came to Europe the agency began to reverse itself. Its 1940 report declared: "As for ourselves, we hate war . . . but we do not believe that the Christian Spirit forbids purely defensive war."[19] The report then justified national defense expenditures to meet the threat of totalitarian regimes. Exercising some restraint, the commission admitted that war could not be equated with the will of God and warned Baptist congregations not to become agents of war propaganda; the 1942 report dropped all such caution and virtually identified the war with the cause of Christianity.[20] Thus, the commission followed the typical pattern of American churches by preaching peace in peacetime and supporting war in time of war.

Undoubtedly the most neglected problem in the commission reports was that of the Negro. Traditional attitudes in the convention concentrated on the spiritual welfare of the individual

---

16. Robert Moats Miller, *American Protestantism and Social Issues,* pp. 337–41.
17. *Annual, SBC, 1940,* p. 96.
18. Editorial, *Christian Frontiers,* II (June, 1947), 171–72.
19. *Annual, SBC, 1940,* p. 87.
20. *Ibid.,* 1942, p. 91.

Negro. When Southern Baptists looked at the social disadvantages of the race, they favored improvements, but always in
conformity with white supremacy. Barton's racial views were
characteristic of Southern white paternalism: in a 1913 address
to the Southern Sociological Congress, he offered the usual
stereotype of the Negro as a childlike creature under the benevolent care of tolerant white superiors.[21]

The Social Service Commission after World War I offered
some hope that Southern Baptists might assume greater obligations for improving the Negro's social position. In 1920 its report
included a lengthy appeal for better education, housing, economic opportunity, and treatment before the law.[22] Unfortunately, the commission scarcely mentioned specific areas of
racial injustice after this auspicious beginning, with the exception of the most scandalous iniquity—mob violence. Almost
every report in the period between the two world wars denounced the lynch evil in the South.

At no time did the commission question the basic race patterns
designed to preserve white supremacy. The 1920 report affirmed
loyalty to racial separation, and as late as 1940 the commission
justified wage differentials and unequal educational facilities
for Negroes because of "differences in social position and living
requirements," even though other portions of the 1940 report
were progressive. One rather exceptional resolution on race
called for "equal and impartial justice before the courts; better and more equitable opportunities in industrial, business,
and professional engagements; and a more equitable share in
public funds and more adequate opportunities in the field of
education."[23]

Southern Baptist opinion on the economic issues of the early
twentieth century reveal a general lack of sympathy for organ-

21. Barton, "The White Man's Task in the Uplift of the Negro," *The South
Mobilizing for Social Service*, pp. 460–76. See also Foy Dan Valentine, "A Historical Study of Southern Baptists and Race Relations, 1917–1947" (Th.D. thesis,
Southwestern Baptist Theological Seminary, 1949), pp. 14, 55, 60–64, 70;
Patrick Henry Hill, pp. 222–48.
22. *Annual, SBC, 1920*, p. 97.
23. *Ibid., 1940*, pp. 85, 95.

ized labor and a failure to grasp the complexity of economic problems in an industrial society.[24] These attitudes resulted from assumptions drawn from a rural economy together with a widely held belief that foreign ideologies dominated the labor movement. The most common reaction to labor-management disputes condemned violence and rebuked the disputants for failing to practice brotherhood and the golden rule. In the absence of informed analysis of the issues involved, such pious talk had almost no relevance to the problem. The Social Service Commission itself at times indulged in generalities equally oversimplified and unrealistic. Its first important statement on labor asserted that both capital and labor had rights that could be reconciled without "serious difficulty" if the industrial system were "permeated with the Christian Spirit." The report did acknowledge that the struggle was "unequal," with the "odds against labor," but then concluded with the exhortation, "Let us preach the gospel of peace and brotherhood and service; and let both Capital and Labor avoid all extremes and each seek the other's good. Thus shall social justice be done, and peace and brotherhood prevail."[25]

The commission said almost nothing further about labor until the Great Depression forced some reappraisals of unemployment problems. The 1930 report included a forthright prolabor declaration inspired by a series of violent disputes over the unionization of textile workers in Tennessee and the Carolinas. The statement supported labor's right to organize in order to obtain a "fair and living wage," advocated better housing, endorsed the nine-hour day, and opposed child labor and night work for women.[26]

24. Robert Moats Miller, "Social Attitudes of American Baptists, 1919–1929," *Chronicle,* XIX (Apr., 1956), 76–78; Hugh A. Brimm, "The Social Consciousness of Southern Baptists in Relation to Some Regional Problems, 1910–1935" (Th.D. thesis, Southern Baptist Theological Seminary, 1944), pp. 118–19; Patrick Henry Hill, pp. 206–21, 282; George D. Kelsey, "The Social Thought of Contemporary Southern Baptists" (Ph.D. diss., Yale University, 1946), pp. 169–88; *Biblical Recorder* (Raleigh), Oct. 3, 1934, p. 7.

25. *Annual, SBC, 1921,* p. 84.

26. *Ibid.,* 1930, pp. 68–69; Samuel Yellen, *American Labor Struggles* (New York, 1936), pp. 292–326.

This report marked only a temporary departure from an otherwise conservative economic outlook, for the views of the commission on the New Deal recovery program were far behind those of most denominational spokesmen. Even though the state Baptist journals, including those previously unsympathetic to labor, praised the New Deal for correcting the anti-Christian features in capitalism,[27] the commission would not endorse any of Roosevelt's economic reforms. Instead, it criticized the Congress for granting excessive power to the president. There was enough New Deal support at the 1933 convention to force Barton to withdraw a resolution critical of the administration, but he successfully incorporated similar objections into the 1938 report, warning that the New Deal marked a dangerous trend toward "centralization" and "regimentation" in violation of individual rights.[28]

This anti-New Deal sentiment almost certainly stemmed from Barton's hostility to Roosevelt for advocating repeal of prohibition. Every commission report from 1926 until repeal had declared that political support should be determined solely on the dry question, and in 1928 Barton had gone so far as to repudiate the Democratic party for its disloyalty to prohibition in nominating Alfred E. Smith, a wet and a Roman Catholic, as its presidential candidate.[29] Roosevelt's inclusion of repeal in his recovery program furnished reason enough for a broadside against the whole New Deal. In articles published in the state Baptist newspapers, Barton expressed only contempt for the claims that Roosevelt's program had inaugurated many needed social reforms; he reasoned that no amount of reform could compensate for the evils that would result from repeal.[30] His political disaffection over the prohibition issue apparently destroyed whatever sympathy he might have had toward attempts of the administration to cure the economic ills of America.

27. Patrick Henry Hill, pp. 274–82.
28. *Annual, SBC, 1933*, pp. 104, 117; *1938*, pp. 101–102, 113.
29. *Ibid., 1928*, p. 88.
30. *Western Recorder* (Louisville), June 14, 1934, p. 12; *Biblical Recorder* (Raleigh), June 20, 1934, p. 1; *Arkansas Baptist* (Little Rock), Apr. 26, 1934, p. 14.

Barton's preoccupation with prohibition was reflected in the work of the commission, and during the dry decade, he called prohibition "our greatest achievement" and its enforcement "our greatest task." After repeal, Barton kept the commission allied to temperance forces through membership in the National Temperance and Prohibition Council. Ignoring the major social crisis of the thirties—the depression—the commission detailed a declining morality that it attributed to repeal; and in one of Barton's last reports, he reaffirmed his devotion to total abstinence and the suppression of the liquor traffic by law.[31]

The emphasis that Barton placed on temperance tells much about the way Southern Baptists generally viewed their social mission. Dry laws offered, in absolute terms, a simplified solution to an evil represented as the primary cause of numerous social ills, from poverty and broken homes to crime and political corruption. Southern Baptists easily united with other church groups against demon rum as the visible agent of the spiritual underworld and engaged in an immense amount of political activity, from their local communities to the high councils of state and federal government. To a people who saw the immediate contest over prohibition as the most crucial in the struggle for the preservation of morality in a changing America, the issues of war, race, and the economic order seemed quite remote. These complex social problems were not susceptible to simple moralistic answers, for they required something few Baptists were prepared to undertake, a careful analysis of social conditions and creative interpretations of traditional religious concepts.

During Barton's chairmanship, the Social Service Commission took up several matters of individual morality in addition to the drink evil. It simply registered disapproval of certain vices, like gambling, obscene literature, and dancing; but on other matters, notably Sabbath desecration, motion pictures, and divorce, the commission advocated corrective legal measures. The commission supported laws curtailing business and public entertain-

31. *Annual, SBC, 1927*, p. 115; *1928*, p. 86; *1934*, pp. 106–12; *1935*, pp. 67–71; *1936*, pp. 28–34; *1940*, p. 98; Edmund A. Moore, *A Catholic Runs for President* (New York, 1956), pp. 169–70.

ment on the Sabbath, justifying such laws on grounds that the state should provide a "Civil Sabbath" not as an aid to religion but as a matter of public welfare. The commission criticized the motion-picture industry because it secularized the Sabbath and offered unwholesome displays of sex and crime, and when the industry failed to police itself satisfactorily, the commission urged government censorship. Statements concerning marriage and divorce offered few suggestions beyond tighter legal requirements. One special report proposed uniform marriage regulations through federal law, and another described as "vicious and immoral" the proposed relaxation of birth-control laws. Reports in other years offered little except condemnation of rising divorce rates.[32]

In view of the general consensus on questions of personal morality, one might expect that some constructive programs would have been carried out, at least in these areas. The state, it was presumed, had a duty to police public morals, but the denomination supported no systematic efforts consistent with this belief. Barton, recognizing this failure, made repeated requests for the expansion of the commission into a full-time agency.[33] In 1925, when the denomination adopted a convention-wide cooperative program for allocating funds, Barton tried unsuccessfully to have the commission included in the unified budget. He then considered the idea of direct financial appeals to the churches, a practice the unified budget was designed to eliminate,[34] but dropped this plan in favor of modest but more dependable support offered by the Sunday School Board, which had its own source of income through the sale of literature. From 1929 onward the board underwrote commission expenses, an arrangement that still left the agency without employed leadership. The board further aided the commission's work by including a week-long Christian Life Conference in its summer assembly program at Ridgecrest, North Carolina.[35] This annual

32. *Annual, SBC, 1921*, pp. 82–84; *1922*, p. 98; *1934*, pp. 102–18; *1936*, pp. 35–36, *1935*, p. 70; *1920*, pp. 127–28.
33. *Ibid., 1924*, p. 118; *1925*, p. 121; *1926*, p. 113.
34. *Ibid., 1930*, p. 76; *1931*, p. 128.
35. *Ibid., 1934*, p. 279.

conference provided the commission its only regular opportunity for extended consideration of social issues.

Although Barton repeatedly requested an enlargement of the commission's operations, his efforts bear a second look. Because he made no effort to organize support but buried his requests in the commission reports, where they would never be considered on the floor of the Southern Baptist Convention, there is reason to believe that his pleas were only halfhearted. And although his decision not to press for convention consideration of the establishment of a full-time commission could have been calculated to avoid the possibility of rejection, the most damaging evidence against Barton's desire for such a commission status comes from his attitude toward a 1933 proposal for a social-action agency entirely unrelated to his own appeals.[36]

E. McNeill Poteat, Jr., pastor in Raleigh and a nephew of William Louis Poteat, introduced an ambitious plan for a fully staffed Social Research Bureau, a full discussion of which will be presented later. Poteat's move is important here because Barton opposed what could have become an authentic social-gospel program. From the beginning, Poteat's social and theological liberalism had caused doubts about the idea, and conservatives made defeat certain by representing the plan as an attempt to foster social reforms at the expense of personal regeneration. In the end, the convention voted on a modified proposal that would simply have expanded the work of Barton's commission. But Barton, unwilling to support a move still identified with Poteat's liberalism, helped defeat the very thing he had been advocating for fifteen years.[37]

The absence of financial backing throughout Barton's years as chairman seriously restricted the operations of the commission. Even so, considering the dimensions of social concern among Southern Baptists before World War I, the agency's activities represented important advancements. The convention

36. *Ibid.*, 1933, p. 118.
37. *Western Recorder* (Louisville), May 16, 1935, p. 1; *Annual, SBC, 1936*, pp. 37–38.

took cognizance of a wide range of social problems; and, what is more important, it acknowledged some responsibility for dealing with them from the Christian perspective. There were times when the commission seemed to discern the necessity of corporate action, as opposed to individual reform, in dealing effectively with social ills. In some instances, the agency supported socially progressive measures.

Regardless of what may be said on the credit side, the commission's failings outnumbered its achievements. Too often its analyses of social problems were superficial and its recommendations oversimplified. Even when noting social injustices, the commission hoped for the peaceful preservation of the present order rather than basic alterations in society. Thus, the agency encouraged disarmament and World Court membership while refusing to champion a new kind of international order, as represented by the League of Nations. It advocated better social conditions for the Negro without demanding full equality, and in its persistent condemnation of mob violence, it seemed more concerned about racial peace than social justice. During the depression years, the commission repeatedly found fault with the New Deal but said almost nothing about the economic distress in the nation.

In view of the commission's many shortcomings, it is difficult to state concisely what the agency represented in Southern Baptist life. Although it demonstrated some new ideas, it was not the product of a full-scale movement nor even of a minor intellectual revolt. A liberal minority indeed existed, but the commission did not represent it. At best, the existence of the commission testified to a neglected area in convention affairs but did little to correct this failing. It lacked vision and insight as a social critic; it lacked resources and leadership as a social-action agency. Caught between two ideological currents—personal evangelism and social Christianity—the commission held completely to neither. Conscious of its precarious position among evangelicals intolerant of any threat to personal religion, the agency always seemed to err on the side of overcaution. Perhaps Jesse B. Weatherspoon, Barton's successor, summarized best the commission's contribution. In offering the proposal that finally gave the commission employed leadership in 1946, he referred to its past work as little more than a "noble gesture and a token of a slightly aroused conscience."[38]

38. *Annual, SBC, 1946,* p. 121.

VII

THE DIVIDED MIND

The full range of Southern Baptist social attitudes found expression in the state conventions' social-service committees. Originally established to promote temperance, these committees were expanded during the 1920's and the 1930's to cover social problems generally. Through them a large representation of church leaders commented on many social issues. More than the Social Service Commission of the Southern Baptist Convention, the state committees revealed fundamental disagreements regarding the church's social ministry. Opinion varied from almost total rejection of the social-gospel ideology to full endorsement of the progressive goals of liberal Protestantism.

Opponents of church involvement in social causes, who sometimes controlled the committees, voiced the old argument that social service detracted from the church's spiritual ministry.[1] They justified their antagonism to practical ministries by downgrading the importance of social work. The Texas Social Service Committee sounded almost contemptuous when it declared: "Social service is temporal and material; the work of the church is eternal and spiritual. Social service seeks to improve the housing problem in the slums; the church points to mansions in the skies. Social service deals in soap as the means to cleanliness; the church contends for the cleansing through the blood of Christ."[2]

1. Charles Price Johnson, p. 71.
2. *Annual, Texas, 1920*, p. 80.

Social gospel critics sometimes accepted the goals of a better society but insisted that evangelism, not reform activity, offered the best way to achieve this end. The Virginia committee of 1920 disposed of social reform in one sweep: "The Baptist attitude towards all social reform work and service is that the unadulterated gospel preached and accepted solves all social problems, rightly adjusts all industrial inequalities, removes domestic frictions, adjourns divorce courts and supplies adequate protection and uplift to the weaker part of humanity."[3] This report warned ministers not to waste their high calling on reform movements. "Right gospel preaching," the committee promised, "will send nine-tenths of these special social service organizations to the scrap heap."[4]

On the other side, some state commitees put up a strong defense of social Christianity.[5] Georgia's Social Service Committee scorned the "transcendental" theology that kept Christians "unspotted from the world" and the church isolated from social problems. Another Georgia report argued that the "full Gospel" must include public health, education, race relations, world peace, and the care of criminals and defectives. The 1933 Virginia committee insisted that the church should engage in social reform until "the organization of society itself shall accord with Christ's will." Likewise, the committee in Alabama urged Baptists to "take the Social Gospel seriously and enter upon a Crusade to achieve its meaning in human society."[6]

Although every state committee gave allegiance to the social gospel at some time or other, none carried on a very active program. Established in recognition of a neglected responsibility, the committees were not equipped to remedy this failing. Most often committees of from three to nine members serving one-

3. *Minutes, Virginia, 1920,* p. 98.
4. *Ibid.* See also *1939,* p. 59; *Annual, Arkansas, 1949,* p. 85; *Annual, Tennessee, 1925,* p. 59; *Annual, Texas, 1944,* pp. 172–73.
5. *Annual, North Carolina, 1921,* pp. 112–13; *1935,* p. 4. *Proceedings, Mississippi, 1923,* p. 76; *Minutes, Virginia, 1936,* p. 62; *Annual, Texas, 1922,* p. 148, *1930,* p. 136; *Annual, Florida, 1936,* p. 131; *Proceedings, Arkansas, 1934,* pp. 30–31.
6. *Minutes, Georgia, 1922,* pp. 22–24; *1927,* p. 30; *Minutes, Virginia, 1933,* p. 95; *Annual, Alabama, 1933,* p. 24.

year terms operated without financial assistance. The work depended on a chairman, whose principal task was to prepare an annual report that might comprise several thousand words. Most chairmen were full-time pastors who headed their committees for one or two years, and while they usually gave serious attention to their assignment, only a few exhibited much originality or strong leadership. Exceptional leadership was exhibited, however, by men like F. Clyde Helms, a South Carolina pastor; W. W. Gaines; and William Louis Poteat, all of whom were chairmen of their respective committees for several years and became outstanding spokesmen for social Christianity.

The state committees illustrate once again the reluctance of Southern Baptists to invest authority in centralized agencies. The state conventions, like the Southern Convention, were made up of those representatives from independent churches who attended the annual meetings. The precarious power of the state organizations made them extremely fearful of controversy that might alienate churches; and, because almost any suggestion for a strong social program was likely to bring charges of infringing on the "autonomy" of local congregations, the committees were not in a position to exercise initiative on social questions or even to provide much effective leadership in molding opinions.[7]

Lacking independent authority, the committees usually recorded the prevailing sentiment of the constituency. They took strong positions when discussing strictly moral issues on which Baptist views were united. On controversial social problems, they avoided progressive stands, preferring instead to speak in safe generalities. The excessive attention given to personal morality was all the more significant because it indicated the prevailing social philosophy that admired responsibility for social welfare but insisted that individual reform was the only method that could effect true improvement. One committee report ar-

7. The South Carolina committee made these limitations explicit when it promised not to assume any "authority to act officially for the convention" or to issue any "official declaration of denominational policies on matters of social concern which involves controversy." See *Minutes, South Carolina,* 1935, p. 142.

gued that the church's "technique" must be "persuasion" rather than "coercion."[8] Another reasoned that the church should render its "most effective social service," not through social reform, but by training its membership in "soul winning and service."[9] By no means a new idea, this position has appeared whenever evangelicals have attempted to answer the claims of social Christianity.

The evangelical position, if carried to its logical end, would have made the specialized work of the social-service committees of minor significance, if not entirely unnecessary. Those with a genuine commitment to social Christianity sought to avoid this contingency by trying to strengthen and enlarge the work of the state committees. The South Carolina committee won authorization to conduct a program of education on social issues and achieved some continuity by means of three-year terms for its members. But these advances failed to correct the most serious deficiencies because the committee's work specifically excluded any "program of action" and had to be carried on without a budget. North Carolina Baptists turned down a request that their committee be named the "authorized agent of the convention in legislative and civic matters" and that it be given the assistance of a full-time worker. Nevertheless, in 1940 this same committee offered the even more radical proposal that the state convention affiliate with the North Carolina Council of Churches in order to "more effectively promote civic righteousness." The best plan for improving a state committee was suggested to the Georgia convention by John E. White, the Savannah pastor and a well-known enthusiast for social causes. White's plan called for a committee with a rotating membership "clothed with responsibility to speak the mind of the convention" and which would have had the finances to engage in research and educational work.[10]

8. *Minutes, Virginia, 1939*, p. 59.
9. *Annual, Alabama, 1923*, p. 131.
10. *Minutes, South Carolina, 1934*, pp. 24–25; *1935*, p. 126; *Annual, North Carolina, 1937*, pp. 37–38; *1940*, pp. 36–37; *1943*, pp. 36–37; *Minutes, Georgia, 1927*, p. 29. For White's activities in the Southern Sociological Congress, see

Hampered by a lack of funds, the work of the committees consisted mostly of preparing their annual reports, the subjects of which usually fell into two general categories: matters of personal morality and social problems of a more complex nature. On questions of personal morality, whether crime, divorce, alcoholism, or Sabbath desecration, widespread agreement permitted the committees to pronounce a categorical ethic that they called upon the state to uphold. The treatment of social problems that involved impersonal relations of groups and institutions proved much more difficult. The committees were less certain, less specific, and less in agreement when they discussed war, race, or the economic order. Many reports could offer only undebatable generalities and moral admonitions drawn from a personal ethic not entirely applicable to maladjustments in society. At the same time, these issues inspired some decidedly progressive social thought from a minority of activists who shared the sentiments of liberal Protestantism on pacifism, racial justice, the rights of labor, and New Deal reforms.

An examination of committee statements on major social issues will make clear the division in the minds of Southern Baptists between the evangelical and the social-gospel traditions. In the discussions on war some reports reflected an underlying suspicion of man-made peace machinery because such devices omitted personal faith. A South Carolina report voiced this ethic when it declared: "The root of the trouble is in the human heart .... The only sure means of world peace is a program of Christian instruction that will change the hearts of the people and make them forget war and think of peace."[11] On the other hand, there were numerous occasions when the committees endorsed international peace efforts. The Georgia committee proved most active in this respect, beginning with a resolution praising the Washington disarmament conference in 1921. This committee

James E. McCullough, ed., *The South Mobilizing for Social Service*, pp. 16–19, 672.

11. *Minutes, South Carolina, 1934*, p. 130. Compare *Minutes, Georgia, 1937*, p. 28; *Minutes, Virginia, 1929*, p. 107; *Annual, Texas, 1941*, p. 182.

supported the League of Nations eight years before the Southern Convention made such a declaration, and it also approved the London Peace Conference, the Kellogg-Briand Pact, and the World Court plan. Moreover, the Georgia agency strongly criticized American isolationism in the late thirties as contributing to the deterioration of international relations.[12]

On a few occasions the state conventions entertained antiwar statements with pacifist overtones. From time to time a state committee report would denounce wars in general, defend conscientious objectors, oppose compulsory military training, support an international police force, or call for the nationalization of the munitions industry.[13] The strongest peace statement was approved by the North Carolina Convention in 1934, when a special committee, headed by E. McNeill Poteat, Jr., presented a Memorial to Congress on the Subject of War, which condemned war as "irreconcilably opposed to the mind of Christ." Influenced no doubt by the congressional investigation into warmongering by munitions makers, the report proposed federal control of the arms industry. Finding the root causes of war in the "competitive economic system," the memorial concluded that capitalism should be modified until it operated "under the domination of the mind of Christ Jesus."[14]

Later the attention of the social-service committees shifted from preserving peace to justifying war, as totalitarian governments which engaged in military aggression and denied civil liberties began to threaten world peace. During World War II, the North Carolina committee, after weakly declaring continued opposition to war as a matter of principle, expressed its willingness to "acquiesce in the present conflict since our liberties and the world's freedom are endangered."[15] For most Baptists, supporting the war posed no moral dilemma at all; the Texas con-

---

12. *Minutes, Georgia, 1921*, p. 15; *1929*, pp. 43–44; *1936*, pp. 31–32; *1938*, p. 33. See similar endorsements in *Minutes, South Carolina, 1923*, p. 154; *1937*, p. 21; *Minutes, Virginia, 1933*, p. 145; *Annual, Alabama, 1921*, p. 67.

13. *Annual, North Carolina, 1935*, p. 43; *1944*, pp. 45–46; *Minutes, South Carolina, 1936*, p. 32; *1937*, p. 21; *Minutes, Virginia, 1941*, p. 119.

14. *Annual, North Carolina, 1935*, p. 41.

15. *Ibid., 1944*, pp. 42–43. See also *Annual, Alabama, 1942*, p. 106.

vention affirmed that the "hand of God" would guide the country to certain military victory and advised Baptist sons that fighting in the war was a Christian duty.[16]

Much as they had in the treatment of war, the committees settled for a compromise between Christian ideals and social realities when they discussed the race problem. They regularly lamented racial injustices and favored improvements in social conditions, but they kept their pronouncements well within the framework of a segregated society. Frequently condemning the relatively few incidents of mob violence, they remained silent about suffrage restrictions throughout the South. They complained about Negro poverty without attacking wage differentials and the farm tenant system and criticized discrimination in the appropriation of public school funds but did not question Jim Crow legislation separating public services. In short, they advocated a better life for the Negro without striking at the root of racial injustice—the Southern caste system.[17]

As a remedy for racial injustice, the social-service committees often found recourse in moral admonitions that they neglected to relate to the practical realities of the problem. To an Oklahoma committee the "Christian ideal" in race relations meant nothing more specific than "peace and good-will among the races." A Virginia committee declared without any elaboration that the "golden rule" offered the only basis for solving the race problem. It was common to blame racial strife on the bad conduct of individuals. Surveying the violence following World War I, the Georgia committee concluded, "Convert the bad ones to Christ and the trouble is over." Those who would reduce the race problem to one of individual morality played down the use of political action as an instrument of social justice. As a result, Christian principles with valid social implications became lofty slogans that obscured the need for action against immediate and specific evils.[18]

16. *Annual, Texas, 1942*, pp. 207, 210.
17. *Minutes, Georgia, 1936*, pp. 30–31; *1939*, p. 45; *1941*, p. 32; *Minutes, South Carolina, 1937*, p. 22; *1938*, p. 122; *1945*, p. 145; *Minutes, Virginia, 1935*, pp. 72–74; *Annual, North Carolina, 1945*, p. 48.
18. *Minutes of the Annual Session of the Baptist Convention of Oklahoma,*

The most progressive racial attitudes came from the special interracial committees that were established in a few state conventions to turn back the rising tide of anti-Negro feeling following World War I. Southern leaders organized the Commission on Inter-racial Cooperation, which had counterparts in many states and local communities. Among the founders was M. Ashby Jones, an Atlanta Baptist minister and the Southern Convention's most outstanding advocate of better race relations. These organizations worked for improved race relations and better social conditions for Negroes with special attention to education, public welfare, economic opportunity, housing, and civil rights. In response to the movement the Baptist conventions in Virginia, North Carolina, and Texas created their own interracial committees.[19]

The Virginia commitee carried on the most active program. It promoted various kinds of interracial meetings and succeeded in obtaining the wide observance of Interracial Goodwill Sunday in white and Negro churches. Going beyond the sponsorship of polite social intercourse, the committee cut to the heart of racial injustice and denominational apathy. In 1938 its report blamed whites for imposing an artificial inequality upon blacks and accused Southern Baptists of helping to perpetuate inequality by compromising Christian principles out of respect for Southern customs. The statement further criticized the denomination for discussing race in "academic and idealistic" terms

---

1944, (n.p., 1944), p. 36; *Minutes, Virginia, 1933*, p. 146; *1935*, pp. 73–74; *Minutes, Georgia, 1921*, p. 15; *1941*, p. 32; *1939*, p. 45; *Minutes, South Carolina, 1932*, p. 53; *1935*, p. 138.

19. Paul E. Baker, *Negro-White Adjustments, An Investigation and Analysis of Methods in the Interracial Movement in the United States* (Pittsfield, Mass., 1934), p. 17. William Louis Poteat was active in the interracial movement of the twenties. A member of the Commission on Inter-racial Cooperation, he was instrumental in getting the Baptists of North Carolina to establish their own interracial commission, which would function along the same lines as the Virginia committee. See T. J. Woofter, Jr., ed., *Cooperation in Southern Communities, Suggested Activities for County and City Inter-racial Committees* (Atlanta, 1921), p. 5; and *Annual, North Carolina, 1929*, pp. 42–43. Texas Baptists set up a Committee on Interracial Relations in 1942. This committee later became a full-time department, carrying on cooperative mission work with Negro Baptists as well as promoting better racial understanding.

without engaging in "positive and constructive action" to effect equality.[20]

The state Baptist conventions witnessed a wide spectrum of opinion on economic issues just as they did on questions related to race and world peace. The social-service committees insisted on the relevance of Christianity to man's economic life, even when their analysis of economic matters was superficial. It was generally recognized that labor had the right to organize and bargain collectively for a fair and living wage, although the committees normally would not support strikes or union-shop contracts. As for capital, the committees complained that certain features of the free-enterprise system conflicted with Christian principles: the exploitation of labor violated the dignity of man, and competition and the profit motive fell short of the higher principles of cooperation and service. However, the committees for the most part would not advocate any fundamental changes in the economic relations between capital and labor. The underlying justification seemed to be that labor's rightful aims could be achieved by peaceful arbitration. The committees often disposed of economic conflicts by sternly admonishing the disputants to practice "brotherhood and the golden rule" in their relationships.[21] The most thorough-going prolabor statements came from the Georgia Social Service Committee's chairman W. W. Gaines, who gave major attention to labor problems in the industrial South.[22] He pointed out that industry was not an unmixed blessing for the region because it often meant low wages, long hours, and Northern ownership. As a partial corrective, Gaines supported the labor movement, especially its fight against child labor and night work for women. Other state committees favored child-labor laws, but the Georgia group stood alone in advocating a federal child-labor constitutional

20. *Minutes, Virginia, 1933*, pp. 70–71; *1938*, p. 79; *1941*, pp. 128–31.
21. *Annual, Alabama, 1927*, p. 136; *Minutes, Georgia, 1929*, p. 45; *Annual, Texas, 1935*, pp. 143–46; *1938*, p. 152; *Annual, North Carolina, 1937*, pp. 31–32; *1934*, p. 45; *Annual, Florida, 1938*, pp. 13–14; *Minutes, Virginia, 1923*, p. 95; *1922*, p. 126; *Minutes, Missouri, 1939*, p. 166.
22. *Minutes, Georgia, 1929*, pp. 44–45.

amendment.[23] Not sharing the usual suspicion of federal power, Gaines's committee even advocated a presidential committee to investigate labor conditions in the cotton-mill industry.[24]

The Great Depression brought a striking change of attitude in the state committees. Unlike the Southern Convention's Social Service Commission, the state committees did not allow the New Deal's stand on the repeal of prohibition to blind them to the achievements of the Roosevelt administration. The Alabama committee report of 1933 declared: "We may not march in the Wet Parade with our courageous President . . . . But we can keep step with him in his efforts . . . to spread wealth; secure higher wages and shorter hours for labor; abolish child labor; to promote a planned industry; to prevent unemployment; [to provide] insurance and old age security; and other means of social justice."[25] The strongest support for economic reforms came from Gaines, who openly questioned the free-enterprise system when private business failed to restore full employment. His criticism of capitalism was so severe that the Georgia convention forced a revision of his 1931 report; yet even after being redrafted, it remained a strong indictment against the "grave imperfections in an economic order" that permitted vast fortunes and food surpluses to exist alongside unemployment and bread lines. Six months before Roosevelt's election, Gaines called for the expansion of welfare services and a planned economy. His 1932 report condemned classical economics because it worked for the benefit of the few in conflict with Christian teachings, which stressed the well-being of all. Refusing to attribute the depression to an "act of God" or to "natural law," Gaines blamed it on "mismanagement" of business and "unwise human politics." He pointed to the "concentration of wealth that has killed the consuming power" as the cause of the depression and the "chief obstacle in the path of recovery." In order to realize a "more equitable distribution of wealth," Gaines favored a vigorous

23. *Minutes, Georgia, 1934*, pp. 42–43; *Minutes, Virginia, 1936*, p. 52; *Annual, North Carolina, 1937*, p. 31; *Annual, Florida, 1938*, pp. 14–15.

24. *Minutes, Georgia, 1929*, p. 45.

25. *Annual, Alabama, 1933*, p. 26. Compare *Minutes, South Carolina, 1933*, p. 141.

federal program to relieve unemployment and to regulate business. As Congress translated the recovery program into law during the First Hundred Days, Gaines praised the New Deal as a combination of "economic justice and social righteousness." "Never in so short a time," he reported, "has so much been done in the interest of social justice."[26]

By the mid-thirties the social-service committees in other states were issuing similar statements. The North Carolina committee declared in 1934: "We advocate such legislation as will secure to each person the opportunity to work at a living wage, prevent unrestricted exploitation of natural resources for private gain, and assure to society as a whole the benefits of our potential wealth." The South Carolina committee charged in 1935 that the majority of the American people were "enslaved" by a "pagan economic system" that placed profit above human need and exploitation above service. In the late thirties this committee endorsed many specific New Deal programs, including the Farm Security Administration, the Federal Housing Administration, and the Rural Electrification Administration. The Virginia committee singled out the Social Security Act as the "most far-reaching piece of humanitarian legislation in modern times."[27]

When the state social-service committees examined the issues of war, race, and the economic order, they were affirming a social responsibility with new dimensions for Southern Baptists. These committees also gave large place to questions of individual morality, which traditionally concerned the constituency. Foremost among these concerns was the archenemy of Baptist morality, intoxicating beverages, and without exception the committees stood for the complete suppression of the liquor traffic. Perhaps their most important service to the cause was to act as liaison between Baptist state conventions and temperance organizations. During the dry decade the committees brought officials of the Anti-Saloon League to the Baptist assemblies and encour-

---

26. *Minutes, Georgia, 1931*, pp. 31–33; *1932*, pp. 29–30; *1933*, pp. 43–44.
27. *Annual, North Carolina, 1934*, p. 44; *Minutes, South Carolina, 1935*, pp. 129–31; *1938*, p. 121; *1939*, p. 125; *1940*, pp. 183–84; *Minutes, Virginia, 1937*, p. 90.

aged churches to finance temperance work. After repeal and the decline of the league, the dry forces reorganized under new names in every state. The Baptist committees maintained a firm alliance with the new organizations, some of which they helped establish. In North Carolina, for example, the state committee helped organize the Allied Church League, to which the state convention appointed representatives and contributed several thousand dollars annually. In a similar fashion Baptists in all states reaffirmed their devotion to prohibition long after it had become a lost cause in the American social order.[28]

Several other matters of personal morality occupied a regular place in the committee reports. Opposing all forms of gambling, the committees protested lax enforcement of anti-gambling laws and lobbied for stronger legislation.[29] They also engaged in political action to preserve the Sabbath against the forces of secularization in an urban society.[30] The committees were extremely disturbed by changing sexual mores, and to preserve a Puritan morality, some committeemen would have even banned dancing and mixed bathing. Mainly, they attacked the loose portrayal of sex in literature and motion pictures.[31] Viewing relaxed standards on sex as certain evidence of national decay, the committees urged government censorship of publications and films.[32] They also looked to the state to maintain the sanctity of marriage through tighter divorce and marriage laws. Overlooking

28. *Annual, Tennessee, 1922*, p. 52; *Annual, Florida, 1924–1925*, p. 46; *Proceedings, Arkansas, 1934*, p. 30; *Annual, Louisiana, 1939*, p. 37; *Minutes, Missouri, 1939*, pp. 165–66; *Minutes, Kentucky, 1944*, pp. 90–91; *Annual, North Carolina, 1940*, p. 36; *1943*, p. 35; *1944*, p. 80; *Annual, Alabama, 1931*, p. 86; *1934*, p. 20; *1936*, p. 101; *1937*, p. 52; *1944*, p. 48; *Minutes, South Carolina, 1945*, pp. 44, 46; *Minutes, Virginia, 1945*, p. 131.

29. *Annual, Alabama, 1935*, p. 53; *Minutes, South Carolina, 1938*, p. 123; *Minutes, Georgia, 1939*, p. 39; *Proceedings, Arkansas, 1940*, p. 91.

30. *Minutes, Georgia, 1929*, p. 39; *Annual, Alabama, 1932*, pp. 51–55; *1934*, pp. 20, 81. *Minutes, South Carolina, 1936*, p. 145.

31. *Minutes, South Carolina, 1921*, p. 182; *Minutes, Virginia, 1922*, p. 125; *Annual, Texas, 1931*, pp. 157–60; *Annual, North Carolina, 1937*, p. 33; *Minutes, Kentucky, 1945*, pp. 105–106; *Annual, Alabama, 1929*, p. 104; *Annual, Tennessee, 1941*, pp. 93–95; *Annual, Florida, 1942*, p. 84.

32. *Annual, Alabama, 1931*, p. 87; *1933*, pp. 51–55; *Annual, South Carolina, 1921*, pp. 181–82; *1934*, pp. 131–33; *1936*, p. 145; *Minutes, Virginia, 1923*, p. 127.

the social and psychological factors affecting family life, the reports represented broken homes almost entirely as products of individual moral failure.[33]

The general subject of crime became a standard feature in committee reports. The typical statement marshaled statistical data on mounting crime rates as evidence of a declining national morality.[34] In only a few instances did committees offer constructive proposals in behalf of the criminal element. One committee, after investigating the needs of parolees, tried without success to initiate a convention-sponsored ministry to ex-convicts.[35] Among the state conventions, Virginia alone supported work with prisoners, an interdenominational ministry for convicts that employed six workers by 1946.[36]

On the basis of the work of the state social-service committees, it is possible to draw some rather firm conclusions regarding the social attitudes of Southern Baptists. The reports offer abundant evidence of the historic Baptist emphasis on the individual, arising from the doctrine of personal regeneration. Attention to individual faith made it difficult for Southern Baptists to recognize the powerful influence of impersonal forces, institutions, and groups not amenable to moral admonitions. Those who addressed social problems often displayed little evidence of understanding the real forces and issues at the center of social conflict. As a result, they tended to reduce complex social problems to questions of personal conduct on which some moral judgments could be made because if high morals alone could assure social peace and justice, as was often claimed, then the church need not become involved in difficult and sometimes morally ambiguous issues.

Practical considerations probably more than a social philos-

33. *Proceedings, Arkansas, 1935,* pp. 73–74; *1937,* p. 82; *1940,* p. 91; *Minutes, South Carolina, 1943,* p. 133; *Minutes, Virginia, 1922,* p. 124; *Annual, Tennessee, 1924,* p. 60; *Annual, Florida, 1936,* p. 105; *Annual, Texas, 1942,* p. 160.
34. *Annual, South Carolina, 1926,* pp. 147–51; *Annual, Texas, 1942,* p. 159; *Annual, Tennessee, 1944,* p. 114.
35. *Annual, North Carolina, 1936,* pp. 26–28. The Texas committee in 1924 and the Georgia committee in 1936 tried to initiate prison-reform movements, but without success.
36. *Minutes, Virginia, 1946,* pp. 157–58.

ophy based on religious individualism dictated the treatment of specific questions. Conventions avoided controversy as a matter of course. To the single-minded evangelical, divisive issues detracted from the main business anyway, and those who might privately have favored a strong stand yielded to the expediency of silence and inaction. The committees, of course, discussed many moral issues that were not controversial, and in these instances the reports became vehicles for expressing righteous indignation against a standardized list of personal vices. The lengths to which Southern Baptists were willing to go to control morality involved them in a basic inconsistency in the use of corporate power for ethical ends: they called for elaborate social controls over private morals and, at the same time, offered simple answers in terms of an individual ethic for the most complex social problems. The inconsistency lies in admitting that personal religion alone could not achieve suitable standards of public morality, but then arguing that an individual ethic could somehow solve all social problems.

The second conclusion recognizes that not all Southern Baptists allowed individualism to determine their social philosophy. Many leaders found in the social gospel much that confronted the realities of faith and life in the modern world. This enlightened and influential minority gained a wide hearing in the state bodies, more so than in the Southern Convention. They challenged the almost sacrosanct idea that personal religion would rectify all social wrongs. Making the necessary distinction between social and individual ethics, they maintained that individual faith alone did not address the moral crises of an age shaped by impersonal forces and collective interests. As W. W. Gaines said, "It is a weak sentimentalist which [sic] would ignore the necessity ever for coercive action. There are evils in society that moral suasion or even a gospel appeal would not reach in a thousand years."[37]

The idea of collective evil came directly from the social-gospel theology, as did the call for corporate action against social ills. It was in the hope of making the denomination a more effective

37. *Minutes, Georgia, 1932,* p. 31.

agent for social reform that the progressives tried to strengthen the state committees. The proponents of more positive action against social evils made clear their own dissatisfaction with the denomination's half-way covenant with social Christianity, even though they were unable to effect substantial corrections at the state level. Southern Baptists were not prepared to employ the means consistent with the social-gospel ends that they generally approved. The question of appropriate methods of social action remained a basic challenge to the social conscience of Southern Baptists. It became the central issue in a full-scale debate over a proposal for a strong social-action agency, which came before the Southern Baptist Convention in the mid-thirties. The controversy over this ambitious but ill-fated plan exposed more clearly than ever the deep ideological division in the minds of Southern Baptists between the evangelical and social-gospel traditions.

VIII

THE SOCIAL GOSPEL UNDER ATTACK

T he contradictory philosophies of personal evangelism and social Christianity coexisted in Southern Baptist life without being engaged in direct confrontation until the mid-thirties, when an attempt to establish the Social Research Bureau touched off a full-scale debate on the social gospel. The attack on the bureau is best understood as an extension of the fundamentalist movement in American Protestantism. Essentially, this conservative reaction to religious liberalism defended the supernatural elements in Christianity. It upheld the verbal inspiration of the Bible against scholarly criticism, denied the social-gospel assumption that man's goodness enabled him to perfect the social order, and opposed the doctrinal compromises of ecumenism.[1]

Fundamentalism included much traditional Calvinist dogma: human depravity, Christ's deity, the atonement, and personal salvation. It also gave new emphasis to eschatology, the doctrine concerning death, resurrection, and the final judgment. Taking Biblical prophecy literally, the fundamentalists propounded a "premillennial" scheme for the end of the age. Accordingly, the kingdom of God (the millennium) would be established on earth after the return of Christ; but until the Second Advent, social and moral conditions would inevitably worsen because of man's fallen state. Such reasoning reduced church work to saving

1. The best general treatment of fundamentalism is Norman F. Furniss, *The Fundamentalist Controversy, 1918–1931* (New Haven, 1954). The theological position of the fundamentalists was originally stated in *The Fundamentals: A Testimony to the Truth* (Chicago, n.d.), 12 vols.

the elect from an evil world, thereby preparing them for the sound of the last trumpet. Fundamentalism thus became the natural ally of personal evangelism and an enemy of social Christianity.[2]

But fundamentalism was more than a theology; it was a social movement concerned with a changing America. It has been explained variously as a rural-urban cultural struggle, a search for certainty by the socially dispossessed, the anti-intellectualism of the common man's religion, and a protest against the loss of nineteenth-century individualism.[3] Those unhappy with modernism, for whatever reason, found a common purpose in upholding the absolutism of revealed religion, which for them constituted the sure foundation for the nation's faith and a sound social order. To the fundamentalists of the 1920's, the greatest source of America's ills was Charles Darwin's theory of evolution, which conflicted with the account of the creation in Genesis.[4] Mass opinion, untouched by earlier debates over evolution in intellectual circles, encountered Darwinism only after it found its way into the public schools.[5] With good reason the fundamentalists made control of the schools their main objective in the war on modernism. In the American experience, the public-supported temples of learning had been expected to preserve right belief and conduct. Darwinism seemed to destroy the most cherished elements of traditional faith: revealed truth, an absolute ethic, a transcendent authority, and a miracle-working deity. Moreover, evolution in the hands of social liberals pro-

2. *The Fundamentals*, XI, 87–99; XII, 108–19.

3. Furniss, pp. 26–29; Herbert Wallace Schneider, *Religion in 20th Century America* (Cambridge, Mass., 1952), pp. 14–15. Paul A. Carter, pp. 46–49, 53–58, stresses the social-reactionary character of fundamentalism. Richard Hofstadter, *Anti-Intellectualism in American Life* (New York, 1963), pp. 117–36, ties fundamentalism to "one-hundred percent" Americanism, the populist-democratic tradition, and right-wing political movements as well as anti-intellectualism.

4. In a 1924 address to the Seventh-Day Adventists, William Jennings Bryan said: "All the ills from which America suffers can be traced back to the teaching of evolution. It would be better to destroy every other book ever written, and save just the first three verses of Genesis." Cited in Maynard Shipley, *The War on Modern Science* (New York, 1927), pp. 254–55.

5. Hofstadter makes this point in *Anti-Intellectualism in American Life*, p. 126.

vided a naturalistic basis for the progressive reforms advocated by the social gospel.[6] The fundamentalist mentality imagined a grand conspiracy by the naturalists, the humanists, and all liberals to undermine the very foundations of national greatness.

Among Southern Baptists the fundamentalist movement contributed to the division already noted between the conservative majority and the progessive minority, with most churchmen sharing the fundamentalist anxieties. The principal antievolution campaigns occurred within Southern Convention territory, where eight states outlawed Darwinism in the public schools. Some Southern Baptists, like publisher John W. Porter of Kentucky, evangelist Thomas T. Martin of Mississippi, and the colorful controversialists J. Frank Norris of Texas and Mordecai Ham of Oklahoma, furnished militant leadership for the antievolution cause.[7] Other prominent churchmen tried to halt the movement against Darwinism. Denominational executive Richard T. Vann of Raleigh; pastors M. Ashby Jones of Atlanta and John E. White of Savannah; and educators Edgar Y. Mullins, president of Southern Seminary, and William Louis Poteat of Wake Forest College all fought attempts to make evolution a test of religious orthodoxy.[8]

Evolution became a divisive issue in the denomination when the fundamentalists charged that Darwin's heresy had made its way into Baptist schools. Using the pulpit, religious journals, and denominational gatherings, the fundamentalists harassed several educators. Although they forced resignations in at least five schools,[9] their triumphs were not complete, for they failed to

6. Eric F. Goldman traces the development of "reform Darwinism" in his *Rendezvous with Destiny, a History of Modern Reform in America*, rev. and abridged ed. (New York, 1961), pp. 72–124, 256, 344.

7. Furniss, pp. 81, 86. Porter was author of *The Menace of Evolution*; Martin wrote *Hell in the High Schools*. Ham's activities are reported in Elbert Watson, "Oklahoma and the Anti-Evolution Movement in the 1920's," *Chronicles of Oklahoma*, XLII (Winter, 1964–65), 396–407.

8. Mims, *The Advancing South*, pp. 12–15, 304–307; Dabney, p. 301; Furniss, pp. 119–21.

9. Furniss, p. 124, notes dismissals at Baylor University and Oklahoma Baptist University. Mims, *The Advancing South*, p. 146, mentions the ouster of Professor Henry Fox at Mercer University. Several resignations, including those of the president and the heads of the Bible and biology departments at Ouachita Col-

unseat the denomination's foremost Darwinist, Wake Forest College President William Poteat. A biologist by training, Poteat had defended evolution for more than two decades in the classroom, in numerous off-campus lectures, and in published statements. The belated move against him, instigated by Martin and Norris, reached the floor of the North Carolina Baptist Convention on two occasions.[10] In an address to the 1922 meeting, Poteat offered a reasoned defense of scientific pursuits. In 1925 —the year that William Jennings Bryan led the antievolution cause at the Scopes trial in Dayton, Tennessee—agitation against Poteat revived after he delivered the McNair Lectures at the University of North Carolina, in which he denounced the Biblical literalists for "compromising Christianity before the intelligence of the world."[11] Poteat's defenders, including the alumni of Wake Forest, the trustees, and the state Baptist journal, blocked an antievolution resolution at the annual convention. Meanwhile, outside the denomination, Poteat was playing a major role in preventing the North Carolina legislature from passing an antievolution law.[12] His battle with the fundamentalists drew high praise from H. L. Mencken, who singled him out as "a sort of liaison officer between the Baptist revelation and human progress."[13]

---

lege in Arkansas, were in part owing to a requirement to sign an antievolution statement. See *Proceedings, Arkansas, 1924*, pp. 64–67; 1925, pp. 52–54. See also James Oliver Whelchel, "The Teaching of Sociology in Southern Baptist Colleges" (M.A. thesis, University of Missouri, 1924), pp. 113–27; and Shipley, pp. 135, 152–53, 177–78.

10. Harriet Suzanne Cameron, "William Louis Poteat and the Evolution Controversy" (M.A. thesis, Wake Forest College, 1962), pp. 11, 21, 26–28, 37, 46–49, 78–89; Paschal, *History of Wake Forest College* (Wake Forest, 1943), III, 119–34; Dabney, p. 301; Mims, *The Advancing South*, p. 15; Cash, pp. 321–54. Miss Cameron's study of Poteat has since been published as Suzanne Cameron Linder, *William Louis Poteat, Prophet of Progress* (Chapel Hill, 1966). The complete story of the evolution fight in North Carolina is in Williard B. Gatewood, Jr., *Preachers, Pedagogues, and Politicians: The Evolution Controversy in North Carolina, 1920–1927* (Chapel Hill, 1966).

11. William Louis Poteat, *Can a Man Be a Christian Today?* (Chapel Hill, 1925).

12. Furniss, p. 85; Howard K. Beale, *Are American Teachers Free?* (New York, 1936), p. 242; Cameron, "William Louis Poteat and the Evolution Controversy," pp. 64–65.

13. Cameron, "William Louis Poteat and the Evolution Controversy," p. 103.

The fundamentalist wing also sought official antievolution action by the Southern Baptist Convention. Edgar Y. Mullins tried to head off a controversy over this question while president of the convention because he sided with Poteat in the belief that evolution could be reconciled with a Biblical faith. Speaking to the 1923 convention, Mullins argued that evolution could be accepted as a "working hypothesis of science" without destroying "the supernatural element in the Christian religion."[14] It appeared that Mullins had satisfactorily disposed of the question when the convention voted to endorse his statement; but, not given to compromise, the fundamentalist faction demanded an unequivocal repudiation of evolution. They twice failed to get a statement before the delegates of the 1924 convention because of opposition from the Committee on Resolutions. In order to silence the ultraconservatives without yielding to their demands, the resolutions committee proposed that a special committee prepare a comprehensive "statement of Baptist faith and message." To prevent the fundamentalists from using this statement for their ends, the recommendation included the names of the proposed committee, a maneuver engineered by John E. White, chairman of the committee and president of Anderson College in South Carolina.[15]

The seven-man committee included only one antievolutionist agitator, Oklahoma editor C. P. Stealy. Mullins, whose attempts to reconcile religion and evolution had made him the target of the fundamentalists, was named chairman. The other members were L. R. Scarborough, president of Southwestern Seminary in Forth Worth; W. J. McGlothlin, president of Furman University; E. C. Dargan, formerly at Southern Seminary; and two editors, both unfriendly to the extreme fundamentalist position. The statement was presented in 1925 and followed closely the historic New Hampshire Confession (1833), to which the committee had added ten new articles, "growing out of present

14. *Annual, SBC*, 1923, pp. 19–20. See also Edgar Y. Mullins, "Evolution and Belief in God," *Biblical Recorder* (Raleigh), Mar. 28, 1923, p. 5.

15. *Annual, SBC*, 1924, pp. 70–71, 80, 95. John E. White opposed the idea of the creed himself. See his "The Baptist Bias on the Creed Question," *Word and Way* (Kansas City), Apr. 16, 1925, p. 6.

needs."[16] Surprisingly, not a single article dealt with the evolution question, an omission justified on grounds that evolution was not a matter of religious doctrine. This explanation did not satisfy the fundamentalists, for committeeman Stealy had tried to include a specific denial of evolution in the statement. Failing in this effort, the antievolutionists prepared to carry their fight to the 1926 convention. An open rift was avoided when the new president, George W. McDaniel, included in his address a remark condemning "every theory, evolution or other, which teaches that man originated in . . . a lower animal ancestry."[17] M. E. Dodd, prominent Louisiana pastor, moved that McDaniel's statement become the "sentiment of this convention." Not a part of the fundamentalist faction, Dodd offered the motion in hope of ending the agitation. The fundamentalists seized upon the approval of the motion as an opportunity to win another point. Before the convention ended they put through a resolution including a "request" that all convention agencies give "hearty and individual acceptance" to the McDaniel statement.[18]

As an organized movement among Southern Baptists, fundamentalism resembled landmarkism of the nineteenth century. Both movements were theologically ultraconservative, attacked agencies of the denomination, fought to control denominational organizations, and produced dissident factions that left the convention. Led by J. Frank Norris, some of the fundamentalists dissociated themselves from the denomination in 1934 and organized the World Baptist Fellowship. As in the case of landmarkism, the reactionary theology exerted a strong influence on many remaining in the convention, with one immediate consequence being the adoption of the convention's first doctrinal statement. However, this statement did not constitute a complete victory for the fundamentalists because, for the most part, it simply reaffirmed traditional Baptist doctrine and said nothing about creation or evolution. Of the ten new articles, only the one about the Second Coming could be credited to fundamen-

16. *Annual, SBC*, 1925, pp. 71, 75–76.
17. *Ibid.*, 1926, p. 18.
18. *Ibid.*, p. 98.

talist influence. On the other hand, at least three articles, those on world peace, social service, and the kingdom of God, could be traced directly to liberal Christianity and the social gospel.

According to the statement, Baptist doctrine included the duty to "seek peace with all men" and to "oppose everything likely to provoke war." The article on social service obligated every Christian to apply the principles of Christ "in his own life and in human society"; to oppose "every form of greed, selfishness, and vice"; and to work for the influence of "righteousness, truth, and brotherly love" in "industry, government, and society." To realize these social goals, Baptists were encouraged to "work with all men of good will in any good cause." The clearest evidence of social-gospel influence appeared in the article that described the kingdom of God as embracing "every human relationship" and "every form and institution of organized human society." Further, the article declared it the "duty of all Christ's people to pray and labor continually that his Kingdom may come and his will be done on earth as it is done in heaven." This interpretation, by assuming that the kingdom included the present social order and that it could be advanced by human effort, was in direct conflict with the fundamentalist premillennial doctrine.[19]

As the 1925 declaration of faith testified, the social-gospel ideology had gained an established place in Southern Baptist thinking. Liberal social ideas found expression in the seminaries even though these institutions were soundly conservative in theology. Archibald Thomas Robertson, a distinguished New Testament scholar at Southern Seminary, called for the "Christianizing of the social order" in a book that drew heavily from the works of social-gospel advocates Washington Gladden and Walter Rauschenbusch.[20] The most important appeals for practical Christianity came from the departments of Christian sociology, which offered courses in sociology, social ethics, social problems, and welfare work.[21]

19. *Ibid.*, p. 74.
20. *The New Citizenship* (New York, 1919), pp. 147–49.
21. *Annual Catalogue of the Southern Baptist Theological Seminary, 1926–*

J. M. Price, who taught sociology for ten years at Southwestern Seminary, reached somewhat beyond the classroom when he published *Christianity and Social Problems* (1928). Describing his reasons for writing the book, Price charged that "the weakest point in Christianity is the application of Christ's teaching to modern conditions." Although he remained basically a conservative, his book incorporated some major social-gospel ideas, such as the kingdom of God as an earthly reality and the duty of the church to Christianize the social order. He favored government regulation of business, justified public ownership of utilities and natural resources, and endorsed measures both voluntary and legislative for improving the conditions of labor.[22]

At Southern Seminary, Charles S. Gardner, using his own text on the social gospel, taught sociology until 1929. His views were more liberal than Price's, as may be noted from writings prior to the advent of the New Deal in which Gardner favored social planning, more government control of the economy, and increased welfare services.[23] Gardner's successor, Jesse B. Weatherspoon, shifted the basic approach of the department from sociology to ethics, but the liberal point of view remained the same. In his inaugural address, Weatherspoon called for a ministry trained to help solve problems related to the industrial economy, race relations, crime, and world peace.[24]

Social Christianity thus remained an important intellectual force among Southern Baptists in contrast to the fundamentalist tradition that made personal evangelism the church's sole mission. Between these two ideologies stood the Social Service Commission, in origin and purpose tied to the social gospel but in performance evangelical and conservative enough not to arouse any complaints from the fundamentalist faction. Then, in the thirties the commission was involuntarily drawn into a

---

1930 (Louisville, 1930), pp. 63–64; *Catalogue of the Southwestern Baptist Theological Seminary, 1923–1924* (Fort Worth, 1924), p. 66.

22. J. M. Price, *Christianity and Social Problems* (Nashville, 1928), preface, pp. 90–103, 224–39.

23. "The Relation of the Individual to Society," pp. 22–25; "The Problem of Democracy from the Psychological Point of View," pp. 320–25.

24. "The Ethical Note in Preaching," pp. 398–406.

controversy over social Christianity in conjunction with a proposal to establish a new social-action agency. The circumstances for this debate began to take shape when the Social Service Commission's 1933 report included a resolution condemning the "extraordinary grants of power" extended to President Roosevelt.[25] When certain delegates objected on grounds that a religious body should not deal with a "political matter," Chairman Barton withdrew the statement. This incident would have had little further significance except that it provided the immediate setting for an amendment that would establish, in addition to the commission, a new "agency for social research," to guide the convention on social questions.[26] Presented by E. McNeill Poteat, Jr., pastor in Raleigh, North Carolina, who had recently returned from missionary work in China, the amendment passed without debate, which may seem surprising in view of the resistance to Barton's resolution. Apparently, Poteat capitalized on the feeling that the commission had overstepped its authority, and the delegates interpreted his move as an effort to prevent future indiscretions.[27] Certainly, the convention as a whole did not understand that Poteat had in mind a full-time agency with powers much greater than those of the commission.

Poteat was named chairman of the five-man committee to study his own proposal. For some time the work of the committee remained obscure; the chairman announced nothing about his plans during the next year and failed to have a report ready for the 1934 convention. The first information about Poteat's intentions appeared in a "tentative report" issued after the 1934 meeting.[28] Although it contained some of the controversial features of the plan that was eventually submitted, it attracted little attention when released. During the next year, only a few state Baptist newspapers discussed the proposal, and conse-

25. *Annual, SBC, 1933*, p. 104.
26. *Ibid.*, p. 118.
27. This interpretation appears in the *Florida Baptist Witness* (Jacksonville), June 15, 1933, p. 5.
28. *Baptist Record* (Jackson), July 12, 1934, p. 6; *Biblical Recorder* (Raleigh), June 27, 1934, p. 1.

quently, the 1935 convention delegates had little prior knowledge of the committee's recommendations.

In the absence of details about the proposed agency, the more conservative members of the convention were probably unfavorably influenced by Poteat's reputation as a social and theological liberal. His name alone could have created doubts in the minds of some. His father, a Northern Baptist, had worked for the ecumenical Interchurch World Movement; his uncle was the famous evolutionist president of Wake Forest College. But more important, Poteat made no secret of his distaste for fundamentalism. In a lecture at Southern Seminary in 1934 on "The Place of the Minister in the Modern World," Poteat claimed that clergymen were failing as social leaders because of religious concepts unrelated to the problems of war, race, and economic justice.[29] Basing his remarks on a survey of lay attitudes, he concluded that if ministers wished to resume intellectual leadership they must revamp their antiquated theology and accept the findings of science and Biblical scholarship. Poteat further separated himself from Southern Baptist orthodoxy in a book published in the same year entitled *Jesus and the Liberal Mind.* The study presented Jesus as a social liberal who placed individual rights above property rights and judged social institutions by their benefit to individuals. The book also chided Baptists for fearing to preach a social gospel and for refusing to cooperate in the ecumenical movement.[30]

By the time Poteat offered his report to the Southern Convention in May, 1935, he was already open to charges of forsaking Baptist traditions. The report itself at nearly every point proved highly objectionable to the guardians of personal evangelism. The social problems outlined for study were about the same as

29. *Review and Expositor,* XXXI (July, 1934), 289–305. The lecture was also given at Duke University and then published in *Reverend John Doe, D.D., A Study of the Ministry in the Modern World* (New York, 1935). See also Poteat's "Religion in the South," in W. T. Couch, ed., *Culture in the South* (Chapel Hill, 1935), which criticizes Southern ministers for their sectarianism and neglect of social issues.

30. Edwin McNeill Poteat, Jr., *Jesus and the Liberal Mind* (Philadelphia, 1934), pp. 222–28.

those formerly covered by the Social Service Commission, but the method for dealing with them was to be entirely different. The proposed agency, to be called the Social Research Bureau, would necessitate the employment of a research director, and this was only the beginning. The plan further anticipated expanding the bureau into an "aggressive and far-reaching denominational program" that would operate independently of all other agencies in the convention in order to ensure its objectivity. For the fundamentalists, the proposal at once stirred the old landmark fears of centralized authority, as well as adding new anxieties about the loss of evangelistic emphasis.[31]

Without so specifying, the bureau would have eliminated any need for the Social Service Commission. The proposal put commission chairman Barton in a difficult position because, at first glance, it appears that the Research Bureau would have fulfilled his repeated request for a full-time agency. But despite the outward similarity of their desires, the two men were far apart in their conception of the function of such an agency. Barton would have studiously avoided progressive social aims in his preoccupation with policing personal morals. Conversely, Poteat envisioned an agency with freedom to criticize both the denomination and the society and sufficiently financed to conduct a comprehensive social reform program. It appears that in conceiving his plan Poteat deliberately by-passed Barton's well-known ambition for an expanded commission and lost any possible chance of cooperation when Barton refused to serve on the committee set up in 1933 to study the proposal.[32]

Barton's reaction foreshadowed the ultimate fate of the bureau. Prior to the 1935 convention, several papers published his articles opposing the bureau as an unwise and unnecessary financial burden,[33] and when Poteat unveiled the plan to the convention, Barton was among the half-dozen who spoke against

31. *Annual, SBC, 1935*, pp. 57–59.
32. *Western Recorder* (Louisville), Apr. 26, 1934, p. 12.
33. *Baptist Standard* (Dallas), May 2, 1935, p. 10; *Alabama Baptist* (Birmingham), Aug. 2, 1934, p. 5; May 9, 1935, p. 9; *Western Recorder* (Louisville), May 16, 1935, p. 1; *Baptist Record* (Jackson), Aug. 2, 1934, p. 4.

it in a brief but heated exchange.[34] The proposal was saved, temporarily at least, by a vote to postpone final action for one year. However, the opponents to the plan succeeded in adding to the original committee of four a member from each state in a move designed to force revision of the plan before the next convention.

The interest generated at the convention touched off an extended debate carried on largely in the state newspapers. Because these weekly publications were official organs of the state conventions, their editors tended to be every bit as sensitive to the popular will as the denominational bodies.[35] Thus, in this newest debate the editors played an important role both in getting the issue before the constituency and in molding opinion regarding it. Editorial opinion varied widely: three newspapers strongly opposed the plan for the bureau; three urged its adoption; two were sympathetic but not strong advocates; and two discussed the subject without taking a position.[36]

But this simple breakdown tells only part of the story, for the three opposition newspapers proved far more influential by assailing the bureau from every side and by publishing almost as much material on the subject as all the other newspapers combined. Victor I. Masters of the *Western Recorder* led the attack. He was well suited for the role, having devoted his twenty years as denominational executive and editor to fighting the forces of modernism.[37] In the campaign against the bureau he published more than fifty articles and editorials by a dozen authors, among

34. *Annual, SBC, 1935*, p. 57; *The Christian Index* (Atlanta), May 23, 1935, p. 6.

35. Patrick Henry Hill, pp. 290–95.

36. Opposing papers were the *Western Recorder* (Louisville), *Baptist Standard* (Dallas), and *Baptist and Reflector* (Nashville). Supporters of the bureau were *The Christian Index* (Atlanta), *Baptist Message* (Shreveport), and *Florida Baptist Witness* (Jacksonville). The two papers that discussed the issue without taking a stand were the *Baptist Record* (Jackson) and *Baptist Courier* (Greenville, S. C.).

37. Compare the role of Masters when he was a Home Mission Board executive, as treated in chap. 5. He edited the Kentucky paper from 1921 to 1942. During the twenties he constantly attacked evolution, ecumenism, the social gospel, and liberal theology.

them James B. Cranfill of Texas, a former editor and one-time vice-presidential candidate on the Prohibition ticket, and G. R. Pettigrew, a South Carolina minister. These two critics wrote several articles heaping ridicule on the bureau, which, in their opinion, would foster investigations by high-salaried experts who would compile useless data about superficial problems. Cranfill delighted in calling the agency the "Poteat Pimple Bureau" and the "South-wide Smelling Committee."[38] Pettigrew, using the dialogue of a backwoods preacher, referred to the bureau as a "fact-findin' detective agency" that would promote the "social gospel" rather than the "plain old Gospel of the Cross."[39]

The most widely used argument against the bureau claimed that it departed from the Biblical mission of the church. Opponents insisted that Christ did not seek to dominate man's "social customs" or "meddle" in his "business or political affairs."[40] Critics argued that the apostles did not preach a "Soap and Soup Salvation" or advocate "cleaning up the slums of Jerusalem."[41] Evangelicals were not apt to examine these contentions very carefully, and those espousing a fundamentalist theology had an apocalyptic vision that left no place for social concern. Masters argued, for example, that while Christianity prompted desires for social betterment, the teachings of Biblical prophecy did not warrant any hope for social progress.[42]

A second criticism pointed to the lack of ecclesiastical authority for such a program. This objection demonstrated the survival of landmarkism, with its emphasis on local church autonomy. Masters, whose whole career had been devoted to promotional work, now claimed that no denominational agency had the authority to formulate policies and urge them upon the churches.[43] F. M. McConnell, the Texas editor, made this ab-

---

38. *Western Recorder* (Louisville), June 20, 1935, p. 5; June 27, 1935, p. 6.
39. *Ibid.*, Oct. 17, 1935, p. 3.
40. *Ibid.*, Dec. 12, 1935, p. 3.
41. *Ibid.*, June 27, 1935, pp. 10–11.
42. *Ibid.*, Oct. 24, 1935, p. 8. See also *Baptist and Reflector* (Nashville), Apr. 30, 1936, p. 5.
43. *Western Recorder* (Louisville), Apr. 23, 1936, p. 8.

sence of authority his principal reason for opposing the bureau. "The business of the Southern Baptist Convention," he wrote, "is primarily and mainly religious rather than social."[44] Efforts toward social improvements, he argued, must be left to the local churches.

Poteat's enemies did not always confine their attack to the plan itself. They associated the bureau with political and theological radicalism, and some saw suspicious similarities between the bureau and New Deal agencies. Cranfill confessed that the "wild riot of political and social insanities emerging from the White House" made him suspect the bureau as a centralizing agency.[45] Others feared that the bureau would compromise the convention's doctrinal conservatism. The Tennessee editor warned that a "few rationalists" might control the agency and "steer Southern Baptists into modernistic, radical ventures."[46] Masters saw an ominous similarity between the aims of the bureau and the emphasis on social action in the Federal Council of Churches. He concluded that Poteat's proposal carried with it the "hidden assumption" that the world could be saved by social reform.[47]

Advocates of more effective social action failed to match the zeal of their opponents, whose attacks on the bureau had, from the start, put its sympathizers on the defensive. It became their principal contention that the new agency would simply expand the work of the Social Service Commission. The Georgia newspaper explained that the bureau would engage in a positive program against social evils that the commission had only condemned.[48] The Louisiana editor also used this point to answer charges that the agency would bring a radical shift in denominational policy.[49] In Virginia the editor expressed surprise at

44. *Baptist Standard* (Dallas), Jan. 9, 1936, p. 3.
45. *Western Recorder* (Louisville), Aug. 15, 1935, p. 11; July 4, 1935, pp. 5, 13; Jan. 20, 1935, pp. 5, 12; and *Baptist and Reflector* (Nashville), Jan. 2, 1936, p. 8.
46. *Baptist and Reflector* (Nashville), Mar. 19, 1936, p. 2; Jan. 2, 1936, p. 8; May 7, 1936, p. 2.
47. *Western Recorder* (Louisville), Apr. 23, 1936, p. 8.
48. *The Christian Index* (Atlanta), June 13, 1935, pp. 8, 9.
49. *Baptist Message* (Shreveport), June 20, 1935, p. 2.

the hysteria displayed over a plan to achieve aims that the convention had long favored. Recognizing the source of these exaggerated fears, the editor accused Masters of misrepresenting the proposal as an attempt to supplant personal regeneration with a social gospel.[50]

The controversy over the bureau caused the committee of twenty-three appointed members to make a new report at the next convention suggesting that the Research Bureau be abandoned altogether. As an alternative, their report suggested transforming the Social Service Commission into a full-time agency with an executive secretary. Its function would consist of investigating social and moral conditions, disseminating information, molding attitudes, and arousing public sentiment on social issues. About one-third of the report argued that the new work would not become a "substitute for the gospel," an obvious attempt to escape the principal criticism against the discarded Research Bureau.[51]

The committee issued its report in October, seven months before the convention, in the hope that the compromise would find general acceptance. Actually, the new plan had little effect on the course of the controversy. The committee itself did little to help the cause, with only three of its twenty-three members writing articles on behalf of the plan.[52] And although the compromise won the approval of half a dozen editors, none of them promoted it with real enthusiasm and only two editors shifted to a favorable position as a result of the report. As for the opposition, most chose to ignore the fact that the issue had been changed to the enlarging the commission's activities. Masters, for example, printed the October report but kept the issue

50. *The Religious Herald* (Richmond), Aug. 15, 1935, p. 20.
51. The report appeared in *Annual, SBC, 1936*, p. 37.
52. Jesse B. Weatherspoon explained in the *Western Recorder* (Louisville), Oct. 24, 1935, pp. 6, 11, that the new plan would merely expand the work of the commission. Ryland Knight stressed the practical value of the agency's services to the local pastor in *The Religious Herald* (Richmond), Oct. 31, 1935, p. 7; *Baptist and Reflector* (Nashville), Nov. 7, 1935, p. 7; *Florida Baptist Witness* (Jacksonville), Oct. 17, 1935, p. 10. Merrill D. Moore argued that the convention needed enlightened leadership in dealing with social issues in *Alabama Baptist* (Birmingham), Nov 28, 1935, pp. 5, 8; and in *Baptist and Reflector* (Nashville), Nov. 7, 1935, p. 5.

confused by continuing to attack the features of the discarded bureau.

Barton must have greeted the new report with mixed feelings, for although the revised plan would achieve his ambition, ironically, it would do so through a series of events not of his making and under circumstances that associated the plan with Poteat's alleged radicalism. Having opposed the Research Bureau, Barton could not bring himself to adopt what would appear to be a reversal of his position, no matter how much the plan resembled his earlier suggestions. His failure to support the October compromise suggests that fear of being identified with unpopular liberalism outweighed any desire for a full-time commission.

The convention met in 1936 expecting a full debate on the committee report, but a motion to table the report, which forestalled any discussion, passed by a slight majority and spelled permanent defeat for the proposal. Most of the editors reporting the incident thought the convention did Poteat's committee an injustice by not voting on the report itself. But there was no doubt that the assembly had spoken its true feelings. On the following day a motion to reconsider the question failed by a wide margin.[53]

The effort to establish a social-action agency failed for several reasons. The most important was the campaign that represented the issue as a choice between either liberal theology and the social gospel or Biblical faith and personal evangelism. The committee can be blamed for making so little effort to sell the idea or to answer the objections to their proposal, and Poteat himself was considerably at fault because he offered the original plan solely as his own idea without advance publicity and used terminology in his proposal that unnecessarily aroused sensitive conservatives. He also did little to promote the idea and allowed his critics to go unanswered. Shifting the issue from the bureau to the commission made little difference, since few understood the distinctions between them. The authors of the compromise plan did not fight for it, the editors failed to explain it, and the

53. *Annual, SBC, 1936*, pp. 37–38; *Baptist Record* (Jackson), May 21, 1936, p. 4; *Baptist and Reflector* (Nashville), May 21, 1936, pp. 1, 3.

opposition preferred to ignore it. As a result, the expansion of the commission was judged, not so much on its own merits, as on its association with Poteat's Research Bureau.

Those who believed that the convention should have a social-action agency did not lose hope after the 1936 defeat. One writer concluded that Southern Baptists in this instance had acted in a "strange and irrational" manner, and he predicted that they would eventually reverse their stand.[54] Subsequent developments would suggest that prejudice, misunderstanding, and ill-founded fears had influenced the convention's action. Just a decade later, in an atmosphere less prejudiced and in consideration of a proposal not linked to past fears, the convention would be able to approve an expanded commission without a dissenting voice.

54. *Florida Baptist Witness* (Jacksonville), June 11, 1936, p. 15.

IX

AN AWAKENED SOCIAL CONSCIENCE

Almost immediately following the 1936 decision not to establish a new social-action agency, Southern Baptists began to realize the practical necessity for more effective means by which they could influence public policies.[1] National and international developments in the thirties and early forties had much to do with this change in attitude. Domestically, certain New Deal programs making public funds available to religious institutions raised the question of church-state separation because, in Baptist eyes, the practice violated freedom of conscience by forcing taxpayers to support religious establishments. The rise of totalitarian states abroad caused added anxiety about religious liberty. During World War II, Southern Baptists worked for a peace settlement that would ensure international adherence to freedom of conscience. The desire to preserve and extend religious liberty offered numerous occasions for direct appeals to secular authority, and such activity went a long way

1. Examples of the continuing influence of the social gospel may be found in Joseph Martin Dawson, *Christ and Social Change* (Philadelphia, 1937), pp. 27–29, 41, 117–19, 135–42; W. R. White, "Is There a Different Gospel for Today?" *Alabama Baptist* (Birmingham), May 23, 1940, p. 5; J. B. Lawrence, "The Church and the Social Order," *Baptist Courier* (Greenville), Aug. 1, 1946, p. 1; Olin T. Binkley, "The Minister's Moral Task," *Review and Expositor*, XLIII (Oct., 1946), 369–83; William O. Carver, "The Function of Christianity in the Making of World Order," *Review and Expositor*, XLIII (July, Oct., 1946), 261–74, 384–402; Wayne Oates, "A Christian Perspective of Social Change," *Review and Expositor*, XLIV (Oct., 1947), 444–54; William Wright Barnes, "The Theological Curriculum of Tomorrow," p. 154.

toward removing reservations about the propriety of political action by church bodies.

Political action in the interest of religious liberty began on a continuous basis with the creation of the Public Relations Committee in 1936.[2] Rufus W. Weaver, executive secretary for the Baptist Convention in the District of Columbia, who had become something of a specialist on church-state relations, conceived the idea for the committee. A former president of Mercer University, a Southern Baptist college in Macon, Georgia, he spent the latter part of his career in Washington first as secretary for the National Advisory Committee on Illiteracy under the Hoover administration, then as pastor of the First Baptist Church, and finally as denominational executive for the Washington area. While he was a Baptist executive, Weaver had been chosen to head the Southern Convention's Committee on Chaplains, which for some years had carried on routine business related to military chaplains in behalf of the convention. At Weaver's request the committee was renamed the Public Relations Committee, and its purpose was broadened to allow it to represent all convention agencies in dealings with the federal government. In the absence of finances and authority to initiate action, the committee was not expected to do more than perform minor services at the request of other agencies. Under Weaver's enterprising leadership, however, the Public Relations Committee became an important source of information for the convention and the denomination's recognized spokesman on legislation and governmental policies affecting church-state relations.

As chairman from 1936 to 1941, Weaver saw himself as the "watchman on the wall" of church-state separation. His first report warned that New Deal welfare services threatened traditional church-state relations. The most serious breach in the wall separating religion and government was the National Youth Administration, a program to aid college students by paying schools to provide jobs in lieu of tuition. Weaver claimed that the participation of church schools, which included every Southern

2. *Annual, SBC, 1936*, p. 96.

Baptist college, violated constitutional prohibitions against aid to religion. He was even more upset about proposals by non-Baptist groups for federal aid to parochial schools. In response to his warnings, the convention authorized him to lobby against all such efforts.[3]

One of Weaver's first steps in strengthening the Public Relations Committee for political action was to arrange for the Home Mission Board to take over the committee's responsibility for chaplains. At the same time he advanced the work of his agency by joining forces with a similar committee created by the Northern Baptist Convention. The combined groups, called the Joint Committee on Public Relations, chose Weaver as chairman and in 1939 admitted representatives from the National Baptist Convention, Incorporated (Negro).[4]

The creation of the Joint Committee, representing ten million Baptists, was no little achievement, even though the agency lacked authority for much independent action. To provide more latitude of operation, Weaver and three other Southern Convention committeemen—United States Senators Walter F. George, M. M. Logan, and Josiah W. Bailey—drafted a Pronouncement on Religious Liberty, which the cooperating conventions approved in 1939. This statement warned that the nation and the world were facing a grave crisis over religious liberty. In addition to the well-known attacks on religion by totalitarian governments, the authors charged that the domestic trend toward a welfare state endangered church-state separation. As an example of the latter, they pointed to recurring efforts to obtain federal tax funds for parochial schools.[5]

The pronouncement dealt with yet a third alleged threat to the separation principle, the extension of special governmental

3. *Ibid.*, *1937*, pp. 102–103; *1938*, pp. 119–20; *1939*, pp. 96–98. The principal bill being considered at the time was the Harrison-Thomas-Fletcher proposal, which grew out of the President's National Advisory Committee on Education report of 1938 The bill received the approval of the Senate Committee on Labor and Education. See Charles A. Quattlebaum, *Federal Aid to Elementary and Secondary Education* (Chicago, 1948), pp. 43–44.

4. *Annual, SBC, 1937*, p. 107; *1938*, pp. 117, 122; *1940*, p. 120; *1941*, p. 318.

5. *Ibid.*, *1939*, pp. 114–17.

courtesies to religious groups.[6] The Roman Catholic Church, it was charged, had received privileged recognition on three recent occasions: the memorial ceremonies for a church dignitary in which federal troops participated, the adjournment of Congress on the death of Pope Pius XI, and the appointment of President Roosevelt's personal representative to the coronation of the new pope. Behind this last complaint was the suspicion that Roman Catholics were pressing for diplomatic recognition of the Vatican. Such a relationship had existed prior to the dissolution of the Papal States in 1870 and could be resumed at any time because the one hundred acres comprising Vatican City technically became a sovereign state in 1929. However harmless this arrangement might have appeared to most observers, among Southern Baptists the prospect of high-level recognition stirred ancient fears of Catholic influence in affairs of state.

The anticipated action occurred in December, 1939, when President Roosevelt appointed Myron C. Taylor as his "personal representative" to the pope for the announced purpose of aiding the cause of world peace. Since Taylor did not hold ambassadorial rank, his appointment, strictly speaking, did not mean diplomatic recognition; but Southern Baptists viewed the distinction in title as a subterfuge, especially after the Vatican assigned Taylor the status of ambassador.[7] Interpreting the recently adopted religious-liberty pronouncement as a "mandate or charter to speak for all Baptists," Weaver denounced the appointment as preferential treatment of a religious group.[8] He protested the action in a letter to the White House and in an interview with the President in the company of four other Protestant representatives.[9] Shortly thereafter, Weaver stated the case against the Vatican envoy in a nationwide radio address.[10]

6. *Ibid.*, p. 116; Rufus W. Weaver, "The Vatican Envoy," a mimeographed copy of an address delivered in Washington, D. C., Oct. 2, 1945, p. 10, located in the Weaver Papers, Dargan-Carver Library, Nashville.

7. *The New York Times*, Feb. 14, 1940, p. 11.

8. *Annual, SBC, 1940*, pp. 120, 123.

9. Weaver, "The Vatican Envoy," p. 12. Appearing with Weaver were United Lutheran and Seventh-Day Adventist officials.

10. Rufus W. Weaver, "Religious Liberty," a mimeographed copy of a radio

Weaver retired from the chairmanship of the Joint Committee in 1941, and his position passed to E. Hilton Jackson, a Southern Baptist layman and constitutional lawyer with experience in church-state questions.[11] The war years gave the Joint Committee a new cause when the Allied powers began laying plans for a postwar international organization. The committee took this opportunity to press for more authority and the financial means to carry on a program of action designed to arouse support of religious liberty as a basic principle in the United Nations. In 1944 the committee received blanket authorization to "use all available means" to extend religious freedom to all mankind. With the aid of a modest budget, supplied mostly by the Southern Convention, the Joint Committee set upon the rather ambitious project. Chairman Jackson kept in touch with the Department of State during the preparatory stages for the initial United Nations meeting in San Francisco. In an interview with Secretary of State Edward R. Stettinius, Jackson argued that religious liberty guarantees should be incorporated in the Charter of the United Nations. The Baptist concern did not, of course, become the State Department's cause, although the department did make its facilities available for distributing the Joint Committee's views to the delegations in San Francisco.[12]

For a people notoriously aloof from worldly affairs, Southern Baptists exhibited a considerable amount of political activism in connection with the peace settlement. Advising the secular world about the way to peace came rather easily because Southern Baptists had, from the beginning, viewed the conflict as a holy war in which their religious interests were almost indis-

---

address delivered over the Columbia Broadcasting System, Jan. 21, 1940, located in the Weaver Papers, Dargan-Weaver Library, Nashville. Opposition to Roosevelt's representative was in vain, but the Protestant protest was sufficient to force President Truman to abandon plans to elevate the post to ambassadorial status in 1949. Southern Baptist reaction to Truman's attempted appointment will be discussed in the next chapter.

11. In the famous Everson v. Board of Education, 330 U. S. 1–74 (1947), Jackson appeared before the Supreme Court to argue against the New Jersey law granting tax money for bus transportation to parochial schools.

12. *Annual, SBC, 1944*, pp. 136–37; *1945*, pp. 58–59; *1946*, p. 57.

tinguishable from national purposes.[13] At some time nearly every state convention had issued a solemn pronouncement on the postwar settlement.[14] In the Southern Baptist Convention a special World Peace Committee under the leadership of Joseph Martin Dawson, pastor in Waco, Texas, worked out a statement of conditions essential to a just and lasting peace: an end to isolationism, the right to self-government, an international organization capable of applying economic and military sanctions, abolition of national trade restrictions, universal respect for human equality, and peace settlements that guaranteed "religious liberty for all mankind." For three years prior to the adoption of the Charter of the United Nations, the committee publicized these six principles. Chairman Dawson communicated the views of the committee to officials of the Department of State during the conferences preceding the San Francisco meeting. In January, 1945, Dawson's committee attended the Cleveland meeting of the Commission for a Just and Durable Peace, an agency of the Federal Council of Churches. In behalf of all the major Baptist bodies in America, Dawson also attended the United Nations Conference on International Organization in San Francisco, where the State Department assigned him the status of official observer.[15]

The activities of the committees on public relations and world peace probably seemed impressive to most Southern Baptists, who were not accustomed to having international affairs occupy a prominent place in their deliberations. Actually, the significance of these committees does not lie in the influence they had on international policies. In this respect, the Federal Council's Commission for a Just and Durable Peace occupied a stronger position because it had the official status of "consultant" to the State Department, and its chairman was the distinguished lay-

13. *Ibid.*, 1940, p. 87; 1942, p. 91; *Annual, North Carolina, 1944*, pp. 42–43; *Annual, Texas, 1942*, pp. 207, 211; *Annual, Alabama, 1942*, p. 106.

14. *Annual, Alabama, 1943*, p. 129; 1949, p. 126; *Annual, North Carolina, 1944*, p. 43; *Minutes, Missouri, 1944*, p. 44; *Annual, Texas, 1945*, p. 178; *Annual, Florida, 1945*, p. 86; *Minutes, South Carolina, 1945*, p. 143.

15. *Annual, SBC, 1944*, pp. 149–50; 1945, p. 61; 1946, p. 64; [Edward R. Stettinius, Jr.] *Charter of the United Nations, Report to the President on the Results of the San Francisco Conference* (n.p., 1945), p. 28.

man and statesman John Foster Dulles, who resigned only at the last minute to serve on the United States delegation.[16] The Southern Baptist committees, by acting independently of other Protestants and concentrating mainly on the one issue of religious freedom, demonstrated some abiding characteristics of the convention's capacity for social action. A high degree of political activism is possible only when there is general agreement on public policy—whether it be religious freedom or prohibition—that can be expressed as an absolute religious principle. As social prophets, Southern Baptists are given to inflexible oversimplifications; as social activists, they are given to single causes, perhaps as a kind of overcompensation for inaction on other issues that are more controversial. But however politically unsophisticated, the work of the two committees was important because it marked a departure from denominational policies usually preoccupied with personal religion. The committees not only nourished the high hopes of a world free from war, they also provided precedents for the future establishment of permanent social-action agencies in the denomination.

The catastrophe of war and the problems of peace finally shook Southern Baptists from a social complacency born of a laissez faire evangelical faith. A review of the convention's wartime record gives the impression of a denomination distressed by its irrelevance to the world crisis. A new sense of social concern was much in evidence at the postwar conventions. It is hardly an exaggeration to say that in the space of two years the Southern Convention took more specific action to advance practical Christianity than in all the years since the social gospel first influenced the denomination. The convention adopted an official declaration of its social responsibilities; it oversubscribed a sizable world relief fund; it drafted a progressive statement on race; and it established both the Joint Committee on Public Relations and the Social Service Commission as full-time agencies.

Baptist editors, remembering the bitter attack on the social gospel that had defeated the Social Research Bureau just a

16. *Charter of the United Nations*, p. 27. See also *Christian Century*, LXII (July 18, 1945), 827–28.

decade earlier, were struck by the change of attitude. Describing the general tone of the 1946 meeting, the Mississippi editor reported, "We have heard proclaimed as never before a whole gospel for the whole man of the whole world."[17] "An epochal convention," said the Texas editor,[18] and the North Carolina newspaper headlined its convention story, "Application of the Gospel to Social and Economic Life."[19] Editor B. J. Murie of Illinois in three separate issues contrasted the new social concern with the convention's past opposition to "anything that suggested an improvement in the social and economic welfare" of mankind.[20] "Baptists are changing," he observed; they are "becoming more conscious of the social gospel. It is high time that they did."[21] Murie made much of the fact that nearly every speaker stressed the convention's obligations to world need in terms of humanitarian service and social uplift, which before the war would certainly have been branded as modernistic heresy. Attention to practical Christianity characterized the 1947 convention as well. The declaration on race and the expansion of the Social Service Commission much impressed one outside observer. Harold E. Fey of the *Christian Century,* a liberal Protestant journal not often friendly to Southern Baptist ways, not only congratulated the convention for its "sprawling vitality," which had pushed membership beyond six million, but also praised what he called "an awakening social conscience." The delegates exhibited "a new state of mind," said Fey, when they approved a statement on race relations "which would be a credit to any denomination."[22]

In one instance especially, the postwar advances could be traced directly to the impact of global conflict on social attitudes. Early in the war the Social Service Commission had viewed the breakdown of world order as an occasion calling for a new "declaration of faith and principle" that would specifically

17. *Baptist Record* (Jackson), May 30, 1946, p. 4.
18. *Baptist Standard* (Dallas), June 6, 1946, p. 4.
19. *Biblical Recorder* (Raleigh), June 5, 1946, p. 6.
20. *Illinois Baptist* (Carbondale), June 14, 1946, p. 4.
21. *Ibid.,* May 24, 1946, p. 4.
22. *Christian Century,* LXIV (May 21, 1947), 649.

instruct Baptists in the relationship of Christian faith to political affairs and economic conditions to the end that the "ideal of brotherhood in social life" might be realized.[23] The convention's authorization of what amounted to a social creed had been in itself something of an admission that personal evangelism had not fulfilled Christianity's social promise. A committee of twenty, headed by Southern Seminary President Ellis Fuller, submitted the statement for final approval at the 1946 convention. Although the declaration began with a set of conventional theological propositions and included a plea for evangelizing the postwar world, the main body of the document dealt with practical Christianity under the heading, "Fields of Application." Here the committee affirmed all the basic ideas in the social gospel: the social value of interchurch cooperation, the earthly nature of the kingdom, the brotherhood of man, the fatherhood of God, and the church's responsibility for human welfare and social justice. "The Christian movement," this section began, "is not isolated from the common concerns and life of mankind but as a declarative, prophetic movement charged with a gospel for men in all relations, is a leavening and instructing agency in the midst of society for the good of the human race and the glory of God in the coming of His Kingdom."[24] If churches were agents of social betterment, then they were "under obligation to seek true Christian unity" in order to promote a world organized on "Christian ideals of brotherhood, justice, and truth" rather than "selfish materialism, arrogant imperialism, and power politics." The church was further commissioned to resist all inequalities arising from "racial prides and prejudices, economic greed, and class distinctions."

The postwar conventions did more than issue social proclamations. The most widely publicized action of the 1946 meeting was the enthusiastic approval of a campaign for world relief. The delegates adopted a $3,500,000 goal and launched the drive on the spot with a $10,000 offering.[25] One editor commented: "I

23. *Annual, SBC, 1942*, pp. 94–95.
24. *Ibid.*, 1946, pp. 38–39.
25. *Ibid.*, p. 75.

have never seen the Southern Baptist Convention undertake an enterprise which had met with such enthusiastic response."[26] During the next year gifts exceeded the goal by more than $200,000. The total offering was equal to the foreign mission budget and twice the home mission expenditure for the same year.[27]

Of much greater significance for the future, this same convention approved the request of the Joint Committee on Public Relations for an employed executive.[28] Southern Baptists accepted the new venture without opposition, thereby embarking on a continuous program of political action on church-state issues. Similar authorization soon came from the other Baptist groups represented by the committee. Operating on a $17,000 budget, more than half of which came from the Southern Convention, the Joint Committee began to carry out its official directive to "enunciate, defend, and extend the historic, traditional Baptist principle of religious freedom with particular application to the separation of church and state."[29] The executive director's principal assignment was to represent the Baptist position on church-state relations at the national and international levels.

Southern Baptists, having inaugurated the work of the Joint Committee and supplied its main leadership, likewise furnished its first executive director. The post went to Joseph Martin Dawson, who had just concluded three years' work as chairman of the Committee on World Peace. Dawson's experience otherwise had been limited largely to pastoral work. Even so, he had already shown an uncommon concern for broadening the church's social ministry. His book, *Christ and Social Change* (1937), affirmed the essential elements in the social gospel. Interpreting the mission of Christ as the establishment of a "new social order," he criticized a one-sided emphasis on individual salvation, urged the church to use its corporate witness in direct social action, and specifically called for socializing the "present

26. *Illinois Baptist* (Carbondale), June 21, 1946, p. 1.
27. *Annual, SBC, 1947*, p. 69.
28. *Ibid., 1946*, p. 75.
29. *Ibid., 1949*, p. 351.

pagan economic system."[30] Although his liberal social views were somewhat obscured while he was director of the Joint Committee because of the agency's attention to the single issue of religious liberty, the social-gospel ideology, together with the work of the World Peace Committee, prepared Dawson for the transition from the pastorate to an effective career in public affairs. In his new position, which he occupied until 1952, Dawson became one of the nation's foremost defenders of the separation principle.

The years of war and peacemaking, which elevated the standing of the Joint Committee, also brought new status to the Social Service Commission. The death of Arthur J. Barton, in addition to the stimulus afforded by world crises, opened the way for a more vigorous program. Jesse B. Weatherspoon, the new chairman, immediately brought new life to the commission, beginning with a fresh appraisal of its purpose.[31] He outlined a working philosophy that would enable the commission to deal with controversial social problems without appearing to stray from the convention's strictly religious purposes, and he made it a definite point to ground the work of the agency on religious principles. His central proposition was that Christian ethics should determine man's social relationships as well as his personal conduct. The commission's purpose was to explore the social implications of Christianity, collect and evaluate information about social conditions, and suggest courses of action against social evils. To avoid charges of substituting social action for evangelism, Weatherspoon explicitly avowed that the "primary" task of the convention was "changing persons" rather than "changing society." Having granted evangelism's priority, Weatherspoon could then affirm the social-gospel doctrine of collective action against corporate evils. In his words, Southern Baptists must make a "direct approach to the powerful economic and political bodies that . . . control our common life."[32]

Weatherspoon next turned to procedures that could be em-

30. *Christ and Social Change*, pp. 28, 119, 142.
31. *Annual, SBC, 1944*, pp. 129–31.
32. *Ibid.*, p. 130.

ployed against social ills, the point at which Southern Baptist
social thought had foundered so often in the past. He made clear
that some problems, such as farm tenancy, race relations, and
labor disputes, were distinctly social in nature and therefore did
not lend themselves to "easy" or "final" solutions drawn from an
absolute ethic. Despite the lack of simple ethical dictums, he
believed that Christians were under a moral imperative to improve man's earthly condition. Weatherspoon's methodology
combined a principled ethic with social pragmatism, thus avoiding one of the long-standing weaknesses of Baptist social
thought. The prevailing tendency had been to look for absolute
answers in terms of personal ethics for all social evils without
recognizing that complex problems arising from an imperfect
social order require the pressure of collective action and the
force of legislation to effect improvements. Weatherspoon
pointed out that Christian ethics directed only to the individual
did not strike at deeply rooted social evils. He thus made institutions as well as individuals subject to judgment and reform.
In taking this position, he entertained no illusions about the per-
fectability of society, the error of some early social-gospel advocates, but he insisted that working for social betterment was an
inescapable obligation of organized Christianity. Weatherspoon
here represents the social liberal who came out of the war chastened but still believing in the possibility of human progress.

Although Weatherspoon's early reports as commission chairman discussed many social problems, it was only in dealing with
race relations that he made significant advancements.[33] His approach to this issue illustrates the combination of realism and
idealism in his social philosophy. As a realist, he spurned all
sweeping moralisms prescribed as the "only" remedy for the
problem of race. However, he also believed that the absence of
"final" answers did not lessen the obligation for immediate action
wherever progress could be made toward racial equality. Weatherspoon specifically called for an end to suffrage restrictions,

33. *Ibid.*, 1944, pp. 132–33; 1945, pp. 96–97.

unequal educational facilities, unfair economic conditions, and discriminatory legislation.

For all his attention to political action, Weatherspoon did not overlook the duty of the individual in race relations. On the contrary, a special report in 1947 on the convention's obligations to the Negro, prepared by a committee headed by Weatherspoon, placed the emphasis on personal attitudes and actions.[34] Generally regarded at the time as the most comprehensive statement on race by Southern Baptists, the report avoided suggesting specific kinds of direct action, but instead set forth certain fundamental "principles and methods of procedures," which presumably would "insure justice to all and establish attitudes of mutual helpfulness and goodwill."[35] After taking into account the essential role of political action in achieving racial justice, the report emphasized that such action did not eliminate the tension, prejudice, and injustices that spring from "fallacious thinking and racial feeling." Correcting these evils would require the inner, personal qualities of "moral understanding and conviction."[36]

As a basis for improving racial attitudes, the study offered a "charter of principles," including the obligation to love one's neighbor, the unity of the human race, the right to social justice, the inherent worth of the individual, and the democratic way of life. From these ideals, the committee formulated certain "principles of conduct" along more practical lines. The Christian must overcome prejudices, protest injustices, insist on equality before the law, pay fair wages, and participate in interracial activities.[37] The committee further argued that its proposals pointed to just and realistic goals clearly demanded by Christian principles. Current analysis would note the absence of practical guidelines for direct action toward specific goals but otherwise would find the declaration a praiseworthy affirmation of Chris-

34. *Ibid., 1946*, p. 127.
35. *Ibid., 1947*, p. 341.
36. *Ibid.*, p. 342.
37. *Ibid.*, pp. 342–43.

tian responsibility for racial justice, especially for the decade of the forties.

In additional to making the social gospel palatable to Southern Baptists, Weatherspoon expanded the work of the Social Service Commission.[38] He involved the commission members in the study of specific problems, and he supplied the Baptist newspapers with articles on social issues. The commission published literature on marriage, industrial problems, race relations, and Christian citizenship; and an annual week-long conference became a regular feature of the convention's summer assembly at Ridgecrest, North Carolina. This stepped-up activity foreshadowed Weatherspoon's ultimate goal of placing the work of the commission in the hands of a paid executive. The ease with which he accomplished this feat is explained partly by the confidence he had earned in the field of social ethics and partly by the general change of attitude in the convention since the defeat of a similar proposal a decade earlier. If the time was right, so was Weatherspoon's approach. He simply requested the powerful Executive Committee of the convention to assess the work of the commission with a view toward expanding its activities. The Executive Committee favored the idea and provided for a commission executive in the convention's 1947 budget. Handled as a routine recommendation, the new program won convention approval without debate from the floor or objection in the Baptist press.[39]

For executive secretary the commission chose Hugh A. Brimm, recently a student under Weatherspoon at Southern Seminary. This choice, added to the leadership Weatherspoon had given the commission since 1943, calls attention to the contribution of the seminarians to denominational social attitudes. Brimm was selected for the new post because, as a student and later as a teacher at Mercer University, his major interest had been the convention's disappointing social record. His doctoral thesis revealed among Southern Baptists a deplorable indifference to the problems of Negroes, farm tenants, migratory

38. *Ibid.*, *1945*, p. 93; *1946*, p. 120.
39. *Ibid.*, *1946*, p. 121; *1947*, pp. 34–35.

workers, and cotton-mill employees. Most distressing was that churches and associations closest to instances of social injustices seemed incapable of dealing with the situations.[40]

Brimm's study in 1944 was only the first of several similar investigations. Students at Southern Seminary under Weatherspoon and Olin T. Binkley analyzed the views of Baptist editors on social issues.[41] At Southwestern Seminary, Thomas B. Maston, head of the ethics department, directed research in the social gospel and race relations.[42] For the first time the convention's response to social problems received critical examination. The results amounted to a unanimous indictment of denominational policies that had either disregarded social evils or lent support to the injustices in the social order.

By far the most outspoken critic of Southern Baptist social conservatism was Das Kelly Barnett, who studied at Southern Seminary during the early forties. In a student commencement address, Barnett attacked the convention leadership for disregarding the social problems in the South and singled out especially those who had opposed the Social Research Bureau.[43] The publication of Barnett's rebuke in the seminary's journal touched off a counter movement against him, initiated by Kentucky editor Victor Masters, that caused Barnett to resign his appointment as a graduate assistant at the school.[44]

Upon completing his seminary work, Barnett took a church in Chapel Hill, North Carolina, where he formed an association of liberal ministers and laymen called the Baptist Book Club. After World War II this group published a small journal, *Christian Frontiers*, which Barnett edited. The title page carried an impressive list of sympathizers: W. O. Carver of Southern Sem-

40. Brimm, "The Social Consciousness of Southern Baptists," pp. vi, 50, 71, 90, 119, 121–35, 139.

41. See Crook, English, and Patrick Henry Hill. Notice should also be given to Davis C. Hill's "Southern Baptist Thought and Action in Race Relations, 1940–1950" (Th.D. thesis, Southern Baptist Theological Seminary, 1952).

42. Charles Price Johnson; Valentine, "A Historical Study of Southern Baptists and Race Relations."

43. Barnett, "The New Theological Frontiers for Southern Baptists," *Review and Expositor*, XXXVIII (July, 1941), 264–76.

44. Information in this paragraph was obtained from correspondence with Barnett, Feb. 5, 1958.

inary, Joseph Martin Dawson of the Joint Committee on Public Relations, William H. Poteat, whose father had proposed the Social Research Bureau, Almonte C. Howell of the English department at the University of North Carolina, and several prominent pastors. Barnett's announced purpose was to provide a journal for the free discussion of controversial issues within the denomination.[45] He complained of the lack of intellectual freedom for anyone who disagreed with traditional theology or denominational policy. The journal gave major emphasis to social questions, on which it invariably took a liberal position: it favored the labor movement in the South, condemned the one-party system, criticized racial discrimination, and supported civil rights legislation. Articles criticizing military spending and defending conscientious objectors gave the publication a pacifist orientation. Most offensive to Southern Baptists generally, the periodical strongly advocated membership in the Federal Council of Churches.[46]

Christian Frontiers was a short-lived example of the presence of a liberal minority in open rebellion against conservatism, social inaction, and isolationism. As a movement, its causes were too unpopular, its criticisms too radical, and its aims too far advanced to develop strong support from a basically conservative denomination. The journal's circulation was never very large, and financial difficulty forced the suspension of publication after three years. Barnett, who turned to teaching, continued for a short time as a minor advocate of liberalism in the convention. He finally concluded that the lack of centralized authority in Baptist ecclesiology made impossible effective convention action against social evils and, along with two other members of the group, eventually joined the Protestant Episcopal Church.

The activities of the North Carolina liberals hold a unique place in Southern Baptist history. They represent the only group specifically organized to promote liberal social and theological ideas within the denomination. Their inability to gain a sub-

45. *Christian Frontiers,* I (Jan., 1946), 6; II (Jan., 1947), 3.
46. The journal was begun as a monthly but appeared irregularly. The issues analyzed ran from Jan., 1946, to Sept., 1948.

stantial following indicates that the increased attention to social problems among Southern Baptists in the forties came about without altering the denomination's fundamental conservatism. With the failure of this movement, the molding of the social conscience of Southern Baptists rested with the more moderate leadership of the convention-controlled seminaries, the Joint Committee on Public Relations, and the Social Service Commission. Upon the Joint Committee and the commission fell the immediate task of interpreting the social goals of the denomination.

X

CHURCH-STATE ISSUES AT MID-CENTURY

The Joint Committee on Public Relations began operating as a full-time agency in 1946.[1] Joseph Martin Dawson, the executive director until 1953, had been a Texas pastor; his successor, C. Emanuel Carlson, was a layman and former dean of Bethel College, a Baptist school in St. Paul, Minnesota. When Dawson accepted the directorship, the Northern and Southern conventions and the two largest Negro Baptist bodies supported the work. Carlson increased the cooperating organizations to eight, representing some twenty million Baptists. The Joint Committee's full membership, consisting of the public affairs committees from each of the affiliated conventions, met twice each year, and an executive committee of seven acted between sessions. The Southern Convention's Public Affairs Committee had fifteen members, who were chosen annually by the convention and included the heads of other major convention agencies, with the remaining members being pastors and laymen who lived near the Joint Committee's headquarters in Washington, D.C. In the early years, the work was carried on by a single executive, but a steady increase in appropriations enabled Carlson to build up a staff of four assistants.[2]

1. At a meeting in 1951, the name of the committee was changed to the Joint Committee on Public Affairs.
2. *Annual, SBC, 1946*, pp. 117–19, 499; *1950*, p. 393; *1964*, p. 253; *1967*, p. 363. Income for the Joint Committee was $126,531 in 1967, of which $104,511 came from the Southern Convention. Carlson's assistants were W. Barry Garrett, former editor in Arizona, in charge of public relations; James Sapp, of the Southern Convention's Brotherhood Commission, in charge of denominational

Authorized to "enunciate, defend, and extend" the principle of church-state separation, the Joint Committee kept watch on legislation, judicial proceedings, and governmental policies.[3] Dawson's greatest efforts were directed against the naming of an ambassador to the Vatican, an issue that, as was mentioned earlier, originated with President Roosevelt's appointment of a personal representative to the Vatican in 1939. Contrary to White House assurances that upon completion of the peace treaties the relationship would be terminated, President Harry S. Truman named General Mark Clark as permanent Vatican envoy in 1951.[4] The Joint Commitee immediately protested. Dawson set forth the Baptist position in *The Ambassador to the Vatican: The Battle for America,* which reached a circulation of half a million copies. His effectiveness in rallying Baptists to this cause made him a key figure in the Protestant uprising that caused Truman to withdraw the nomination.[5]

Over the years, the most persistent question before the committee concerned the use of public funds by religious institutions. Nearly every issue of the agency's bulletin discussed some governmental program, proposed legislation, or judicial ruling related to state aid to religious establishments; and on these matters, the director became recognized as the Baptist spokesman by public officials and the national press. The public affairs com-

relations; Walfred Peterson, a political scientist from Bethel College, St. Paul, Minn., director of research; and Alice Moody, administrative assistant.

3. *Annual, SBC, 1949,* p. 351. A new constitution gave the committee greater freedom to act. See *Annual, SBC, 1956,* pp. 353–56. The responsibility of the committee included promoting religious liberty abroad. The 1946 request for a paid director made much of the opportunities to extend religious freedom through the United Nations organization. Dawson attended several conferences sponsored by UNESCO in connection with the provision for religious freedom in the international Bill of Human Rights adopted in 1948. On several occasions the Joint Committee protested denials of religious liberty in Latin American countries, Russia, Italy, Spain, and Egypt. See *Annual, SBC, 1946,* p. 118; *1952,* p. 429; and *Report from the Capital,* June, 1955; Jan., 1956; Feb., 1956; June, 1956; July, 1956; Aug., 1957; Jan., 1963; May, 1965 (hereafter cited as *Report*).

4. Presidential Secretary Charles G. Ross to William B. Lippard, recording secretary for the Joint Committee, Aug. 4, 1948, reproduced in *Report,* Dec., 1951. For other assurances see *Annual, SBC, 1947,* p. 41; *Christian Century,* LXVIII (Nov. 7, 1951), 1270; *The New York Times,* Jan. 19, 1951, p. 10.

5. *Annual, SBC, 1952,* pp. 428–29; *Time,* LVIII (Oct. 29, 1951), 20; *Christian Century,* LXVIII (Oct. 31, 1951), 1243.

mittee also kept the Baptist constituency informed about the growing number of government programs offering aid to church institutions. A 1953 survey found that half the states furnished textbooks or bus transportation or both for parochial school students and that federal grants to sectarian hospitals totaled $87,000,000. A similar study a decade later revealed 115 separate programs in health, education, research, housing, foreign aid, and the war on poverty in which church agencies were participating.[6]

Carlson and his associates presented the case against government aid to religious groups in numerous appearances before congressional committees and federal agencies. The committee opposed extending social security to ministers under terms that required church participation.[7] In respect to this position, which was held by many Protestants, the 1954 law included ministers on a voluntary, self-employed basis.[8] The committee's objections did not prevent an extension of the Hill-Burton hospital grants in 1958; however, an amendment offering federal funds as loans was a direct result of Baptist objections to outright grants.[9] On the perennial question of federal aid to education, the committee lobbied against the inclusion of parochial schools. It is of some credit to the Baptists that the 1965 Elementary and Secondary Act adopted the child-benefit principle by which aid went to pupils rather than to schools. The Joint Committee specifically approved the provision that aid to private school students was to be administered through public agencies.[10]

6. *Annual, SBC, 1953,* p. 435. A summary of Bryant's findings was published by the Joint Committee under the title, "In Review and Evaluation of the C. E. Bryant Research into the Allotment of Federal Funds to Churches" (n.p., n.d.). In support of Bryant's conclusions, see *The Nation,* CLXXIII (Sept. 8, 1951), 192; *Christianity Today,* III (Feb. 2, 1959), 31–33. Alice Moody, "Church Agencies Eligible in 115 Government Programs," *Report,* July, 1965, pp. 5–7.

7. *Report,* Mar., 1953; Apr., 1954; *Annual, SBC, 1953,* p. 56; *1954,* p. 41.

8. *68 U. S. Statutes at Large* (1955), pp. 1052–99.

9. *Report,* May, 1957; Oct., 1958; *Church and State,* X (May, 1957), 4. The Executive Committee of the Southern Baptist Convention, acting on a recommendation from the Public Affairs Committee, petitioned Congress to offer hospital funds as loans rather than grants. The new bill allowed both loans and grants. See *Word and Way* (Jefferson City), July 12, 1956, p. 4.

10. Emanuel Carlson, "Baptists and Dual Enrollment," *Baptist Program* (Nov., 1965), pp. 7, 16; *Report,* Jan., 1966, p. 5; Mar.–Apr., 1966, p.

As a regular practice, the Joint Committee on Public Affairs followed church-state questions in the courts, giving particular attention to Supreme Court cases on the use of public school facilities for religious purposes.[11] In the *Everson* v. *Board of Education* (1947) case, the committee submitted a brief to the Court, and one of the committee members, E. Hilton Jackson, served as counsel for the appellant in an unsuccessful attempt to invalidate a New Jersey law that paid transportation costs for parochial students. In *McCollum* v. *Board of Education* (1948), the Court's decision agreed with the brief presented by Jackson in which he argued that the use of public school buildings for religious instruction by church-appointed teachers on a "released time" basis violated the Constitution. The Supreme Court again faced the religion-in-the-schools issue in the "prayer cases" of 1962–63, in which the Court first outlawed a prayer prescribed by the New York Board of Regents, then overruled state laws requiring Bible reading and the Lord's Prayer. While many evangelicals, including Southern Baptist evangelist Billy Graham and Southern Seminary President Duke McCall, objected to the decisions, most Southern Convention sentiment supported the Court. The Joint Committee not only upheld the Court but did much to clarify the decision and then opposed efforts in Congress to nullify the ruling by a constitutional amendment.[12]

The Joint Committee's contribution to the cause of separation extended beyond Baptist circles. When Dawson became director, he immediately began organizing Protestants and Other

---

5. The Joint Committee approved the bill in its report to the Southern Convention in *Annual, SBC, 1965*, p. 273. The committee subsequently criticized administrative procedures in local communities that did not respect the intention of the law at the point of distinguishing between aid to students and aid to schools. See *Report*, May, 1966, p. 7.

11. Everson v. Board of Education, 330 U. S., pp. 1–74 (1947); McCollum v. Board of Education, 33 U. S., pp. 203–56 (1948). For the Joint Committee's action, see *Annual, SBC, 1947*, p. 308; *1948*, p. 359.

12. *Report*, July–Aug., 1962, pp. 1, 5; Sept.–Oct.–Nov., 1965, p. 4; June, 1966, pp. 1–3, 5–6. For the approval of Baptist editors, see *Report*, July–Aug., 1962, p. 2. On Graham's and McCall's stands, see *The Religious Herald* (Richmond), July 4, 1963, p. 3; and *Maryland Baptist* (Baltimore), Jan. 27, 1966, p. 3. The Joint Committee went on record against the Becker amendment in *Report*, June, 1962, pp. 1, 6; Mar., 1964, pp. 1–4. Carlson testified against the Dirksen amendment. See *Report*, Aug., 1966, pp. 6–7.

Americans United for the Separation of Church and State (POAU). For several months the Joint Committee members carried on most of the work of POAU until it attracted support from Protestants across the nation. By 1948 the organization had its own staff, headquartered in Washington, D. C. Registered as a lobby, POAU published a monthly bulletin, *Church and State*, aided in litigation against state aid to religion, and extended its influence to local communities through affiliated chapters. Its officers included prominent figures in the Protestant world: Methodist Bishop G. Bromley Oxnam; John A. Mackay, president of Princeton Theological Seminary; Edwin McNeill Poteat, Jr., then president of Colgate-Rochester Divinity School; and Charles Clayton Morrison, former editor of *Christian Century*. Southern Baptists among its officers were convention president Louie D. Newton and Joseph Martin Dawson of the Joint Committee.[13]

The Joint Committee fulfilled the intention of its founders when it defended the wall of separation without compromise. Dawson carried out this purpose heroically, as his speeches, articles, and books testify.[14] He so aroused fears of Catholic violations of the First Amendment that Southern Baptists were willing to cooperate with other religious groups in the cause of separation.

When Carlson took over the office, the work underwent an important shift of emphasis. The new chairmen faithfully opposed all forms of direct public aid to religion, but he sought a more positive mission for the agency. Viewing the basic principle in church-state relations to be religious freedom rather than Thomas Jefferson's wall-of-separation metaphor, Carlson called for a fresh examination of the Baptist position. He wanted the agency's operations to be well grounded on principles with-

13. *Annual, SBC, 1947*, p. 34; *1948*, p. 359; *1949*, p. 351; *1950*, p. 393. The POAU "manifesto" appeared in *Christian Century*, LXV (Jan. 21, 1948), 79–82. Luke Ebersole, *Church Lobbying in the Nation's Capital* (New York, 1951), pp. 67–73, gives a full account of the background of POAU and the roles of Southern Baptists Weaver and Dawson. POAU was regularly included in the budgets of state conventions and many district associations.

14. The best statement of Dawson's views is in his *Separate Church and State Now* (New York, 1948).

out offering doctrinaire answers to church-state problems. An educator by training and an intellectual by temperament, Carlson led Baptists in a continuing study of the meaning of religious liberty in the light of the changing roles of church and state in modern society.

Carlson's most significant innovation was the establishment of an annual religious-liberty conference. Educators, denominational executives, and pastors were invited to discuss religious freedom as it related to expanding governmental services in areas served by the church. Not designed to arouse political action, the sessions exposed the participants to varying points of view, with the conferences so structured that church-state issues became points of departure for the study of larger social problems. Recent conferences have examined social welfare, international relations, population control, the guaranteed income, and conscientious objection to war. Resource people, some of whom were not Baptists, included scholars, public officials, and churchmen experienced in public affairs. The conferences afforded Southern Baptists an almost unique opportunity for creative thinking about the church's social mission as well as church-state relations.[15]

That the committee's work also became less anti-Catholic in character is another example of Carlson's influence. The agency did not join Southern Baptists in opposing Senator John F. Kennedy's presidential campaign; in fact, Carlson's published analysis concluded that of all the candidates Kennedy had the most acceptable position on church-state matters.[16] One example of greater tolerance for Roman Catholicism appeared in connec-

15. For Carlson's views on the work of the agency, see his "The Biblical Basis of Religious Liberty," a mimeographed study paper for the 1958 Religious Liberty Conference, and his "The Baptist Genius in Today's World," a mimeographed copy of an address to the American Baptist Convention, June 16, 1958. Carlson reviewed the ten conferences, 1957–66, in Report, July, 1966, pp. 2, 6. His goals for the agency are difficult to pin down from his writings, but his many references to the value of "interaction" of different points of view, to the "sharing" of insights, and to the "rethinking" of the Baptist position suggest something of his desire to make the agency more than a defender of separation.

16. Report, Apr.–May, 1960, p. 2. Reuben Alley, editor of The Religious Herald (Richmond), criticized the Joint Committee's "spirit of accommodation" toward Roman Catholicism during the 1960 campaign (Jan. 5, 1961, p. 10).

tion with Pope John XXIII's call for church renewal and the subsequent Ecumenical Council (1962–65). Most Southern Baptists viewed with skepticism the evidence that the Church of Rome might liberalize its stand on interfaith marriages, birth control, centralized authority, Christian unity, religious freedom, and other points of dogma offensive to Protestants; and Baptists were among the few communions who refused to send an official observer to Vatican II.[17] The Joint Committee reacted differently. Viewing the council as a hopeful sign that Catholics might make concessions toward freedom of conscience, the committee sent Associate Director W. Barry Garrett to Rome with credentials as a newsman. His accounts represented something new in Southern Baptist reportings on the Catholic church. While clearly specifying deficiencies in the council's decrees, Garrett confirmed the reports from religious and secular observers that Vatican II marked a historic victory for liberal forces in the church.[18]

Carlson's policies exposed the Joint Committee to charges of following a "soft line" on church-state separation. Displeasure first developed over his treatment of the religious issue in the 1960 election, and criticism became more widespread following the Joint Committee's 1965 report, which endorsed the Elementary and Secondary Education Act, providing funds to students in private schools. Even more distressing to the separationists, this report took no position on the Higher Education Facilities Act, which made federal money available to church colleges.

17. W. Barry Garrett, "Baptists Need Report on Vatican Council II," *Report,* Aug.–Sept.–Oct., 1963, p. 3; Nov.–Dec., 1963, p. 1. The Southern Baptist Executive Committee refused to act on a recommended expression of gratitude for the Council's statement on religious freedom. See the *Maryland Baptist* (Baltimore), Oct. 7, 1965, p. 1.

18. *Report,* Nov.–Dec., 1963, pp. 1–8. In an address to a Pastor's Conference in Texas, Garrett condemned "isolated Christianity" and called for "a new day in conversations between Catholics and Baptists." See the *Maryland Baptist* (Baltimore), July 21, 1966, p. 2. Other Southern Baptists who attended the final session were Maryland editor Gainer Bryan and Claude Broach, a North Carolina pastor. See the *Maryland Baptist* (Baltimore), Sept. 16, 1965, p. 8. Broach, in "A Baptist Pastor at Vatican II," *Baptist Program* (Nashville), Apr., 1966, p. 20, said that Vatican II "smashed the myth . . . that Rome never changes."

Carlson justified the omission on grounds that the "Baptist positions have not yet crystallized."[19]

The presentation of Carlson's 1965 report to the Southern Convention seemed to emphasize the committee's apparent deviation from strict separation. Appearing with Carlson was William Moyers, an ordained Southern Baptist minister and a member of President Lyndon B. Johnson's staff. In his address, Moyers called for greater cooperation between churches and government in solving the problems of war, civil rights, education, and poverty. The plea for church-state cooperation sounded strange to a Baptist audience. Immediately following Moyers on the program was Glenn Archer, an executive of POAU. In striking contrast to Moyers's remarks, Archer reviewed Baptist devotion to separation and warned against those who would "barter their birthright" for a "mess of pottage" from a state that would destroy the distinctive purposes of religious institutions.[20]

Archer's accusations about disloyalty to separation were in reference to current discussions among Southern Baptists on the question of public assistance to religious institutions. The issue was being debated primarily at the state-convention level because those bodies controlled most of the medical, educational, and child-care institutions that were in a position to receive public assistance. The practice of accepting various forms of government aid had become widespread in the postwar years. A survey of aid to Southern Baptist institutions from major federal sources alone is revealing.[21] Grants under the Hill-Burton Act in the amount of $12,757,535 went to eighteen hospitals in seven states, while the Public Health Service in the years 1959–61 awarded Baptist schools $9,146,793 for research. The National

19. *The Religious Herald* (Richmond), Jan. 5, 1961, p. 10; June 17, 1965, pp. 10–11; the *Maryland Baptist* (Baltimore), June 24, 1965, p. 8; *Annual, SBC, 1965*, p. 273.

20. Archer's address, "Will Baptists Barter Their Birthright," appeared in the *Baptist Messenger* (Oklahoma City), June 24, 1965, pp. 8–9, 12–13.

21. I am indebted to William Meredith Pinson, Jr., for the data in this paragraph. See his "Contemporary Southern Baptist Involvement with the State" (Th.D. thesis, Southwestern Baptist Theological Seminary, 1963), pp. 59, 64–65, 77–79, 81.

Science Foundation through 1961 gave Baptist schools half a million dollars in grants; and in the fifteen-year period following World War II, $3,262,157 in government surplus land, buildings, and equipment were transferred to Baptist ownership for token payments. Federal loans through 1962 amounted to $36,580,000 for college dormitories and $4,668,058 for students. Finally, the Johnson administration's higher education acts of 1963 and 1965 made federal funds available on an unprecedented scale to private schools for classrooms, libraries, laboratories, teaching equipment, and student aid.

Strong reaction to the acceptance of public money developed in the fifties, and by 1963 at least ten state conventions had made extensive examinations of institutional practices.[22] Perhaps the most typical policy statement was adopted by Texas Baptists in 1961 after a year-long study by a special committee. The report ruled out all direct financial assistance, including grants and loans at below commercial interest rates, although loans to students were allowed. Government property could be purchased but only at a "fair market value." Research grants met approval if they were contracted in return for "services rendered." The committee found no objection to ministers serving as chaplains and saw no practical way to avoid the benefits of second-class mailing privileges for church newspapers. Tax exemption for church property was approved, although the committee suggested that "voluntary fees" might be paid for local fire and police protection.[23]

Separationists were at work in other states during the year of the Texas study. The Missouri Convention severed a seventy-year-old affiliation with Baptist Hospital in St. Louis when its board would not return Hill-Burton funds. Oklahoma Baptists

22. *Ibid.*, p. 286. Investigations were carried on by the conventions in Georgia, Kentucky, Mississippi, Missouri, North Carolina, Oklahoma, South Carolina, Tennessee, Texas, and Washington, D. C. For examples see *Annual, North Carolina, 1950*, pp. 24I–24P; *1956*, pp. 58–62; *Journal, Virginia, 1956* (n.p., n.d.), pp. 68–75; *Minutes of the Baptist General Convention of Oklahoma, 1962* (n.p., n.d.), pp. 85–91.
23. *Annual, Texas, 1961*, pp. 85–93.

re-examined their relationship to six hospitals that had been built with federal grants and then leased to the state convention. They voted not to renew the existing leases and not to allow acceptance of future grants by any convention-related institution. Arkansas Baptists by a narrow vote leased a Little Rock hospital built with federal funds, but the certainty of convention disapproval of future grants led the hospital board to seek a release from denominational control.[24]

During the 1960's convention debates on federal aid turned almost entirely to the denomination's thirty colleges and universities.[25] Rising educational costs set against increased appropriations to state schools created a critical financial disadvantage for church schools. Furthermore, the funds available through the higher education acts of 1963 and 1965 brought little relief to Southern Baptist schools because of the prevailing belief in the denomination that such aid violated religious principle. In every state where the issue came to a vote, conventions disapproved of all federal aid, the only exception being for research grants, which were regarded as payments for "services rendered" rather than as aid to schools. Conventions in California, Kentucky, Texas, and Virginia forbade both grants and loans for school facilities; North Carolina Baptists refused a Wake Forest College request for the removal of all restrictions against federal aid; the South Carolina Convention forced Furman University to turn back a building grant; and the Georgia Convention, which earlier had allowed loans, barred all building grants and loans in 1965. Only two schools successfully defied the separationists. The newly formed Atlanta Baptist College, controlled by a local association, was allowed to receive federal aid by a narrow vote; and Stetson University in Florida,

24. *Word and Way* (Jefferson City), Jan. 19, 1961, p. 4; *Minutes, Oklahoma, 1961*, pp. 93–98; *1962*, pp. 85–91; *The Religious Herald* (Richmond), Nov. 28, 1963, p. 10; *Maryland Baptist* (Baltimore), Sept. 15, 1966, pp. 1–2.

25. *Southern Baptist Educator*, XXX (Jan., 1966), 11–12, reported that in 1965 alone sixteen of the twenty-nine state conventions dealt with the federal-aid question. Special committees were set up to study the problem in Arkansas, Arizona, Florida, Mississippi, and South Carolina. Kentucky held a special state convention in 1966, which decided against loans and grants.

governed by an independent board, accepted more than one million dollars in grants and loans in 1966 against the expressed wishes of the state convention.[26]

The denial of federal aid to convention-controlled schools was not decided without a fight, for never in their history have Southern Baptists disagreed so strongly on the meaning of church-state separation. Vigorously prosecuting the case for public funds, the Southern Association of Baptist Colleges, composed of school administrators, assailed the traditional view of church-station relations in both 1961 and 1965.[27] The denomination's most distinguished educators, representing the best schools, led the fight: J. Ollie Edmunds of Stetson, Harold Tribble of Wake Forest, Francis Bonner of Furman, Rufus Harris of Mercer, Abner McCall of Baylor. McCall was the most outspoken and persistent critic of the separation doctrine.[28] A layman himself, he chided the clerical separationists for denying aid to schools while serving tax-free churches subsidized by public services. McCall also quarreled with the Baptist editors, who opposed aid for schools while accepting mailing privileges at substantial cost to the taxpayer.[29] The main concern of the educators was the practical matter of competition. To them,

26. *Baptist Messenger* (Oklahoma City), June 24, 1965, p. 5; *Southern Baptist Educator*, XXX (Jan., 1966), 15–16; (July–Aug., 1966), 11–12; *Maryland Baptist* (Baltimore), Apr. 21, 1966, p. 2.

27. *Baptist Messenger* (Oklahoma City), June 22, 1961, p. 4; *Southern Baptist Educator*, XXIX (July–Aug., 1965), 11.

28. Abner McCall, "A Discussion of Two Federal Aid Objections," *Southern Baptist Educator*, XXX (Nov., 1966), 8–10. One of McCall's statements was made to the Christian Life Workshop at Southwestern Seminary, Mar. 10, 1964. This address, "Another View of Tax Support," appeared in the *Ouachita Baptist Alumni Magazine*, June, 1965. Ouachita College President Ralph Phelps also favored federal aid. See the *Southern Baptist Educator*, XXX (Jan., 1966), 9. Two college presidents defended strict separation. G. Earl Guinn of Louisiana College opposed federal aid in "Can Baptist Colleges Afford to Accept Federal Aid?" *Southern Baptist Educator*, XXIX (July–Aug., 1965), 3–6. Five college presidents joined in answering Guinn in "Can Baptist Colleges Afford Isolation Instead of Cooperation," *Southern Baptist Educator* (Sept.–Oct., 1965), 3–4. The separationist views of Loyed R. Simmons of California Baptist College were published by POAU in *Southern Baptists and Federal Aid* (Washington, D. C., 1968).

29. McCall charged that the *Baptist Standard* (Dallas) alone enjoyed a one-million-dollar subsidy annually. See the *Maryland Baptist* (Baltimore), July 14, 1966, p. 1, and Alley's answer, in the *Maryland Baptist*, Aug. 4, 1966, p. 8.

government control and the loss of religious freedom were quite remote from the real issue in Baptist higher education—finding the resources to maintain existing educational programs.

The vast majority of the pastors, editors, and state-convention executives opposed federal aid. They built their case on loyalty to Baptist principle, no matter what the financial sacrifice, and would deny to their own schools funds that institutions of every other religious affiliation gladly accepted. Although their arguments made much of preserving religious freedom, a careful reading of the debate suggests that their main fear was not government control but loss of denominational control. Many of the determined separationists were among those who worried most about whether liberalism in the classroom might be undermining the faith taught in the churches. Federal money, it was feared, would only make the schools less dependent on denominational support. Texas editor E. S. James warned that federal aid would result in the loss of Baptist schools and with them "our heritage, our distinctives, our spiritual influence." The separationists thus made federal aid an issue on which turned the very survival of the Baptist faith as a religious force in America.[30]

The work of the Joint Committee on Public Affairs and the debate over federal aid demonstrated that Southern Baptists were more likely to be aroused to political action by a church-state question than by any other public issue. This observation is well illustrated by the 1960 presidential election. Southern Baptist leaders entered the campaign in massive force because they viewed the election as a contest to maintain a state free from church control. Fear of clerical interference in public affairs was rooted deep in the Baptist experience in Europe and colonial America. This fear had come to center on the Roman church because Baptists believed that the Catholic hierarchy

30. *Maryland Baptist* (Baltimore), Mar. 10, 1966, p. 2; *Southern Baptist Educator*, XXX (July–Aug., 1966), 6. James's remarks were made at a pastor's conference at Southwestern Seminary in the summer of 1966. McCall, speaking to the same group, criticized those "extremists who preach complete separation of church and state." The Virginia newspaper, no less than the Texas weekly, fought federal aid. See Alley's editorials in *The Religious Herald* (Richmond), Sept. 12, 1963, p. 10; Sept. 16, 1965, pp. 10–11; Sept. 23, 1965, pp. 10–11.

had never fully accepted religious freedom in the American sense. Catholic attempts to obtain a Vatican representative and state aid to church schools were viewed as certain evidence of Rome's disregard for the separation principle.[31]

Behind the ideological differences over church-state relations was the hard reality of the growing numbers of Catholics in the nation's urban centers, which at mid-century furnished the controlling blocs in American politics. The election of President Truman, himself a Southern Baptist, revealed something of the political significance of twentieth-century demographic trends. The 1948 contest made clear that the politically solid and heavily Protestant South could no longer exercise a decisive voice in the Democratic party, for Truman's strength among Northern urban voters had more than compensated for the Dixiecrat defection.

The religious implications of the population shift were dramatically illustrated by the emergence of John F. Kennedy as a presidential aspirant. The youthful Roman Catholic from New England narrowly missed the vice-presidential nomination at the 1956 Democratic convention, and from that moment the likelihood of a Catholic presidential candidate in the next election could not be dismissed from the national consciousness. Southern Baptist opposition to Kennedy's nomination appeared long before the delegates met for the quadrennial ballot; in 1958 and 1959, Baptist state conventions declared that no Roman Catholic could be an acceptable candidate.[32] The presidential primaries in the spring of 1960 brought the religious issue to national attention. Kennedy won in Wisconsin, but the evidence that voting had split along religious lines placed an ominous forecast on a Catholic's chances for nomination. Kennedy met the issue squarely in heavily Protestant West Virginia, where he

31. For an analysis of the basis for Protestant disquietude regarding Catholic teachings, written in an atmosphere removed from the 1960 election by one who could hardly be labeled as anti-Catholic, see Harvey Cox, "A Baptist Intellectual's View of Catholicism," *Harper's Magazine*, CCXXV (Dec., 1962), 47–50.

32. *Annual, Alabama, 1958*, pp. 136–37; *1959*, pp. 39, 128–32. The *Word and Way* (Jefferson City, Mo.), Dec. 17, 1959, p. 3, reported anti-Catholic actions in the state conventions in Arizona and Oklahoma.

convinced voters in the hills and small towns that his religion did not make him unfit for the high office.[33]

Meanwhile, the full force of Southern Baptist opposition began to take shape. Early in the election year Texas editor E. S. James called Baptists to battle against Catholic dominance in American political life. During the spring primaries, James urged his readers to put their views before the Democratic party leadership.[34] From that point on, every issue of the weekly newspaper carried the case against the Catholic candidate, establishing a pattern soon to be followed by all twenty-eight Baptist periodicals. The most authoritative statement on the denomination's position was adopted by the 13,612 messengers to the Southern Baptist Convention in May. The resolution upheld the constitutional prohibition against religious tests for public office but then proceeded to argue that no Roman Catholic should be elected president because his church's position on religious liberty, prenuptial marriage contracts, and state aid to church schools were in "open conflict with our established and constituted American pattern of life." Since a Catholic was "inescapably bound by the dogma and demands of his church," a public official of that faith could not make "independent decisions consistent with the rights and privileges of all citizens."[35]

It is important to identify here the essential reason for Southern Baptist opposition to Kennedy, whose church-state views were, ironically, closer to their own than those of any other candidate. The casual observer might easily dismiss Baptist campaigning as religious bigotry, cultural bias, political conservatism, or even, perhaps, a disguise for racism.[36] These considerations undoubtedly do explain some of their political activism. However, the evidence bearing directly on the cam-

33. Theodore H. White, *The Making of the President, 1960* (New York, 1961), 113–14, 121, 127–30.

34. *Baptist Standard* (Dallas), Feb. 17, 1960, p. 4; Apr. 20, 1960, p. 5. This newspaper had a weekly circulation of 364,548, three times more than any other state Baptist newspaper.

35. *Annual, SBC, 1960*, p. 71.

36. *The New York Times*, Oct. 29, 1960, p. 12, suggested political conservatism as a motive.

paign puts the emphasis more precisely on the issue of possible ecclesiastical influence in affairs of state. Public statements did not reflect a bias against the person of the urbane New Englander; in fact, there was much admiration for the man. Arguments were not directed against the senator's liberal political record. In sermons, articles, and resolutions the issue was not Kennedy himself but, rather, his church and its claims to absolute authority over the spiritual and secular, over private conduct and public policy. That this view of the church was drawn more from medieval times and Catholic countries than from American experience mattered little. The convention's theologians and church historians in numerous campaign articles gave scholarly backing to the popular notion that Romanism was a monolithic system, unchanging in its aims, absolute in its authority, and devious in its methods.[37]

The theme of ecclesiastical political influence received the widest possible circulation in the denominational press. In its most extreme form, the argument ran that Kennedy's election would bring immediate clerical pressure for public policies dictated by the church. One editor predicted that American liberties would be "whittled away" and the nation "enslaved" by a "ruthless religious totalitarianism controlled from Rome."[38] The Missouri newspaper asked: "Will the American people place in the highest office in the land a man whose first allegiance and whose final accountability may be to a foreign potentate, and to a hierarchy which demands utter obedience from its adherents?"[39] And James of the *Baptist Standard* issued this sweeping demand to the nation's Catholic voters: "There must be a renunciation of allegiance to the foreign religio-political state of the Vatican, and there must be a declaration of freedom from the domination of the clergy by American Catholic citizens."[40]

37. The *Baptist Standard* (Dallas) published eight articles by seminarians during the campaign. It might be noted that the Baptist opposition to Kennedy was essentially the same as that raised against Al Smith in 1928. See Moore, pp. 45, 59–79.
38. *Arkansas Baptist* (Little Rock), Sept. 8, 1960, p. 8.
39. *Word and Way* (Jefferson City, Mo.), Aug. 25, 1960, p. 4.
40. Feb. 17, 1960, p. 4.

It was just this unshakable belief in the political aims of a church with absolute authority over its members that made Kennedy's disavowals of no consequence. His fourteen years in Congress presented a near-flawless record on church-state questions. In the campaign he opposed federal aid to parochial schools, promised no representative to the Vatican, and disagreed with his church on governmental distribution of birth-control information.[41] In a televised appearance before Protestant ministers in Houston, Texas, he affirmed church-state separation, upheld the independence of the presidency, declared his primary loyalty to national interests, and even promised to work for religious freedom in Catholic countries.[42]

But Baptists at Houston pressed Kennedy on the point of hierarchial authority. Kennedy was asked to obtain official approval of his stand on church-state issues from his ecclesiastical superior, Richard Cardinal Cushing of Boston. Kennedy's response—"I am the one that is running for the office of the presidency and not Cardinal Cushing"—struck at the taproot of Baptist anti-Catholicism. The petition might have outraged a less skillful performer, but Kennedy knew the importance of the request. He could not defend or apologize for his church's dogma and history; he could only try to remove his church as a campaign issue.[43]

To most observers Kennedy had answered every possible objection. Why, then, did he fail to convince his Baptist critics? Because they refused to believe that a loyal son of the Roman church could exercise the freedom Kennedy claimed without endangering his very soul. The Arkansas editor discounted Kennedy's promises because "We have not the slightest word from his superior, Pope John in Rome, to indicate he would be per-

41. *U. S. News and World Report*, XLVIII (Apr. 21, 1960), 90–92, gives Kennedy's address to the American Society of Newspaper Editors, which dealt with the religious issue. See also *ibid.*, May 2, 1960, p. 91.

42. *Ibid.*, Sept. 26, 1960, pp. 74–78, contains the Houston speech.

43. *Ibid.*, p. 79. Kennedy had tried to separate himself from his church leaders earlier in the address when he said, "I do not speak for my church on public matters—and the church does not speak for me." This similarity to the 1928 campaign is striking; Smith was also asked to obtain church approval of his views. See Moore, p. 79.

mitted to carry out his pledges."[44] A Southern Convention executive said that Kennedy's "right answers" at Houston meant nothing because the threat of papal excommunication ensured that once in office the candidate would put the church ahead of the nation's welfare.[45]

The fear of the Catholic hierarchy's political interference magnified some otherwise minor incidents related to the campaign. Wide publicity was given to Daniel Poling's account of Kennedy's refusal to participate in the dedication of a chapel honoring the famed World II chaplains who went down with the *Dorchester* after giving their life jackets to enlisted men. According to Poling, the father of one of the chaplains, the church hierarchy caused Senator Kennedy to decline attendance at the interfaith gathering. Kennedy explained that he withdrew on his own decision after learning that he was to represent his church and that the chapel was located inside a Protestant church.[46] Kennedy's explanation had no perceptible influence on Baptist leaders, who persisted in representing the incident as proof that a Catholic in public office takes orders from his spiritual superiors.

The election year provided hard evidence from abroad that the Roman church indeed did still claim authority over individual political actions. During the Italian elections in May, the Vatican newspaper, attempting to keep Catholics from supporting Communist candidates, reaffirmed the church's authority over political affairs. A hasty denial that the editorial applied to the American election did nothing to change the fact of clerical intervention.[47] W. A. Criswell of Dallas, in a widely distributed sermon, insisted that the Vatican editorial was published "in order that John Kennedy himself might know that, despite his avowals, he cannot be disassociated from and free from the directives of the Roman Catholic Church."[48] A similar example of

44. *Arkansas Gazette* (Little Rock), Oct. 19, 1960, p. 2A.
45. Paul Stevens, head of the Radio and Television Commission, in *The Beam*, XI (Oct., 1960), 5. See also *Baptist Standard* (Dallas), Oct. 5, 1960, p. 7.
46. *U.S. News and World Report*, XLVII (Sept. 26, 1960), 76–78.
47. *Ibid.*, May 30, 1960, pp. 73–74.
48. The sermon, originally delivered in June, 1960, appeared in *The Beam*,

church interposition occurred in the Puerto Rican elections when bishops ordered Catholics not to vote for the anticlerical but popular Governor Luis Muños Marín. Although of little effect on Puerto Rican voters, the directive, issued just days before the American election, served to corroborate the warnings from Baptist pulpits.[49]

Judging from the national coverage, Southern Baptists seemed to represent a solid bloc of anti-Catholicism. However, some corrective observations are in order. For example, several of the smaller, more fundamentalist groups associated with the National Association of Evangelicals (NAE) were more militantly anti-Catholic than the Southern Baptists, and there is little evidence that the latter engaged in the ministry of hate of the sort carried on in the Protestant underworld.[50] Almost unnoticed were those leaders who were out of sympathy with the denomination's anti-Kennedy stance. A group of North Carolina ministers and laymen published a statement condemning denominational leaders for being partisan and unfair.[51] Blake Smith, pastor of University Church in Austin, described the Kennedy critics as "irresponsible apostles of discord."[52] Gainer Bryan, the Maryland editor, objected to the Southern Convention's resolution because it in effect imposed a religious test for office-holding.[53] James R. Scales, vice-president of Oklahoma Baptist University, worked for the Democratic ticket in his state.[54] The

XI (Oct., 1960), 13. Texas millionaire H. L. Hunt paid for the printing of at least 100,000 copies of the address, according to one report. John Wicklein, religious reporter for *The New York Times*, said that Criswell's sermon was one of the most widely distributed pieces of literature of the whole campaign. See *The New York Times*, Oct. 17, 1960, p. 24.

49. *Ibid.*, Oct. 26, 1960, p. 26; Nov. 9, 1960, p. 25.

50. *The New York Times*, Oct. 16, 1960, p. 52; Oct. 17, 1960, p. 24; Oct. 21, 1960, pp. 1, 13, classified Southern Convention President Ramsey Pollard and W. A. Criswell among the extreme anti-Catholics, along with the organizations NAE and POAU.

51. "A Declaration of Conscience for Baptists to Consider," undated mimeographed copy.

52. *Baptist Beacon* (Phoenix), Sept. 29, 1960, p. 6.

53. *Maryland Baptist* (Baltimore), Sept. 1, 1960, p. 3.

54. James Ralph Scales, "Southern Baptists in the Elections of 1960 and 1964," mimeographed copy of an address delivered to the Christian Citizenship Seminar in Washington, D.C., in 1964, p. 1.

Joint Committee on Public Affairs, which might have been expected to be at the forefront of the action, took a very moderate position. Walter Pope Binns, chairman of the Joint Committee, felt that the politicking clerics had lost sight of the issue of church-state separation.[55] Executive Director C. Emanuel Carlson published data relevant to the religious issues, including the Declaration on Religious Liberty, prepared by a group of Catholic laymen in support of the American church-state tradition. The Joint Committee's bulletin credited Kennedy with an excellent record on church-state issues.[56]

The election results themselves throw some light on the actual influence Kennedy's Catholicism had on the voting. The best authority has concluded that the religious issue was the "strongest single factor" in voter behavior.[57] The University of Michigan Research Center's analysis reported that 10.8 percent of the voters crossed party lines because of religious considerations, with Kennedy suffering a net loss of 2.2 percent. The religious factor was most noticeable in the South, where the Democratic vote (51.2 percent) was off by 17 percent. Overall, the election was so close that the degree to which Baptist voters followed their church leaders could have made the critical difference.[58] Undoubtedly, Baptist opposition to Kennedy helped give the traditionally Democratic states of Florida, Kentucky, Oklahoma, Tennessee, and Virginia to the Republicans. By the same token, Democratic victories in Alabama, Arkansas, Georgia, Louisiana, Missouri, and the Carolinas suggest that Kennedy could not have won without large numbers of Baptist votes. One

55. Letter to the author, Jan. 25, 1961.
56. *Report*, Apr.–May, 1960, p. 2; Oct., 1960, pp. 2–4. See also the report on Carlson's interview with Kennedy in the *Baptist Standard* (Dallas), Aug. 31, 1960, p. 12.
57. Philip E. Converse *et al.*, "Stability and Change in 1960: A Reinstating Election," *The American Political Science Review*, LV (June, 1961), 275, 278.
58. Theodore H. White, pp. 461–63, using the Associated Press tabulation with corrections for the Hawaii recount, gave the total vote as 68,832,778. Of the total, Nixon received 49.6 percent and Kennedy received 49.7 percent. Kennedy's margin was 113,057 votes, and he carried six Southern and border states by 2 percent or less: Arkansas, 50.2 percent; Louisiana, 50.4 percent; Missouri, 50.3 percent; North Carolina, 52.1 percent; South Carolina, 51.2 percent; and Texas, 50.5 percent. Nixon's margin was close in Florida: 51.5 percent; Kentucky, 53.6 percent; Tennessee, 52.9 percent; and Virginia, 52.4 percent.

observer concluded that while the campaign produced a "Baptist position," it did not produce a "Baptist vote."[59] In other words, there was a defection of the Baptist leadership from the Democratic party, but there was a much greater defection of lay people from the Baptist leadership.

However much religion affected voter behavior, it is unlikely that Catholicism will be an important issue in future national elections, for even Southern Baptists are never again likely to muster a campaign that would begin to equal their 1960 engagement. None of the dark campaign predictions materialized during Kennedy's presidential years, and Vatican II did much to relieve Protestant fears of Rome's unbending absolutism. Church-state issues do not seem to be crucial national questions for most Americans and probably not for the average Southern Baptist churchgoer. It would be well to note here that Southern Baptist church-state attitudes took on the appearance of rigidity and unanimity partly because the clergy easily controlled the church conventions which positioned the denomination in the public mind. Moreover, there is good reason to believe that clerical leaders themselves were chastened by the election. During the next several months Baptist editorials and convention resolutions publicly praised President Kennedy's loyalty to separation.[60] No Baptist spokesman did more of an about face than the crusading separationist from Texas, E. S. James, who accepted an invitation to the White House in March, 1963, after which he declared, "It was a pleasure to tell the President that he has disillusioned many of us who felt that a Roman Catholic could not make a good President."[61]

If Baptist leaders came to accept a Catholic President, it was only because Kennedy observed the separation principle more carefully than did his Protestant predecessors. The majority of Southern Baptist churchmen were as devoted as ever to preserving the wall of separation, even while the nation as a whole

59. Scales, p. 4.
60. Annual, SBC, 1961, p. 81; Annual, North Carolina, 1960, pp. 67, 69; Minutes, Georgia, 1960, p. 45; Word and Way (Jefferson City), Dec. 6, 1960, p. 3; Mar. 16, 1961, p. 2; Baptist Messenger (Oklahoma City), June 8, 1961, p. 2.
61. Newsweek, LXI (Mar. 4, 1963), 77.

seemed ready to make some accommodation for the public support of private institutions in a welfare state. It was not the first time Southern Baptists had found themselves standing against the current of national history. Would the issue of strict separation, like slavery and prohibition, become another occasion of over-commitment to a lost cause? Unfortunately, that habit of mind which saw public issues in terms of absolute principles served to shut out the creative contribution to social policy to which their numbers should have entitled them.

XI

PROCEED WITH CAUTION

With the elevation of the Social Service Commission to full-time status in 1947, Southern Baptists were in a position to demonstrate their willingness to undertake a religion of social relevance. The stated purposes of the commission were sufficiently broad—promotion of "morality in social relations" with specific reference to race relations, the industrial order, international affairs, the family, and the whole area of personal behavior.[1] The problem lay in the practical restrictions imposed by a denomination that remained evangelical in its primary commitments. Financially, the work depended on annual allocations from the Southern Baptist Convention, as recommended by its powerful Executive Committee. But the appropriations, which had multiplied almost twenty times by 1969, never permitted a very extensive program, especially when compared to the outlay for church expansion and missionary enterprises.[2] In addition, the agency's operations were closely supervised by a commission appointed by the Southern Convention and representing each state in the convention. Although the commission

---

1. *Annual, SBC, 1947,* p. 34.
2. *Annual, SBC, 1947,* p. 35; *1968,* p. 115. A summary of convention income appeared in *The Quarterly Review,* XXII (Third Quarter, 1962), 54–55. Gifts to convention causes multiplied eleven times from 1940 to 1960. The commission's budget increased at about the same rate. Its share of the Cooperative Program appropriations remained extremely low, rising from about 0.13 percent in 1948 to 0.44 percent in 1966. The Foreign Mission Board received more than half and the Home Mission Board about 20 percent of the Cooperative Program receipts.

members were usually enthusiastic boosters for the work, they represented the convention's ultimate control over the executive secretary and his staff.

The success of the commission's expanded activities depended on the development of a convincing rationale for denominational involvement in social problems. From the first, commission spokesmen took pains to establish the work on firm theological grounds by representing Christianity as a religion of ethical behavior as well as one of personal faith. A religion that embraced all of man's life made legitimate a church-sponsored program dealing with social and political questions. Much more difficult was the task of devising effective methods of social action by a centralized agency that would not offend Baptist concepts of religious individualism or arouse too much resistance in the democratic churches. Essentially, the commission chose to emphasize an educational-prophetic ministry rather than direct social action. That is, it gave first attention to Christian principles with social implications in the hope of changing attitudes in the convention instead of promoting specific programs of social betterment.

Jesse B. Weatherspoon set forth the agency's operating philosophy, envisioning a three-fold work: collecting and reporting information, interpreting Christian responsibilities toward social ills, and recommending position statements for convention approval.[3] In such work, he cautioned, "the base line of all our social judgments and proposals" should be "Christian moral teachings." On the question of methods, he reasoned that direct political action should be secondary because "Christianity contemplates inward, moral control," and advised the commission to appeal to the "Christian constituency in the churches, to awaken them and teach them the moral duties of Christian citizens." He likened the agency to the minister who "works behind the lines," inspiring his people to fight for social justice.

Such a procedure could obviously produce the same ineffec-

---

3. The original appeared in *Annual, SBC, 1944*, pp. 129–31. It was reprinted in *Annual, SBC, 1950*, pp. 371–72.

tiveness that had characterized Southern Baptist social concern in the past. By deferring to local church sentiment and stressing general principles, the commission could easily evade the most vital issues calling for firm commitments and moral leadership. Foreseeing this situation, Weatherspoon insisted that the agency must not be restricted to "problems remote from Southern life or only those on which a final Christian answer is evident." Since "some progress is possible" even on the most complex problems, the "Christian position is beyond where we now stand." Weatherspoon fully understood the inherent dangers in activities along these lines. Lingering suspicions remained about the social gospel, and the voluntary nature of church cooperation in the convention acted as an ever-present restraint against engagement in controversial matters. Weatherspoon therefore conceded that the commission, of necessity, must "proceed with caution" when confronting divisive issues.[4]

Weatherspoon's admonition became the commission's guideline. In the years following, great care was exercised in dealing with sensitive questions in order to remain in good standing with the constituency. Lacking the freedom to initiate a more positive program, the commission did the next best thing. It tried to relate ethical teachings to the social issues raised to national consciousness by forces outside the church. Its role was more one of reaction to social crises than one of leadership in exploring the social implications of faith.

After appointing an executive secretary in 1947, the commission continued under the influence of Weatherspoon, who served as its chairman until 1955. Hugh A. Brimm, the new secretary, worked from an office on the campus of the Southern Baptist Theological Seminary, where he had studied under Weatherspoon a few years earlier. He and his successors, Acker C. Miller and Foy Dan Valentine, stressed both the ethical foundations for social action and a commission program directed at improving attitudes in the churches. In Miller's words, the commission was to "develop within our people an awareness of the ethical

4. *Ibid.*, p. 373.

content of the gospel and the social responsibility of the Christian life."[5] Valentine had been trained in the field of social ethics at Southwestern Seminary. Of the three executives, he was the most effective public speaker in behalf of the commission's work. His sermon "Relevant Religion," delivered before many Baptist audiences, developed his favorite theme—the practical implementation of faith in personal and social life.[6]

Emphasis on ethical religion and local church attitudes affected the treatment of controversial questions. That is, such matters, when not avoided altogether, were discussed in very general terms. One report, for example, voiced appreciation for the work of President Truman's civil rights committee without endorsing any of its suggested legislation against racial discrimination.[7] The same report analyzed the Taft-Hartley labor law, but offered no judgments about its provisions. The commission discussed right-to-work legislation at its annual conference in Ridgecrest, North Carolina, but took no position on compulsory unionism.[8] The agency sympathized with federal welfare programs but would not advocate specific measures on housing, medical care, or education. Commission statements repeatedly opposed discrimination in education, employment, housing, and voting rights but would not back proposed civil rights legislation.

However, the desire to avoid partisan political quarrels did not produce a policy of neutrality on the great public issues of the mid-twentieth century. All three directors privately possessed social philosophies sympathetic to internationalism, government welfare, and civil rights; and on such matters they were not very different from other Protestant social-action leaders. In view of the agency's inherent limitations, it would seem that the leadership operated near the tolerable limits of involvement in vital national issues. Indeed, in the minds of some, they went beyond permissible limits on a few occasions. The first criticism against the commission occurred when Hugh Brimm promoted

5. *Ibid.*, 1953, p. 427.
6. Foy Dan Valentine, "Relevant Religion," *Believe and Behave* (n.d.), pp. 111–25; *Annual, SBC, 1961*, p. 298; *1963*, p. 236.
7. *Annual, SBC, 1948*, p. 337.
8. *Ibid.*, 1957, p. 365.

certain liberal social ideas in the agency's official bulletin. He denounced the concentration of wealth, supported cooperatives, and condemned unfair labor practices; and he repeatedly complained about racial discrimination and backed the proposals of Truman's civil rights committee. The bulletin also carried articles favorable to federal housing and medical care.[9]

Complaints about Brimm's views brought an investigation by the commission's executive committee and a general statement of policy on the treatment of controversial matters. The inquiry concluded that Brimm had erred in publishing material that was not "factual and objective." When discussing solutions to social ills in the future, it was decided, the commission should keep the over-all "Christian objective in view" but take care not to "endorse completely one method as opposed to another." The agency's literature should be informative, but it should not be used for "advocation and agitation" of particular points of view. The final admonition noted that while the commission should be "out in front" of Baptist social thought, it must "always be connected with our people." Such was the narrow latitude within which the commission could operate because of its dependence on the good will of local churches.[10]

The practice of noninvolvement in specific questions of social betterment had some justification, for by withholding endorsements, the commission preserved a freedom to evaluate social policies. Also, one might question whether a church agency should become embroiled over means, particularly when the supporting denomination has not declared itself on the matter. When the commission did speak, its views usually represented rather accurately the sentiments of the thousands active in convention affairs. In this respect the commission differed greatly from most other Protestant social-action agencies, which stressed legislative programs promoted by a liberal minority.[11]

9. *Light*, Nov., 1948; Dec., 1948; Mar., 1949; October, 1949; Nov. 1949; Jan., 1950; Oct., 1950, Dec., 1950; Oct., 1951.

10. Minutes of the Executive Committee of the Social Service Commission, Feb. 10, 1951, on file at the Christian Life Commission in Nashville, Tenn.

11. Carter points out this difference in *The Decline and Revival of the Social Gospel*, pp. 172–79. For a specific example, see Cyrus Ransom Pangborn, "Free

With its potential for social action minimized, the commission was left with the task of influencing social attitudes. An educational ministry called for a vast program reaching down to the churches, a monumental undertaking under the most auspicious circumstances. Never equipped to minister directly to the more than thirty thousand churches, the commission nevertheless made effective use of its limited resources. Brimm sought to educate a following through literature and conferences. He edited the monthly bulletin, wrote for denominational publications, and supplied reports for use in the state conventions and district associations. Annual conferences became a major enterprise and dealt with Christian citizenship, church-state problems, race relations, the family, and alcoholism.[12]

After five years, Brimm left the commission to return to the classroom. His successor, Acker C. Miller, had many years of experience in the pastorate and in denominational work in Texas. In fact, Miller had helped to create and then had headed a Texas Baptist agency similar to the Southern Convention's Social Service Commission.[13] At the time of Miller's new appointment the name of the Social Service Commission was changed to the Christian Life Commission, and its headquarters were moved to Nashville, the location for several other convention agencies. In Nashville, Miller was able to integrate his work with other convention programs and thus partly overcome the commission's budget limitations. He participated in top-level planning of the total convention program and made use of the vast resources of the Sunday School Board, which housed the commission's offices. Beginning in 1958, Miller sat on the Inter-Agency Council, which coordinated plans for all convention agencies, and from time to time he aided other agencies in special projects. He devoted one Ridgecrest conference to the problems of dependent children as a service to the twenty-three child-care institutions in the state conventions. Working with the Sunday School Board,

Churches and Social Change, a Critical Study of the Council for Social Action of the Congregational Churches of the United States" (Ph.D. diss., Columbia University, 1951), pp. 40, 62, 66–68, 80–83, 109, 124, 141, 163, 205.

12. Annual, SBC, 1949, pp. 336–38; 1951, p. 424; Light, Sept., 1949.

13. Annual, Texas, 1949, pp. 27, 174; 1950, pp. 180–88.

Miller led conferences on problems of the aged and a clinic on pastoral counseling. In all, the executive secretary considerably improved the standing of his agency in the denomination.[14]

The commission continued its educational work much as before. It sponsored summer conferences at Ridgecrest and the new assembly at Glorieta, New Mexico. For conference leaders, Miller chose labor representatives, businessmen, educators, and public officials. He published literature on topics ranging from marriage, alcoholism, and obscenity to race, labor, and world peace. Mailings for the commission's monthly bulletin reached thirty thousand.[15]

Following Miller's retirement in 1959, Foy Dan Valentine became the third executive secretary, and like his predecessor, he was taken from the Texas Christian Life Commission. Only ten years out of Southwestern Seminary, where he had studied social ethics under Thomas B. Maston, Valentine soon won a solid standing in the inner circles of convention leadership. Effective public appearances gained support for the work, and promising new ventures included annual seminars on Christian citizenship in Washington, D.C., and on the work of the United Nations in New York.[16] The commission also assigned a Baptist observer to the United Nations during meetings of the General Assembly. Valentine moved the agency's offices to more spacious accommodations in the new Southern Baptist Convention building and expanded the work on all fronts. His staff assistants, totaling four by 1968, were men experienced in denominational service, particularly foreign mission work. Their idealism coupled with judicious restraint earned general respect for them and some genuine enthusiasm for the work of the commission.[17]

14. *Annual, SBC,* 1953, pp. 426–27, 429–30; *1954,* p. 401; *1956,* pp. 334–35; *1958,* pp. 57–58; Acker C. Miller, "What Is the Christian Life Commission?" *Baptist Program* (Aug.–Sept., 1953), p. 7; *Baptist Program* (May, 1956), p. 5; Feb., 1958, p. 11.

15. *Baptist Program,* 1957, pp. 362–65; *1965,* p. 244. *Christian Life Bulletin,* Nov., 1957 (hereafter cited as *Bulletin*). Attendance at the conferences reached 250 in 1956 and 3,290 in 1964.

16. *Annual, SBC,* 1959, p. 541; *1964,* p. 227.

17. *Ibid.,* 1959, p. 450; *1962,* p. 221; *1963,* p. 237; *1964,* p. 227; *1965,* p. 244. Valentine's first assistants, William Dyal and Ross Coggins, were former

Although the commission viewed its task as an educational one, it assumed a definite position on many issues. Consistent with the agency's tradition, the most categorical pronouncements dealt with personal morals.[18] The agency's literature, conferences, and reports offered much evidence that Baptist dedication to high morals, outwardly at least, had changed little from that of earlier generations. On the other hand, it is equally clear from the agency's publications and reports that the promotion of a Puritan morality did not dominate the commission as it had in the twenties and thirties, a change also in evidence outside the commission. State conventions periodically waged battle against gambling, obscenity, and intoxicants but not with the fervor, frequency, or enterprise of former days. Apparently, even Southern Baptists were caught up in the national drift away from a prohibitive morality imposed by law.

If the commission gave less emphasis to personal morality, it did not endorse the contemporary trend in Christian ethics toward a morality that allowed the individual situation to determine behavior. Refusing to embrace the "new morality," the Christian Life Commission declared: "Modern man is in deep moral trouble, not because the Ten Commandments are no longer valid . . . but because he has ignored the everlastingly valid law of God."[19] The commission's 1967 Ridgecrest conference featured a critique of situational ethics by Kyle Haselden, editor of the nondenominational *Christian Century.*

Local Baptist churches likewise tried to uphold the authoritarian ethic, but however much clergymen condemned the sins of the flesh, their capacity to shape public morality seemed to be on the wane. The proscriptive morality of the pulpit not only

---

missionaries. They left the commission in 1967 for administrative posts in the Peace Corps and Volunteers in the Service to America (VISTA). The commission's present staff members are Elmer West, W. L. Howse III, and Floyd Craig.

18. *Annual, SBC, 1950*, pp. 374–76; *1951*, p. 53; *1954*, p. 403–407; *1956*, p. 332; *Bulletin*, Jan.–Feb., 1958; Mar.–Apr., 1958.

19. *Annual, SBC, 1965*, p. 245. On the "new morality," see Harvey Cox, *The Secular City* (New York, 1965), pp. 205–16; Joseph Fletcher, *Situation Ethics, the New Morality* (Philadelphia, 1966); John A. T. Robinson, *Honest to God* (Philadelphia, 1963), pp. 105–21; and Kyle Haselden, *Morality and the Mass Media* (Nashville, 1968).

found less loyalty in the pew, it also had the unfortunate effect of alienating those in greatest need of spiritual help. Moreover, the uncompromising ethic left little opportunity for Baptist moralists to contribute to the search for an ethic with greater existential relevance.

The commission exercised more initiative and leadership in dealing with the social questions of world peace, the economic order, and civil rights. Annual reports rallied support for the United Nations as the best hope for world peace, urged international agreements on arms reductions, and favored nuclear arms controls.[20] At no time did the agency support a more militant anticommunist foreign policy, and it consistently opposed a national defense policy requiring universal military training.[21] One report included a lengthy discussion sympathetic to pacifism.[22] Another supported President Truman's Point Four program to assist backward nations and denounced the "isolationist lobby" that was trying to block a continuation of the aid.[23] The most imaginative peace move was the appointment of an observer to the United Nations in 1959. The commission avoided the Vietnam issue until 1967, when it brought war critic Senator Mark O. Hatfield to address the Southern Convention. A strong peace statement in the annual report questioned United States involvement, but the convention compromised the dovelike report by adopting a resolution from the floor against withdrawal without an "honorable" settlement.[24]

The commission's analysis of economic issues was probably less profound than its treatment of any other major social problem. The agency emphasized that all economic systems were under divine judgment, meaning that capitalism, like all other

20. *Annual, SBC,* 1951, p. 54; 1952, p. 409; 1955, pp. 330–35.
21. *Ibid.,* 1948, p. 338; 1951, pp. 411–17; 1952, pp. 412–14.
22. *Ibid.,* 1951, pp. 414–17.
23. *Ibid.,* 1952, pp. 409–12; 1955, p. 330.
24. *Ibid.,* 1967, pp. 72, 294. Although a few Southern Baptists spoke against the war—Henlee Barnette of Southern Seminary and the California and Arkansas editors—a poll at the 1967 convention revealed that two thirds of the delegates favored doing whatever was necessary to win. See *Maryland Baptist* (Baltimore), June 15, 1967, pp. 1, 3, 8; June 22, 1967, pp. 2, 3; Sept. 7, 1967, p. 1; Sept. 28, 1967, pp. 1, 8; Feb. 29, 1968, pp. 1, 6.

human creations, shared in man's depravity. Even so, economic pronouncements never seemed to question the essential soundness of the existing American system. Capital had a right to a fair profit; labor had the right to unionize for better wages; collective bargaining presumably would settle all disputes unless the parties were guilty of "unworthy motives and objectives."[25] In any case, the church should not get involved in labor-management quarrels. Its role, rather, was limited to inspiring individuals in labor and management to carry "the ideals of the Christian life into their economic professions."[26]

The above quotation points up fundamental aspects of Baptist economic thought. The chief concerns have been, not corporate institutions, but the demands that the Christian faith makes upon the economic life of the individual. The idea of Christian stewardship has been one of the dominant themes in church life. Derived from the Puritan notion of a secular calling, the stewardship of one's possessions has been more than a social ethic. The Baptist view not only has taught laymen to glorify God in their daily work, but it also has demanded regular financial support of the church and its missionary program. Clergymen have interpreted the Old Testament practice of tithing as the minimal requirement for Christian contributions to religious work, and the Christian Life Commission has helped develop the doctrinal basis for giving by making stewardship one of the practical expressions of faith.[27] Viewed in terms of its social implications, the stewardship doctrine has been essentially conservative in character. It has undergirded the religious establishment while giving the churches a stake in the existing economic system. As churches and conventions have begun to operate

25. *Annual, SBC, 1948*, p. 336; *1951*, pp. 417–20.
26. *Ibid.*, *1952*, p. 417.
27. *Ibid.*, *1955*, p. 331; *1956*, p. 333. The commission published tracts under the titles *Christian Principles Applied to Daily Work* (Nashville, n.d.) and *The Bible Speaks on Economics* (Nashville, n.d.). Promotional materials on tithing, stewardship, and church finance abound. A key figure in developing the doctrine of stewardship was J. E. Dillard. One of the creators of the Cooperative Program in 1925, Dillard devoted his career to financing denominational work as president of the Executive Committee, 1927–36, and director of promotion for the Cooperative Program, 1936–47. See his *Good Stewards* (Nashville, 1953); *Bible Stewardship* (Nashville, n.d.); *Building a Stewardship Church* (Nashville, n.d.).

more and more like business enterprises, with budgets, financial campaigns, and expanding programs all dependent upon systematic contributions, they inevitably have lost something of their potential as social critics.[28]

The commission made its greatest contribution in the treatment of the race question. Long before the civil rights movement developed, Southern Baptists admitted the conflicts between Christian ethics and Southern race practices. The commission widely publicized the Charter of Principles on Race Relations, adopted at the 1947 convention.[29] In keeping with this declaration, the agency praised desegregation in colleges, professional organizations, and labor unions and opposed discrimination in voting, education, and employment. With regard to the report of President Truman's civil rights committee, the commission said that its "major objectives are in keeping with the American way of life as guaranteed by the Bill of Rights."[30]

These statements established firm precedents for supporting the 1954 Supreme Court ruling against segregation in public schools. Before declaring its position, the commission deliberated carefully, knowing full well the constituency's strong feelings against racial integration. Still, the commission could not escape the fact that Christian principles, as well as its own past statements, called for approval of the Court's order. A further consideration was the peculiar responsibility resting upon the commission because it represented the largest religious body in the South. In the end, moral obligations dictated a stand that would certainly meet opposition in much of the convention

28. The successful promotion of church causes may be measured by the increase in annual contributions. From 1940 to 1960, total gifts increased from $40,359,038 to $480,608,972, with gifts to "missions" (all causes outside the local church) advancing from $6,787,627 to $81,924,906. The increase for both categories was about 1,100 percent, while the number of churches grew by 27.7 percent and the membership by 96.5 percent. In considering church ties to the economic system, it is also significant that the value of church property increased 900 percent during the two decades. Church debts in 1960 reached $475,220,000, an amount nearly equal to the total church gifts for one year. See *The Quarterly Review*, XXII (Third Quarter, 1962), 38–39, 54–55.

29. Printed in *Light*, Sept., 1949, and in Jesse B. Weatherspoon's *Southern Baptists and Race Relations* (Louisville, 1949).

30. *Annual, SBC, 1948*, p. 337; *1951*, pp. 420–21; *1950*, p. 376.

territory.[31] Fortunately, the 1954 convention met in St. Louis, somewhat removed from the areas most bitterly opposed to desegregation. The commission's report presented a lengthy justification of the ruling, accompanied by a moderate but unequivocal resolution declaring, "That we recognize the fact that this Supreme Court decision is in harmony with the constitutional guarantee of equal freedom to all citizens, and with the Christian principles of equal justice and love for all men."[32] Opponents tried to strike the resolution from the report. Jesse B. Weatherspoon, the commission chairman, rose to defend the statement, urging the delegates to decide the question on the basis of Christian principles. The vote surprised even the members of the commission. Only a handful in an assembly of nine thousand opposed the resolution.[33] In the months following, Executive Secretary Miller began an educational campaign against the rising tide of hostility to desegregation. Commission literature not only defended the Court but also represented segregation as contrary to Christian teachings. To publish and distribute additional literature, Miller procured a grant from the Ford Foundation's Fund for the Republic in an amount larger than the commission's annual budget.[34]

The near-unanimous approval of the commission's resolution at the 1954 convention was not an accurate measure of Southern Baptist feeling about desegregation.[35] Some pastors openly criticized the Court's ruling, the most prominent being W. A. Cris-

31. Based on interviews with Acker C. Miller. May 31, 1956, and July 1, 1957.
32. *Annual, SBC, 1954*, pp. 56, 403–404. The Baptist statement was similar to declarations made by other religious groups. See Don Shoemaker, ed., *With All Deliberate Speed, Segregation-Desegregation in Southern Schools* (New York, 1957), p. 24.
33. *Christian Century*, LXXI (June 16, 1954), 723.
34. *The Fund for the Republic, a Report on Three Years' Work* (New York, 1956), p. 9; *Bulletin*, Jan.–Feb., 1958.
35. *Christian Century*, LXXIII (March 14, 1956), 325, 328; *Newsweek*, Mar. 12, 1956, p. 64. Information on Southern Baptist reaction to the desegregation decision came from the files of Acker C. Miller and Guy Ranson, professor of Christian Ethics at Southern Seminary. Ranson's collection included an unpublished research paper, "Reaction of Southern Baptists to the Supreme Court Decision of May 17, 1954," by Lewis C. McKinney, which contained much helpful information. The pastors in Orangeburg and Batesburg, S. C., were

well of Dallas, Texas, pastor of the convention's largest church. A few churches forced resignations from ministers supporting integration, and some in the Deep South denounced the commission and threatened to withdraw financial support from the convention. Miller and the authors of the commission's literature were severely attacked from various quarters. Two state editors condemned the commission's action, and one advocated abolishing the agency.[36] Other critics circulated charges of subversion against the Fund for the Republic. But for all the noisy agitation, the minority seeking to discredit the commission failed to attract a substantial following. In a showdown at the 1958 convention, opponents gained small support in an effort to compel the return of the grant from the Fund for the Republic.[37]

The convention president and the heads of the Home and Foreign Mission boards endorsed the court decision.[38] Foy Valentine, then head of the Texas Christian Life Commission, associated himself with those working for the integration of the Dallas schools.[39] Officials at Southern Seminary helped achieve the peaceful integration of Louisville schools,[40] and several seminary professors published articles urging compliance with the ruling.[41] When segregationists began to organize resistance, twenty-eight officials representing every denominational agency

---

forced to resign because they supported integration. One reported that some fifteen churches in the state had taken some kind of formal action against the commission.

36. *Baptist Message* (Alexandria, La.), Aug. 8, 1957, p. 2; Aug. 29, 1957, p. 2; *The Religious Herald* (Richmond), June 6, 1957, p. 14; Sept. 26, 1957, p. 10.

37. *Annual, SBC, 1958*, p. 53; *The Houston Post*, May 23, 1958, p. 1; *Bulletin*, Jan.–Feb., 1958; Robert M. Hutchins, *Freedom, Education, and the Fund, Essays and Addresses, 1946–1956* (New York, 1956), pp. 199–232.

38. *Christian Century*, LXXI (June 9, 1954), 691–92.

39. *Ibid.*, LXXV (May 21, 1958), 619–20; Foy Dan Valentine, "The Court, the Church, and the Community," *Review and Expositor*, LII (Oct., 1956), 536–50.

40. Omer Carmichael and Weldon James, *The Louisville Story* (New York, 1957), p. 55.

41. Henlee Barnette, "What Can Southern Baptists Do?" *Christianity Today*, I (June 24, 1957), 14–16; Guy H. Ranson, pp. 528–37. The commission published tracts supporting integration by Jesse B. Weatherspoon and Thomas B. Maston. Maston also wrote two books arguing in favor of integration: *Segregation and Desegregation* (New York, 1959) and *The Bible and Race* (Nashville, 1959).

published a statement dissociating the convention from efforts to defy federal authority.[42]

Congressman Brooks Hays, veteran Arkansas lawmaker with a reputation as a racial moderate in Congress, became chairman of the Christian Life Commission in 1955 and president of the convention in 1957. While in this latter office, he acted as mediator between President Dwight D. Eisenhower and Governor Orval Faubus during the desegregation dispute in Little Rock, located in Hays's congressional district. Without personally endorsing the Court's ruling, Hays advocated adherence to it as the law of the land. His plea for moderation during the Little Rock crisis carried a high price: a write-in vote gave his congressional seat to a rabid segregationist in 1958. Within the convention, however, Hays fared somewhat better. He easily won re-election as convention president against a minor effort to deprive him of the customary second term. Following his congressional defeat, five state conventions commended Hays for his efforts toward peaceful integration.[43]

Many local pastors worked for an orderly adjustment to integration. The views of some were published in national Protestant journals and by the Christian Life Commission.[44] One minister was physically assaulted by whites after escorting Negro children to a newly integrated school in Clinton, Tennessee.[45] Others, in less spectacular ways, called for racial justice and compliance to the court order. Notable examples of this group

42. *Bulletin*, Apr., 1956.

43. For Hays's role in the integration dispute, see *The New York Times*, Sept. 13, 1957, pp. 1, 10; Nov. 8, 1958, pp. 1, 23, 44; *Christian Century*, LXXV (Dec. 3, 1958), 1390; *Annual, SBC, 1958*, pp. 50–51, 79; Brooks Hays, *This World: A Christian's Workshop* (Nashville, 1958), pp. 92–100; Brooks Hays, *A Southern Moderate Speaks* (Chapel Hill, 1959), pp. 130–94, 200–14.

44. D. Perry Ginn, "Christians and Desegregation," *The Pulpit*, XXVII (Nov., 1956), 20, 22–23; G. Avery Lee, "Some Quiet Thoughts on a Turbulent Issue," *Pulpit Digest*, XXXVII (May, 1957), 25–30; Carlyle Marney, "The Emancipation of a White," *Christian Century*, LXXI (Nov. 17, 1954), 1397–98. The commission published R. Lofton Hudson's *Is Segregation Christian?* (Nashville, n.d.) and John Hall Jones's *The Unity of Humanity* (Nashville, 1956).

45. *The New York Times*, Dec. 5, 1956, p. 44; George Barrett, "Study in Desegregation: The Clinton Story," *New York Times Magazine*, Sept. 16, 1956, pp. 11, 71–72, 76.

were Dale Cowling and W. O. Vaught, the two leading Southern Baptist ministers in Little Rock.[46] Cowling supported the plan for desegregating the Little Rock schools two days before Governor Faubus used troops to block integration. Vaught publicly assailed the leaders of organized resistance as "unscrupulous" fomenters of racial prejudice and strife.

The desegregation order was but the beginning of a much larger civil rights movement. During the next decade as the controversy raged, the Christian Life Commission exercised great restraint. Its annual reports did not begin to reflect the intensity of the revolution that produced the Montgomery bus boycott, the Nashville sit-ins, and the freedom rides, that brought federal force to university campuses and voter-rights demonstrations to Southern communities. By the mid-sixties, however, the inherent justice of the movement and the violence of the resistance moved the commission to action. Executive Secretary Valentine conducted a Christian citizenship seminar for denominational leaders in Washington in the spring of 1964. President Johnson entertained the delegation at the White House and made a plea for Baptist support of the civil rights bill then being considered in Congress. The next month, Valentine asked the Southern Convention to endorse a statement backing civil rights laws and urging Southern Baptists "to go beyond these laws by practicing Christian love and reconciliation in all human relations." An extended debate on the resolution divided the convention. In the end, a substitute motion declaring that the solution to the race problems must be left to the local churches was adopted by a close vote.[47]

46. Cowling and Vaught are to be distinguished from the segregationist Baptist ministers in fundamentalist churches not affiliated with the Southern Baptist Convention. Only one convention minister in Little Rock would not support school integration. See *The New York Times*, Oct. 7, 1956, pp. 1, 12; Oct. 9, 1957, p. 22; Oct. 12, 1957, pp. 1, 17; Ernest Q. Campbell and Thomas F. Pettigrew, *Christians in Racial Crisis: A Study of the Little Rock Ministry* (Washington, D.C., 1959), pp. 19, 30–35, 71; Cowling, *A Pastor Looks at Integration in Little Rock* (Nashville, 1957).

47. *Annual, SBC, 1964*, pp. 72–73; *1965*, p. 244; *Maryland Baptist* (Baltimore), Apr. 2, 1964, pp. 1, 2, 4.

Not deterred, Valentine devoted the summer conferences at Ridgecrest and Glorieta to the Negro revolt and returned to next year's convention with an even stronger statement on race. This report called on Southern Baptists to confess their guilt in conforming to immoral secular race patterns and condemned the convention's "silence and fear" in the midst of the struggle for racial justice. In direct answer to the substitute motion of the previous year, the report declared that for all their autonomy Baptist churches were subject to the Lordship of Christ and as such should "bear witness to the truth that the doors of salvation, fellowship, and ministry are open to all men." Going even further, the commission urged Southern Baptists to become "involved actively and redemptively in seeking specific cures for such specific racial ailments as personal prejudice, unfair housing practices, discriminatory employment, unequal justice under the law, and denial of voting rights." Most heartening, the convention accepted the censure of its own failings. The best that opponents could do was to affix an innocuous amendment about local church autonomy and the priority of evangelism. They failed completely in the most significant test, a motion to block a 25 percent increase in the commission's budget.[48]

The civil rights movement offered the first real test of the commission's ability to enter a serious controversy and supply relevant guidance that Southern Baptists would accept. The commission's ultimate success was an important measure of the denomination's gains toward greater social responsibility. It must be admitted, of course, that the largest religious body in the South could claim no credit for initiating or even offering much direct assistance to the Negro revolt. No convention executive publicly associated himself with the movement, and the desegregation of the denomination's schools was most notable in that in nearly every instance it was delayed until after the

48. *Maryland Baptist* (Baltimore), 1965, pp. 84, 90, 247. Editorial comment in denominational and secular newspapers placed great significance on the adoption of the commission's statement on race. Baptist editors in Georgia, Arkansas, and even Mississippi praised the statement. See *Baptist Program* (Aug., 1965), pp. 18–19; *Newsweek*, June 14, 1965, p. 94; *Maryland Baptist* (Baltimore), June 24, 1965, p. 3.

integration of secular institutions.[49] The publicity given to Negroes who were turned away from prominent churches exposed the true feelings of many white Baptists toward integration.[50]

But on the other side, more churches integrated peacefully than turned away Negro members.[51] Some ministers, even at the risk of their careers, worked for integrated memberships and concessions to Negro demands outside the church.[52] If Southern Baptists did not welcome civil rights demonstrations, they de-

49. *Maryland Baptist* (Baltimore), Apr. 29, 1965, p. 3, reported that 70 percent of the denomination's colleges and universities had signed the nondiscriminatory agreements required by the Civil Rights Act of 1964.

50. Some of the more celebrated incidents during the early sixties occurred at the First Baptist churches in Atlanta; Oklahoma City; Montgomery; Houston; and Albany, Ga.; and at the Tattnal Square Church in Macon, Ga.

51. Baptist state newspapers reported that many churches adopted an integrated policy on membership during the early 1960's including: the First Baptist Churches in Atlanta; Richmond; Cambridge, Mass.; Oklahoma City; Arkadelphia, Ark.; Winston-Salem; Belle View Church in Alexandria, Va.; Memorial Church in Baltimore, Md.; Valley Baptist Church in Lutherville, Md.; Allen Memorial in Salisbury, Md.; and all 13 Southern Baptist churches in metropolitan New York. A survey by the Home Mission Board in 1968, based on returns from 408 of 752 district associations contacted, revealed 510 integrated churches, 3,724 churches willing to receive Negro members, and 57 all-Negro churches affiliated with white associations.

52. Numerous instances of ministers who opposed segregation in their churches and communities were reported in religious and secular papers during the 1960's. "A Long, Hot August," *Baptist Program* (Aug., 1965), pp. 3–5, is an anonymous account of a pastor's frustration in trying to lead a Georgia church to permit the attendance of Negro worshippers. Liberal attitudes on race was the issue in the forced resignations of Thomas J. Holmes and two assistants of Macon, Ga.; Paul L. Stagg of Front Royal, Va.; and Charles Webster, Jr., Baptist Student Union director at Clemson College. Jerry Chance had to resign after he and a fellow minister, Paul Gillespie, attempted to bring Brooks Hays to Bogalusa, La., for an address on the Civil Rights Act of 1964. Two white students at New Orleans Seminary enrolled their children in a newly integrated school in defiance of a white boycott but after a few days succumbed to segregationist abuse and withdrew their children.

Not all involvement in racial crises brought reprisals. Charles A. Trentham of the First Baptist Church in Knoxville, Tenn., was active in the peaceful integration of that community, and he served on the clergymen's White House committee on race. Leland Higginbotham of Towson, Md., participated in a civil rights rally in that city. Brooks Ramsey openly disagreed with his church's policy of denying the admittance of Negroes, but he won a unanimous vote of confidence after he tried to mediate racial unrest in Albany, Ga. John R. Claypool of the Crescent Hill Baptist Church in Louisville and chairman of the Christian Life Commission, William Dyal of the Christian Life Commission, and the faculty of Oklahoma Baptist University sent messages to religious and political leaders in Alabama urging racial justice and peace during the Selma crisis of 1965. In 1969, Claypool participated in a public rally for open housing in Louisville.

plored white violence even more. Disorder moved many state conventions to address the racial crisis. In 1965 alone nearly half the state meetings took some official action inspired by the civil rights movement. Resolutions condemned bigotry, injustice, and violence and praised the work of the Christian Life Commission. A North Carolina report in 1963 advocated open membership in all the churches.[53]

The most celebrated declaration on race came in response to the violence that swept the nation's cities in the late sixties. Following the assassination of Martin Luther King, Jr., and the ensuing riots of April, 1968, the top denominational officers and executives prepared a Statement Concerning the Crisis in Our Nation, which the Southern Baptist Convention adopted on the day Senator Robert F. Kennedy was assassinated. The declaration was a somber confession of responsibility for the social ills that produced the urban riots. It also committed the eight thousand messengers to greater involvement in public issues in order to combat racism, violence, and injustice and to bring about equality in jobs, education, and public services. Convention spokesmen attached high significance to the action, describing it as a historic turning point in the treatment of race. Baptist editors made it the top news story of the year.[54] A candid appraisal must note that the document was toned down considerably before adoption and that the urgent plea for action resulted only in requests for existing agencies to deal with the crisis through existing programs.[55] Although disappointing in

53. *Maryland Baptist* (Baltimore), Nov. 28, 1963, p. 4; Dec. 5, 1963, p. 1; Dec. 2, 1965, pp. 2, 8; *The Religious Herald* (Richmond), Oct. 8, 1964, p. 7.

54. *Annual, SBC, 1968*, pp. 66–69; *Maryland Baptist* (Baltimore), June 20, 1968, pp. 1–5; June 27, 1968, pp. 1–3; *Baptist Standard* (Dallas), June 12, 1968, p. 4; June 19, 1968, pp. 6, 16; June 26, 1968, pp. 6, 9; Dec. 18, 1968, p. 3; Jan. 8, 1969, p. 5.

55. In the minds of some, the convention further compromised its stand by electing W. A. Criswell as president. The longtime critic of social Christianity endorsed the statement and publicly repudiated his earlier segregationist views. Beyond this he yielded little from his conservative stance. His principal innovation as president was to conclude the next annual meeting with an evangelistic rally in order to "balance" the new attention to social issues. Before the year was out some Southern Baptists were expressing apprehension lest the new social concern might dissipate evangelistic efforts. See *Baptist Messenger* (Oklahoma

some respects, the statement remained the strongest declaration for racial justice in the convention's history.

Baptists editors generally viewed the crisis statement as an overdue recognition of social responsibility. Most of them had made some effort during the decade to still racial passions. Although no paper would endorse the strategy of public confrontations to expose injustices, once the issue was drawn, editors never encouraged white resistance to Negro demands. Deep South editors resented outside interference, but they generally conceded the justice of the Negro's cause and usually urged compliance to civil rights legislation. Erwin McDonald of Arkansas; John J. Hurt, Jr., of Georgia; Reuben Alley of Virginia; J. Marse Grant of North Carolina; C. R. Daley of Kentucky; Terry Young of California; Bryan of Maryland; and James of Texas not only proclaimed the virtues of Christian love and brotherhood but also denounced violence and urged respect for the Negro's legal rights.[56] The twenty-nine editors at the Southern Baptist Press Association meeting in 1965 called upon "each Southern Baptist to take immediate steps to assist all citizens to attain the full privileges of U. S. citizenship."[57] Acts of terrorism and destruction directed at Negro churches during the summer of 1964 outraged Mississippi editor Joe T. Odle. His editorials on the burning of churches won national commendation; and with the aid of other convention officials, Odle organized an interfaith Committee of Concern that rebuilt forty-one Negro churches.[58]

The best that most ministers could do was call for justice, brotherhood, and peace; and a good many did. Such a ministry

---

City), Nov. 28, 1968, p. 3; *Baptist Program* (Jan. 1969), pp. 4, 23; *Maryland Baptist* (Baltimore), Dec. 19, 1968, p. 8.

56. *Word and Way* (Jefferson City), Feb. 2, 1961, p. 2; *Maryland Baptist* (Baltimore), Sept. 6, 1962, p. 4; June 20, 1963, p. 8; Sept. 5, 1963, p. 4; Mar. 4, 1965, p. 3; *The Religious Herald* (Richmond), July 9, 1964, p. 10.

57. *Maryland Baptist* (Baltimore), Mar. 4, 1965, p. 3.

58. Anne Washburn McWilliams, "Out of the Mississippi Ashes . . . ," *Baptist Program* (Nov., 1965), pp. 3–4. Odle won awards from the Evangelical Press Association and the Associated Church Press for his editorial, "Smoke over Mississippi."

was far from irrelevant in tense Southern communities and, in some situations, required a measure of courage. The Southern clergy has been blamed for more than a century for its singular failure of moral leadership in matters of race. That judgment stands, but it is a bit uncharitable to condemn even teachers of morality without some consideration of the circumstances that controlled their actions. Baptist pastors in particular, lacking bishops or presbyteries, had little protection from hostile congregations.[59] It is understandable, if not entirely justifiable, that a clergyman with the usual family and community obligations would not champion a cause that would almost certainly disrupt both community and church and perhaps cost him his job.

To shift the blame from ministers to members still does not absolve the church. Whether a democratic church can exercise loyalty to an authority that transcends its cultural environment remains an open question. But, as demonstrated by the civil rights controversy, when a question with clear moral implications demands commitments, Southern Baptists can be led to translate Christian principles into practical declarations.

The Christian Life Commission and the Joint Committee on Public Affairs, in recent years, have enjoyed greater freedom to confront social issues with intelligence and prophetic insight. A group called Baptist Students Concerned attracted much favorable comment at the Southern Baptist Convention in 1968 when they staged a "silent vigil" with placards calling attention to the problems of race, poverty, and war; and a group of like-minded professors organized the E. Y. Mullins Fellowship, dedicated to achieving greater intellectual freedom and social relevance in the denomination. The Sunday School Board's *Baptist Student* magazine adopted an impressive new format and enlisted writers who could deal with the topics of greatest contemporary concern on the nation's campuses; and for use in the churches, the board prepared special material on the national ills of pov-

59. This fact is pointed out by Ernest White in "Baptist Churches and Race Problems," *Baptist Program* (Oct., 1964), p. 4; and in Reuben Alley's editorial "Progress in Race Relations," *Religious Herald* (Richmond), Oct. 4, 1963, p. 10.

erty, urbanization, the ghetto, and racism, the content of which was in keeping with the more progressive thought in the nation.[60]

Concern for social relevance inspired the Home Mission Board to reappraise its mission in 1965, when the board's new executive secretary, Arthur B. Rutledge, called for a "creative approach" in meeting the secular crises of the sixties. The agency gave greater attention to work with Negro Baptists and work in metropolitan areas. A reorganization created a new department of Social Ministries with nearly two hundred workers who went beyond evangelism in ministering to juveniles, migrants, illiterates, former prisoners, alcoholics, and drug addicts. The board's monthly magazine emphasized what editor Walker L. Knight called "social evangelism." By the end of the decade the journal was given almost wholly to the social dimension of the church's mission, with the editor urging more discussion of controversial social problems in pulpits. A wide range of competently written articles examined social disorder, church integration, the inner city, population control, poverty, and hunger.[61]

If Southern Baptists have made advances, they have done so within an institutional and ideological framework that remains unchanged. Their conservative theology, religious individualism, and congregational government continue to restrict progressive social expression. The main source of hope is the ever-growing number of enlightened leaders who are vocal, influential, and strategically located in pastorates, schools, and denominational positions. For the character of Southern Baptist influence in the secular world will be determined largely by the extent to which leaders of this sort are allowed to shape denominational social attitudes and action.

60. *Maryland Baptist* (Lutherville), May 15, 1969, p. 1; Norman Bowman et al., *We Hold These Truths* (Nashville, 1968).

61. *Annual, SBC, 1965*, p. 159; *1966*, p. 162; *1967*, p. 226; *Home Missions* (Atlanta), Jan., 1968, p. 4; July, 1968, p. 4.

No regional subculture in the United States has been so distinctive as that of the South. To a remarkably intense degree, the context of the South as area and culture has provided both individual citizens and the general culture with dominant values, perceptions, assumptions, and goals. Perhaps this condition is best demonstrated by the lengths to which Southerners have gone in constructing regional myths, such as plantation elegance and "New South" progress in its various versions. Whereas residents of Kansas or Wisconsin, for example, also live in a culture with well-defined patterns, typically they have not felt the need to construct a defense of it and invest it with some kind of transcendent sanction—in other words, to create a Midwest mythology. The South stands alone among American regions in manifesting this penchant.

Accordingly, we may speak of Southerners as a regionally self-conscious people. Historically and culturally, they have known who they are; they have identified themselves as members of a particular society covering the large and diverse area extending from the Potomac to the Rio Grande, a type of thinking that has held on for two centuries. The cultural similarity within this territory, bordering at times on uniformity, reflects a highly developed societal awareness. After all, it is remarkable that a society should continue to be bound to slavery as an institution, should fight a civil war rather than dissolve it, and then practice official racial segregation for nearly another century in order to preserve its traditions during a period in Western civilization when opposite currents, such as the egalitarian and democratic, were running so strong.

For a long time Southerners lived significantly apart from major developments in the world of the nineteenth and twentieth centuries. Theirs was identity by contrast, by dissociation from other cultures. White citizens by their own design and black citizens by enforced abdication knew that residents of the region were a special people and that their corporate culture was different. In this sense, societal consciousness was a staple of Southern identity.

Turning to the religious dimensions of that culture, there is some kind of irony in the fact that a people live with such a hearty awareness of their larger secular context but have not assimilated a corresponding social awareness in their religious patterns of thought. Their ordinary mode of self-perception has been corporate; they have conceived of themselves not as discrete individuals, but as persons associated with, formed by, and contributing to the perpetuation of a cultural heritage far wider than their individual lives. Yet they seem not to have taken clues from ordinary living in constructing their interpretation of the Christian message, despite its fundamental contribution to their world view. Rather, as all studies on the religion practiced by Southern people conclude, the primary presuppositions and concerns of popular religion are individualistic, centering on the salvation of each soul. This book itself confirms that fact, by highlighting the way in which social interpretations of Christianity are irruptions into standard regional religious patterns and by noting the narrowness of the range of social concerns which Southern churches have institutionalized. Whether the issue is social responsibility, the nature of the church, basic theology, or the meaning of salvation, Southern Protestants think dominantly in individualistic terms. Images of theology and mission are thus not social in character.

What can be said about the incompatibility between the social nature of cultural perception and the individualism of religious understanding? Are the two reconcilable? Interestingly, what first appears to be ironic turns out, on closer scrutiny, to be quite straightforward. That is to say, in a very special way the popular religion of the South possesses strong social and corporate qualities. For it has functioned as a primary means of preserving the region's cultural unity. In the process of holding on to the individualistic theology of saving souls, the churches have served, usually unwittingly, as agents of reinforcement. This has been the case because both Christianity and Southernness have been effective frameworks of meaning—cultural systems, in the language of anthropologists, providing symbols for communicating, perpetuating, and developing knowledge and attitudes. The overwhelming majority of white people have learned their identity and have acquired their uncritical assumptions about life from both these sources.

Moreover, the religion of the Southern people and their culture have been linked by the tightest bonds. That culture, particularly in its moral aspects, could not have survived without the legitimating impetus provided by religion. Their co-existence helped enable Southern values and institutions to survive in the face of internal spiritual contradictions and external political pressures. For the South to stand, its people had to be religious and its churches the purest anywhere. If versions of the social gospel vigorously advocating racial integration and a general transformation of the churches' social responsibility had ever penetrated the South to the degree sought by Northern clergymen, the region's cultural ways would have been called into question and the moral legitimacy of the society undermined.

Eighmy's work proves that the social gospel did "come South," and that it was generated by the Southern Christian consciousness. But he makes it very clear that the social Christianity practiced by Southern whites has been social in a specific and designedly limited sense. Thus, the principal achievement of the main text is to exhibit the *growing* sense of responsiveness to broader social issues in the Southern Baptist Convention as cultural epoch followed cultural epoch.

One of the major merits of this longitudinal study is its clarification of companion developments: on one track, the convention has improved its levels of awareness and activity, while on another Southern Baptist life has proceeded without major, vital alterations occurring as a result of social gospel influence. On some issues, Baptists have come to give high priority to matters other than the salvation of souls and the aggrandizement of church institutions. They have been selective about their new concerns and commitments, emphasizing such causes as prohibition and the separation of church and state. Also, they have shown an increasing interest in civil rights and the matter of white supremacy, particularly in the years after World War II. Social service issues in general have become of sufficient importance for denominational committees and agencies to be created to consider them, to seek to educate the churches, and to make annual reports and recommendations to the convention. As a rule, the social—actually *public* is the more accurate term— concerns of the Southern Baptists have dealt with the legislation, or control, of personal morality extended into the public arena, for example, sabbath conduct, temperance, legalized gambling, and obscenity. The Southern Baptists have, in fact, "sought to control the morals of the whole community." But this is emphatically not to say that the Baptists (or Protestant churches generally) have confronted the regnant values of society on race or economics and the basic social structures which institutionalized those values.

That formal recognition of social problems has increased may be seen in various proposals made by both state and convention-wide social service agencies. Those bodies have frequently addressed such goals as better health, education, and housing; improved economic conditions; care for dependent children; recreation facilities; and rehabilitation of criminals. As the foregoing indicates, however, these pronouncements have contained "undebatable generalities." Whenever Baptist agencies have ventured to speak to more complicated and fundamental matters —like urbanization, the decline of the rural South, labor organization and agitation, and laissez faire economics and property rights—they have done so through general, noncommittal statements lacking in concrete proposals.

The data compiled in Professor Eighmy's work make it plain that leadership in the formal life of the Southern Baptist Convention came overwhelmingly from the ranks of the clergy. Social historians of the South are now discovering that from the establishment of the American republic forward Southern clergymen have been major instruments for the creation, first, of community-consciousness on the part of a scattered, rural population, and later, of regional consciousness by leading the denominations to form pan-South denominational bodies, within which Southern values could be perpetuated and given moral sanction. From the 1790's through the 1960's, religious professionals exercised a powerful role in Southern society. They provided social leadership, as we have seen, in that they helped to create and legitimize Southern solidarity. By virtue of rendering that service, however, they also truncated the Southern Convention's commitments to social ministries. The "bourbon" mentality long prevailed among pastors and denominational officials, perhaps until World War II. From Reconstruction until then, most of the more socially conscious ministers were "genteel"; they were adept at forging informal alliances with the outstanding business and professional leaders of their communities. Often charming, even courtly in manner, they practiced tolerance and eschewed crudeness or bombast. But they were wed to the *status quo*, or at the very most were gradualists in their desire for change in church and community. They were much admired by most Southerners, who had scant opportunity to see persons with so cultivated a style anywhere in their society. These were men who supplied desperately felt needs among Southern whites for dignity, refinement, and consolation.

Baptist leadership in the later decades of this era ranged from Arthur J. Barton on the right to Edwin McNeill Poteat on the left. Barton seems to have been the proto-typical bourbon in mentality. Moreover, he stands as a kind of bridge figure between older and newer types of leaders in the convention, a point to which I shall return. Poteat was nearly the ultimate in refinement and cosmopolitan qualities, a truly distinguished man by universal (as distinct from regional) standards. But he was hardly the archetypal Southern Baptist. Nor was he inclined to "play politics," to formulate his policies in such language and with such tactics as would win support of a Southern Baptist constituency. For this reason, as a galvanizer of social change, he was largely ineffective. At the same time, he provided superior leadership for the society at large, standing as a model of humanistic statesmanship for some in his own day and for many more in subsequent periods. Between Barton and Poteat looms the figure of J. B. Weatherspoon, one of the grandest men ever. Similar to Poteat in manner, he was distinguishable from him in that his identity was Southern Baptist. They were Weatherspoon's people; he was one of them. His context was their tradition, with all of its evil and its great potential. He was in a position to afford them prophetic leadership, and he yearned for nothing higher. He knew that nothing else would work than to "proceed with caution," but vigorously advocated that the convention proceed. To my mind, Weatherspoon is the principal figure in the progress Southern Baptists have made to date in social ministries.

Barton's position as a bridge between older and newer types of leadership points to the emergence of a different sense of denominational identification. The data presented suggest that Barton's attitude was primarily one of denominational "loyalty," of predominant interest in the upbuilding of the institution while acknowledging no other frame of reference than the Southern Baptist Convention. Part and parcel with this commitment in his life, however, was the willingness to expend years of energy on social ministries. Later "loyalists" were to be far more self-consciously Southern Baptist and obsessed with the evangelistic program of the convention to the exclusion of social ministries.

The newer types of leadership came to preeminent visibility in the 1950's and 1960's. For persons of this orientation, the Southern Baptist Convention is the norm for all considerations and the sole reference group. In the eyes of these people, its institutional life must be aggrandized, its traditions retained, its unity preserved. During this period, three principal forms of leadership managed to gain power and become responsible for steering this ship of faith through uncharted or turbulent waters: (1) Those classifiable as "organization men," whose passion is for keeping the body together, solvent, and moving. Accordingly, they give skillful energies to formulating compromise measures and encouraging subscription to the denomination's programs. (2) Those who stress "spiritual" qualities more than institutional concerns, by seeking to heal and reconcile. These men work assiduously to point up the spiritual unity which binds those of different persuasions. Treatment of issues is subordinated to the cultivation of sentiments, such as peace, brotherhood, and the common undertaking of Christian tasks. (3) Those charismatic personages who by absorbing the shock of warring parties into their own expansive personalities succeed in shifting the convention's focus away from potentially divisive issues. Through their golden oratory, or humorist gifts, or unimpeachable pietism, variously, they cool tempers and calm troubled waters. It bears repeating that these three types belong to the newer forms of denominational leadership in that for them all the Southern Baptist Convention frames the context of their experience and concerns.

The foregoing analysis of the convention's current leadership up to date confirms the general conclusion evident in the main text that the social gospel "moved South" in a limited and specialized sense. For instance, a review of the data presented in chapter four reveals scarcely a mention of the Southern Baptists. Other denominations surpassed them in receptiveness to the new ideas filtering in from the more industrialized North. But the salient point here is that secular humanitarian organizations were more active than were Baptist churches in considering the social ills of the Southern people and the means with which to cure them. There were numbers of Southerners who responded to the gnawing problems of health, education, poverty, race relations, industrial development, and the like. Among them, one suspects, were few who owned no church affiliation and even fewer who challenged the traditional values of Christianity. Not many Southerners, after all, knew of or acknowledged alternative value systems. Nor have many felt any inclination to reject the moral philosophy of the regional civilization. This intriguing fact has several sources, no doubt, including the inherent attractiveness of Christianity's call to love, justice, and sacrificial service, as well as the generally held conviction that Christianity provides the culture-ethic so necessary for stability and order. Yet the churches themselves, whether "liberal" or "conservative," rarely afforded means by which social concerns could be implemented. Accordingly, organized efforts have come most often through governmental and humanitarian agencies, for example, the Southern Sociological Congress, the Commission on Interracial Cooperation, and the Works Progress Administration. The churches were never primarily and rarely heavily devoted to the alleviation of personal and social distress in the public arena.

This book possesses two major thrusts. First it points to the paucity of evidence for any claim of significant penetration of social-gospel influences among Southern Baptists. Those manifestations of concern to ameliorate conditions in the public arena which did emerge were friendly to the individualistic impulses of Southern Baptist theology and predictable on that basis. Yet it is equally clear that Southern Baptists did invest in causes having to do with public morality and welfare, with the impetus for those involvements sometimes being indigenous and sometimes imported. Second, it offers an exhaustive examination and evaluation of the fact that from the period of Reconstruction forward—especially after 1913 and with larger bursts of activity following World War II, the Southern Baptist Convention deepened its commitments to social ministries. This fact is exhibited rather dramatically by the increasing attention given to the civil rights and black revolution movements, even though these developments were profoundly antagonistic to Southern cultural values, and were volatile aspects of Southern life during the 1950's and 1960's.

The convention's growing attentiveness to the South's (and the nation's) racial crisis in the 1960's serves to highlight this study's main thesis, namely, that Southern Baptist churches tend to reflect the values held by their surrounding culture rather than to prompt critical assessment of those values. For example, not until legislative and legal requirements made it all but mandatory did the Southern Baptists exert much leadership in implementing humane treatment of those blacks who share the same geographical space. "Churches in cultural captivity" is a strong accusation, but it is borne out by the facts detailed; for as regards ministry to the public areas of their existence, Southern Baptists have not managed typically to transcend themselves or to become prophetic visionaries.

One of the distinguishing marks of Southern life historically has been the paucity of options available to its people, whether one thinks of cultural patterns or values or political affiliations or styles of leadership. In religion, too, the South has been a limited-option culture. Accordingly, the term "solid South," for all its ambiguity, has continued to have some meaning, at least until very recently. One of the finest achievements of this book is its illumination of the gradual loosening of the solidarity of traditional theology. Since 1900 social interpretations of Christianity have emerged, thereby providing churchmen with an extra option or two. In the process a few challenges have been delivered to the prevailing order, and they have continued into the second third of the century, though perhaps somewhat less amply in the Baptist ranks than among other denominations.

As I write in 1971, options are proliferating in the South, partly within the churches (with Baptist churches still least among the major groups), where by now many new currents are visible, especially among younger churchmen. But the new elements lie mostly outside the churches, since for larger and larger numbers secularity is an attractive position. The really new situation pertains to the crumbling of a single-option culture, in religion as in other things. Needless to say, Christianity remains the sole religious tradition for upwards of 95 percent of the Southern population. But formal rejection of Christianity or resolute and socially acknowledged indifference to it bulks large in the picture of the present and future South.

As we look to the future, what may we expect concerning the leadership of the Southern Baptist Convention? Who will its leaders be, and what will it have to offer to Southern society at large? Can it be counted on to provide progressive, humane visions and benefits for the people who are affected by its dominant presence? Under the impact of rapid social change during the past ten or so years, some in its constituency have become reactionary. Being vocal and determined, this minority will tolerate nothing but the most absolutist rigor. At the other extreme, many of the younger Southern Baptists will affiliate with other denominations or leave the church altogether if the Convention is not responsive to new social and cultural conditions. In other words, its unity is being threatened from multiple directions.

I think that the crisis in leadership is acute. It seems to me that the denomination still has only a handful of leaders possessing significant influence or power, who are capable of being responsive to the emerging cultural situation, so dramatically pervasive in the 1970's, as symbolized by the new presence of pluralism in all facets of life. By now much of the cream of the under-forty generation has been siphoned off into other Christian bodies or into "secular," humanitarian vocations. Moreover, I do not see the denominational seminaries attracting or producing men who are alert to the necessary transformation of the churches' perceptions and goals. In a companion development, the young men and women who comprise the potential for lay leadership in the future show decreasing interest in the life of the church. There is occasion to wonder if the leadership of Southern society before and after the year 2000 will include the church within the span of its attention.

Notwithstanding these developments and prospects, convention decisions and actions continue to exhibit a preoccupation with institutional unity and aggrandizement and a disposition to cater to the most audible fundamentalist voices. If the social gospel is a force to be reckoned with in the South in the 1970's, I do not see effective evidence in the institutional life of the Southern Baptist Convention. Until the reigning interpretations of evangelism and Christian responsibility are altered, moreover, there appears to be little chance of serious openness to the social obligations of the church.

From their beginnings, Baptist people in the American South, like responsible people everywhere, have been aware of their obligations to contribute to the quality of their civilization. They have been neither blind nor remiss concerning the need to foster visions of life in society which ennoble and enhance. Their sense of social responsibility in the past has taken a number of forms: the founding and support of colleges for the proper instruction of the young, the preservation of orthodoxy in the interest of social stability and the strength which derives from having a viable culture-ethic, and the purification of public morality through antiliquor and antigambling legislation. These endeavors they have made, often without prior policy commitments, because they have sensed that Christian responsibility is not really exhausted in individualistic and other-worldly ministries.

Today's greatest occasion for hope is provided by that significant minority of Baptist leaders, both lay and clergy, who recognize that the stakes are very high over the matter of the denomination's responsiveness to the new cultural situation. These people know that the religious idiom is a primary and meaningful one for millions of Southern people. Accordingly, the quality of the civilization is recognized as closely coordinated with the integrity and creativity of the people's religious life. Many Southern Christians in various communions perceive that the churches have a staggering responsibility to empower lives with strength, liberation, and optimal development, and to assist in constructing a healthy public order.

B y far the most helpful source materials on the subject of this volume are located in the Dargan-Carver Library, Nashville, which is operated jointly by the Southern Baptist Historical Commission and the Sunday School Board. The minutes of the Southern Baptist Convention and the state conventions, which contain the annual proceedings and the reports of committees, agencies, and institutions associated with the respective conventions, were invaluable for my purpose; and I would recommend to those who would pursue this subject further that they begin there. Because the titles and places of publication of the minutes, proceedings, and reports varied widely, especially in the early years, the titles given here are the ones most consistently used. The place of publication often did not appear, but usually the volumes were issued from the convention headquarters, the locations of which are included in the individual citations. The most complete collection of convention annuals is in the Dargan-Carver Library. The annuals consulted in most cases were those held in this collection. The inclusive dates cover the annuals examined, although within each series some volumes were missing. For the other major primary source, the state newspapers, official organs of the various state conventions, the Dargan-Carver Library was again the principal repository.

Other useful papers housed in the Dargan-Carver Library are those of Brooks Hays, including correspondence and miscellaneous papers pertaining to his position as chairman of the Christian Life Commission and president of the Southern Baptist Convention, and those of Rufus W. Weaver, including newspaper clippings, unpublished manuscripts, and letters on religious freedom and the work of the Baptist Joint Committee on Public Relations.

Guy H. Ranson, erstwhile professor of Christian ethics at Southern Baptist Theological Seminary, made available his collection of some fifty items, including letters, newspaper clippings, and addresses relating to the reaction of Southern Baptists to the Supreme Court desegregation order. And the letters and newspaper clippings of the Christian Life Commission regarding the commission's statements on race in 1954–57 and in 1964–65 were also helpful.

[EDITOR'S NOTE: I have added a score of items to the list of books, articles, periodicals, and theses prepared by the author. Nearly all of these have appeared since the completion of Eighmy's major research. Within the past half-dozen years a growing number of scholars have begun to focus attention on the religious dimensions of Southern culture. Thus, Eighmy's work is a part of a major new literature being produced on an aspect of Southern culture long neglected.]

SOUTHERN BAPTIST PUBLICATIONS

Convention Annuals and Newspapers

Alabama. *Annual of the Alabama Baptist State Convention.* Birmingham. 1839–1961.

———. *Alabama Baptist* (Birmingham), 1881, 1888, 1933–36, 1946–47, 1963–64.

———. *South Western Baptist* (Tuskegee), 1860–61, 1870, 1879.

Arizona. *Annual of the Baptist General Convention of Arizona.* Phoenix. 1946–55.

———. *Baptist Beacon* (Phoenix), 1957, 1960, 1964.

Arkansas. *Proceedings of the Arkansas Baptist State Convention.* Little Rock. 1848–1960.

———. *Arkansas Baptist* (Little Rock), 1934, 1936, 1947, 1957, 1958, 1960, 1964.

California. *Annual of the Southern Baptist General Convention of California.* Fresno. 1954–59.

———. *The California Baptist* (Fresno), 1964.

Colorado. *Rocky Mountain Baptist* (Denver), 1960.

District of Columbia. *Minutes of the District of Columbia Baptist Convention.* Washington, D. C. 1914–61.

Florida. *Annual of the Florida Baptist Convention.* Jacksonville. 1860–1954.

———. *Florida Baptist Witness* (Jacksonville), 1933–36, 1964.

Georgia. *Minutes of the Baptist Convention of the State of Georgia.* Atlanta. 1841–1960.

———. *The Christian Index* (Atlanta), 1837, 1844, 1860, 1862, 1882, 1888, 1894, 1933–36, 1946–47, 1964.

Illinois. *Annual of the Illinois Baptist State Convention.* Carbondale. 1917–54.

———. *Illinois Baptist* (Carbondale), 1946–47, 1964.

Kentucky. *Minutes of the General Association of Baptists in Kentucky.* Louisville. 1832–1960.

———. *Western Recorder* (Louisville), 1860–62, 1881–82, 1886, 1921, 1925, 1933–36, 1946–47, 1964.

Louisiana. *Annual of the Louisiana Baptist Convention.* Shreveport. 1920–61.

———. *Baptist Message* (Alexandria), 1933–36, 1957, 1960.

Maryland. *Annual of the Maryland Baptist Union.* Baltimore. 1840–66, 1929–58.

———. *Maryland Baptist* (Baltimore), 1960, 1962–66.

Mississippi. *Proceedings of the Mississippi Baptist Convention.* Jackson. 1838–1960.

———. *Baptist Record* (Jackson), 1933–36, 1946–47, 1957, 1962, 1964.

Missouri. *Minutes of the Missouri Baptist General Association.* Jefferson City. 1908–60.

———. *Word and Way* (Jefferson City), 1920, 1925, 1952–61, 1964.

New Mexico. *The New Mexico Baptist Annual.* Albuquerque. 1920–21.

———. *The Baptist New Mexican* (Albuquerque), 1960.

North Carolina. *Annual of the North Carolina Baptist State Convention.* Raleigh. 1831–1960.

———. *Biblical Recorder* (Raleigh), 1834, 1844, 1933–36, 1946–47, 1964.

Oklahoma. *Minutes of the Baptist General Convention of Oklahoma.* Oklahoma City. 1926–65.

———. *Baptist Messenger* (Oklahoma City), 1961–66.

Oregon-Washington. *Pacific Coast Baptist* (Portland), 1960.

South Carolina. *Minutes of the State Convention of the Baptist Denomination in South Carolina.* Greenville. 1840–88, 1911–60.

———. *Baptist Courier* (Greenville), 1879, 1933–36, 1946–47, 1952, 1957, 1963.

———. *Southern Baptist* (Charleston), 1860.

Southern Baptist Convention. *Annual of the Southern Baptist Convention.* Nashville. 1845–1970.

Tennessee. *Annual of the Tennessee Baptist Convention.* Nashville. 1834–1959.

———. *Proceedings of the General Association of East Tennessee.* Knoxville. 1845–84.

———. *Proceedings of the West Tennessee Baptist Association.* Nashville. 1837–74.

———. *Baptist and Reflector* (Nashville), 1890, 1894, 1933–36, 1946, 1960, 1964.

———. *Tennessee Baptist* (Nashville), 1860.

Texas. *Annual of the Baptist Convention of Texas.* Dallas. 1834–1959.

———. *Baptist Standard* (Dallas), 1933–36, 1946–47, 1960, 1964.

———. *Texas Baptist* (Anderson), 1860–61.

Virginia. *Minutes of the Baptist General Association of Virginia.* Richmond. 1824–1961.

———. *The Religious Herald* (Richmond), 1831–33, 1835, 1846–48, 1854, 1856, 1860, 1870–72, 1876, 1878, 1880, 1882, 1885, 1887, 1892, 1894, 1923, 1933–36, 1946–47, 1957–58, 1960–65.

Miscellaneous

Baptist Program, 1952–66. [A monthly journal published by the Executive Committee of the Southern Baptist Conevntion.]

Catalogue of the New Orleans Baptist Theological Seminary, 1919–57.

Catalogue of the Southern Baptist Theological Seminary, 1895–1946.

Catalogue of the Southwestern Baptist Theological Seminary, 1912–49.

Christian Frontiers, I (1946)–III (1948). [Monthly journal of the Baptist Book Club.]

Christian Life Bulletin, July, 1955 to Mar.–Apr., 1958. [Monthly organ of the Christian Life Commission, published with some irregularity.]

Light, Oct., 1948 to Mar.–Apr., 1960. [Monthly organ of the Social Service Commission and the Christian Life Commission, published with some irregularity.]

The Quarterly Review, VII (1947)–XXVI (1966). [Quarterly journal of the Sunday School Board.]

Report from the Capital, Sept., 1951 to Sept.–Oct., 1966. [Monthly organ of the Baptist Joint Committee on Public Affairs.]

Southern Baptist Educator, XVI (1952)–XXX (1966). [Monthly organ of the Education Commission of the Southern Baptist Convention.]

BOOKS, ARTICLES, PERIODICALS, AND THESES

Abell, Aaron Ignatius. *The Urban Impact on American Protestantism, 1865–1900.* Cambridge, Mass., 1943.

Alderman, Edwin A. *The Growing South.* New York, 1908.

Alexander, Walter R. *Doing Likewise, Three Vital Southern Baptist Ministries.* Nashville, 1947.

Alley, Reuben. "Progress in Race Relations," *The Religious Herald* (Richmond), Oct. 4, 1963, p. 10.

Anderson, Henry Lee. "The Ecclesiology of Ante-Bellum Baptist Churches in the South." Th.D. thesis, New Orleans Baptist Theological Seminary, 1960.

Annual Reports of the Board of Managers of the Baptist General Convention, 1815, 1816, 1818, 1822, 1827, 1828, 1830, 1831, 1833, 1834, 1837, 1842, 1843. [The exact title varies considerably. Published in Boston, Philadelphia, and Washington, D. C.]

Archer, Glenn A. "Will Baptists Barter Their Birthright?" *The Baptist Messenger* (Oklahoma City), June 24, 1965, pp. 8–9, 12–13.

The Arkansas Gazette (Little Rock), Oct. 19, 1960.

Asbury, Herbert. *The Great Illusion, an Informal History of Prohibition.* Garden City, N. Y., 1950.

Atwood, Jason Jones, Jr. "Southern Baptist Attitudes Toward Church-State Cooperation in Religious Instruction, 1930–1952." Th.D. thesis, Southwestern Baptist Theological Seminary, 1956.

Autrey, C. E. "Home Mission Program of Evangelism," *Encyclopedia of Southern Baptists*, I (1958), 419–24.

Axt, Richard G. *The Federal Government and Financing Higher Education*. New York, 1952.

Bailey, Eldon W. "Southern Baptist Reactions to Diplomatic Relations with the Vatican (1939–1953)." Th.D. thesis, Southwestern Baptist Theological Seminary, 1955.

Bailey, Joseph Cannon. *Seaman A. Knapp, Schoolmaster of American Agriculture*. New York, 1945.

Bailey, Kenneth K. *Southern White Protestantism in the Twentieth Century*. New York, 1964.

Bailey, T. J. *Prohibition in Mississippi*. Jackson, 1917.

Baker, Paul E. *Negro-White Adjustments, an Investigation and Analysis of Methods in the Interracial Movement in the United States*. Pittsfield, Mass., 1934.

Baker, Robert A. *Relations between Northern and Southern Baptists*. N.p., 1948.

———. *A Baptist Source Book*. Nashville, 1966.

Baldwin, Alice V. *The New England Clergy and the American Revolution*. Durham, 1923.

Baptist Home Missions in North America. New York, 1883.

Baptist Joint Committee on Public Affairs. "In Review and Evaluation of the C. E. Bryant Research into Allotment of Federal Funds to Churches." Washington, D. C., n.d.

———. "The Biblical Basis of Religious Liberty." Washington, D. C., 1958. Mimeographed.

———. "5th Annual Religious Liberty Conference. Study Papers on Church-State Aspects of the Churches' Involvement in Human Need." Washington, D. C., 1961. Mimeographed.

Baptist Missionary Magazine, XVI (1836)–XXVI (1846). Boston. [Monthly journal of the Board of Managers of the General Convention. Contains the reports of the board and the proceedings of the Triennial Conventions.]

The Baptist World Alliance, Second Congress, 1911. Philadelphia, 1911.

Barnes, Gilbert Hobbes. *The Antislavery Impulse, 1830–1844*. Gloucester, Mass., 1957.

Barnes, William Wright. *The Southern Baptist Convention, A Study in the Development of Ecclesiology*. Fort Worth, 1934.

————. "Why the Southern Baptist Convention Was Formed," *Review and Expositor*, XLI (Jan., 1944), 3–17.

————. "The Theological Curriculum of Tomorrow in the Light of the Past," *Review and Expositor*, XLIV (Apr., 1947), 136–57.

————. *The Southern Baptist Convention, 1845–1953*. Nashville, 1954.

————. "Home Mission Board of the Southern Baptist Convention," *Encyclopedia of Southern Baptists*, I (1958), 635–49.

Barnett, Das Kelly. "The New Theological Frontiers for Southern Baptists," *Review and Expositor*, XXXVIII (July, 1941), 264–76.

Barnette, Henlee. "The Challenge of Southern Cities," *Review and Expositor*, XLV (Oct., 1948), 423–34.

————. "The Role of the Church in the Conservation of Youth," *Review and Expositor*, XLVII (Apr., 1950), 173–77.

————. "Urbanization and Southern Churches," *Review and Expositor*, L (Oct., 1953), 430–42.

————. "What Can Southern Baptists Do?" *Christianity Today*, I (June 24, 1957), 14–16.

Barrett, George. "Study in Desegregation: The Clinton Story," *New York Times Magazine*, Sept. 16, 1956, pp. 11, 71–72, 76.

Barton, Arthur J. "The White Man's Task in the Uplift of the Negro." In *The South Mobilizing for Social Service, Addresses Delivered at the Southern Sociological Congress, Atlanta, Georgia, April 25–29, 1913*, edited by James E. McCullough, pp. 460–76. Nashville, 1913.

————. "Wine, Women and the New Deal," *Arkansas Baptist* (Little Rock), Apr. 26, 1934, p. 14.

————. "Practical Application of the Principles of Christ's Teachings," *The Biblical Recorder* (Raleigh), June 20, 1934, p. 1.

————. "The Attitude of Society Must Be Vicarious," *Biblical Recorder* (Raleigh), Oct. 24, 1934, p. 1.

————. "Southern Baptists Finding Their Voice for Civic Righteousness and Social Service," *Baptist and Reflector* (Nashville), Oct. 31, 1935, p. 6.

————. "Southern Baptists Decide to Have a Standing Committee on Temperance," *Baptist and Reflector* (Nashville), Nov. 17, 1935, p. 5.

————. "Meeting 'Mr Speaker' 'Uncle Joe' Cannon," *Alabama Baptist* (Birmingham), Dec. 5, 1935, pp. 5, 9.

Barton, Henderson. "Arthur James Barton," *Encyclopedia of Southern Baptists*, I (1958), 146.

Bassett, John S. "Editor's Announcement," *The South Atlantic Quarterly*, I (Jan., 1902), 2–3.

Batten, Samuel Zane. *The Social Task of Christianity*. New York, 1911.

————. "The Church and Social Service." In *The Call of the New South, Addresses Delivered at the Southern Sociological Congress, Nashville, Tennessee, May 7 to 10, 1912*, edited by James E. McCullough, pp. 275–92. Nashville, 1912.

————. "Social Service and the Church." In *The South Mobilizing for Social Service, Addresses Delivered at the Southern Sociological Congress, Atlanta, Georgia, April 25–29, 1913*, edited by James E. McCullough, pp. 13–15. Nashville, 1913.

Beale, Howard K. *Are American Teachers Free?* New York, 1936.

The Beam, XI (Oct., 1960).

Bencham, Dewitt M. "Methods of City Evangelization," *Union Seminary Magazine*, XV (Dec., 1903–Jan., 1904), 105–18.

Benedict, David. *A General History of the Baptist Denomination in America*. 2 vols. Boston, 1813.

The Bible Speaks on Economics. Nashville, n.d.

Binkley, Olin T. "The Minister's Moral Task," *Review and Expositor*, XLIII (Oct., 1946), 369–83.

————. *The Churches and the Social Conscience*. Indianapolis, 1948.

————. "C[hristian] S[ociology] 19 Lectures." Mimeographed notes on Binkley's lectures taken by Millard R. Brown, June, 1949. Located at Southern Baptist Theological Seminary.

"Bishops' Address," *Journal of the General Conference of the Methodist Episcopal Church, South, 1910*, p. 40.

Blanshard, Paul. *American Freedom and Catholic Power*. Boston, 1949.

————. *God and Man in Washington*. Boston, 1960.

Bodo, John R. *The Protestant Clergy and Public Issues, 1812–1848*. Princeton, 1954.

Bond, Horace Mann. *The Education of the Negro in the American Social Order*. New York, 1934.

Bowman, Norman *et al. We Hold These Truths*. Nashville, 1968.

Boyd, Jesse L. *A History of Baptists in America*. New York, 1957.

[Boykin, Samuel.] *History of the Baptist Denomination in Georgia.* Atlanta, 1881.

Bragg, George F. *History of the Afro-American Group of the Episcopal Church.* Baltimore, 1922.

Brimm, Hugh A. "The Social Consciousness of Southern Baptists in Relation to Some Regional Problems, 1910–1935." Th.D. thesis, Southern Baptist Theological Seminary, 1944.

————. "The Social Service Commission of the Southern Baptist Convention," *The Quarterly Review,* VIII (Third Quarter, 1948), 24–27.

————. "The Christian Task of Moral Education," *Review and Expositor,* XLVI (Jan., 1949), 43–55.

Broach, Claude U. "A Baptist Pastor at Vatican II," *Baptist Program* (Apr., 1966), p. 20.

Bundy, Edgar C. *Collectivism in the Churches, a Documentary Account of the Political Activities of the Federal, National and World Council of Churches.* Wheaton, Ill., 1961.

Bureau of Research and Survey, National Council of Churches. *Churches and Church Membership in the United States.* New York, 1957.

Burton, Joe W. *Epochs of Home Missions.* Atlanta, 1945.

Bushnell, Horace. *Christian Nurture.* New Haven, 1953.

Cable, George W. *The Silent South.* New York, 1885.

Campbell, Ernest Q., and Thomas F. Pettigrew. *Christians in Racial Crisis: A Study of the Little Rock Ministry.* Washington, D. C., 1959.

Cameron, Harriet Suzanne. "William Louis Poteat and the Evolution Controversy." M.A. thesis, Wake Forest College, 1962.

"Can Baptist Colleges Afford Isolation Instead of Cooperation," *Southern Baptist Educator,* XXIX (Sept.–Oct., 1965), 3–4.

Carlson, C. Emanuel. "Religious Liberty and Baptist Organization." Mimeographed paper prepared for the 1957 Religious Liberty Conference.

————. "The Baptist Genius in Today's World." Mimeographed copy of an address delivered to the American Baptist Convention, June 16, 1958.

————. "The Meaning of the Baptist Position." Mimeographed discussion materials for the 1958 Religious Liberty Conference.

————. "The Biblical Basis of Religious Liberty." Mimeographed study paper for the 1958 Religious Liberty Conference.

————. "Baptists and Dual Enrollment," *Baptist Program* (Nov., 1965), pp. 7, 16.

Carmichael, Omer, and Weldon James. *The Louisville Story.* New York, 1957.

Carter, Hodding, III. *The South Strikes Back.* Garden City, N. Y., 1959.

Carter, Paul A. *The Decline and Revival of the Social Gospel: Social and Political Liberalism in American Protestant Churches, 1920–1940.* Ithaca, 1954.

Carver, William O. "The Function of Christianity in the Making of World Order," *Review and Expositor,* XLIII (July, Oct., 1946), 261–74, 384–402.

Cash, Wilbur J. *The Mind of the South.* New York, 1941.

Cathcart, William. *The Baptists and the American Revolution.* Philadelphia, 1876.

————. *The Baptist Encyclopedia.* Philadelphia, 1881.

Chatfield, E. Charles, Jr. "The Southern Sociological Congress: Organization of Uplift," *Tennessee Historical Quarterly,* XIX (Dec., 1960), 328–47.

————. "The Southern Sociological Congress: Rationale of Uplift," *Tennessee Historical Quarterly,* XX (Mar., 1961), 51–64.

Cherrington, Ernest H. *The Evolution of Prohibition in the United States of America.* Westerville, Ohio, 1920.

Christian, John T. *A History of the Baptists of the United States from the First Settlement of the Country to the Year 1845.* Nashville, 1926.

Christian Century, LV (Mar. 16, 1938), LXII (Jan. 31, 1945; July 18, 1945), LXIV (May 21, 1947), LXV (Jan. 21, 1948), LXVIII (Oct. 31, 1951; Nov. 7, 1951; Nov. 14, 1951), LXIX (Jan. 23, 1952), LXXI (June 9, 1954; June 16, 1954; June 23, 1954; Nov. 17, 1954), LXXII (July 27, 1955), LXXIII (Mar. 14, 1956), LXXIV (Oct. 9, 1957), LXXV (May 21, 1958; Dec. 3, 1958). [A nondenominational weekly.]

Christian Principles Applied to Daily Work. Nashville, n.d.

Christianity Today, III (Feb. 2, 1959).

Church and State, VIII (1955)–XIII (1960). [A monthly journal of Protestants and other Americans united for the separation of church and state.]

Clark, Thomas D., and Albert Kirwan. *The South Since Appomattox.* New York, 1967.

Cole, Charles C., Jr. *The Social Ideas of the Northern Evangelists, 1826–1860.* New York, 1954.

Cole, Stewart G. *The History of Fundamentalism.* New York, 1931.

The Coming Peace. Nashville, 1944.

Commission on Interracial Co-operation. *Progress in Race Relations, 1924–25.* Atlanta, n.d.

The Commonweal, LXIX (1959)–LXXIII (1960). [A lay Catholic weekly.]

Converse, Philip E. *et al.* "Stability and Change in 1960: A Reinstating Election," *The American Political Science Review,* LV (June, 1961), 269–80.

Council of Christian Social Progress of the American Baptist Convention. *Resolutions Adopted by the Northern Baptist Convention.* New York, 1950.

Cowling, Dale. *A Pastor Looks at Integration in Little Rock.* Nashville, 1957.

Cox, Harvey. "A Baptist Intellectual's View of Catholicism," *Harper's Magazine,* CCXXV (Dec., 1962), 47–50.

———. *The Secular City.* New York, 1965.

Crafts, Wilbur F. "The Potential Resources of the South for Leadership in Social Science." In *The Call of the New South, Addresses Delivered at the Southern Sociological Congress, Nashville, Tennessee, May 7 to 10, 1912,* edited by James E. McCullough, pp. 311–12. Nashville, 1912.

"A Creed for a Crusade." In *The New Chivalry—Health, Southern Sociological Congress, Houston, Texas, May 8–11, 1915,* edited by James E. McCullough, p. 11. Nashville, 1915.

Criswell, W. A. "Religious Freedom, the Church, the State, and Senator Kennedy," *The Beam,* XI (Oct., 1960), 8–13.

Crook, Roger H. "The Ethical Emphasis of the Editors of Baptist Journals Published in the Southeastern Region of the United States up to 1865." Th.D. thesis, Southern Baptist Theological Seminary, 1947.

Culver, Dwight W. *Negro Segregation in the Methodist Church.* New Haven, 1953.

Curry, J. T. "What Is Higher Criticism?" *Methodist Review,* LIV (Jan., 1905), 472–78.

Cushman, Robert E. *Civil Liberties, a Guide to Current Problems and Experiences.* Ithaca, 1956.

Dabney, Virginius. *Liberalism in the South.* Chapel Hill, 1932.

————. *The Dry Messiah, the Life of Bishop Cannon.* New York, 1949.

Dargan, Edwin C. "The Teaching of Sociology in the Seminary," *Seminary Magazine* (Mar., 1900), pp. 295–99.

————. *Society, Kingdom, and Church.* Philadelphia, 1907.

Davidson, Elizabeth H. *Child Labor Legislation in the Southern Textile States.* Chapel Hill, 1939.

Davis, Hugh C. "Edwin T. Winkler, Baptist Bayard," *Alabama Review* (Jan., 1965), pp. 33–44.

Dawson, Joseph Martin. *Christ and Social Change.* Philadelphia, 1937.

————. "Religious Liberty Restated," *Review and Expositor,* XLI (Oct., 1944), 337–49.

————. *The Road to Real Freedom.* Atlanta, 1947.

————. "Can a Public Relations Secretary Speak for the Baptists?" *The Religious Herald* (Richmond), Jan. 2, 1947, pp. 20, 24.

————. *Separate Church and State Now.* New York, 1948.

————. *America's Way in Church and State.* New York, 1953.

————. "The Church and Religious Liberty," *Review and Expositor,* L (Apr., 1953), 144–59.

"A Declaration of Conscience for Baptists." N.p., 1960. Mimeographed.

De Witt, Benjamin Parke. *The Progressive Movement.* New York, 1915.

Dick, Everett. *The Dixie Frontier.* New York, 1948.

Dillard, J. E. *Good Stewards.* Nashville, 1953.

————. *Bible Stewardship.* Nashville, n.d.

————. *Building a Stewardship Church.* Nashville, n.d.

The Doctrine and Discipline of the Methodist Episcopal Church, South, 1914. Nashville, 1914.

————. *1918.* Nashville, 1920.

Doherty, Herbert J., Jr. "Voices of Protest from the New South, 1875–1910," *The Mississippi Valley Historical Review,* XLII (June, 1955), 45–66.

————. "Alexander J. McKelway: Preacher to Progressives," *The Journal of Southern History,* XXIV (May, 1958), 177–90.

Domestic Slavery Considered as a Scriptural Institution. New York, 1845.

DuBois, W. E. Burghardt, ed. *The Negro Church.* Atlanta, 1903.

Duff, Edward. *The Social Thought of the World Council of Churches.* New York, 1956.

Dumond, Dwight Lowell. *Antislavery Origins of the Civil War in the United States.* Ann Arbor, 1959.

————. *Antislavery: The Crusade for Freedom in America.* Ann Arbor, 1961.

Dyer, G. W. "Southern Problems That Challenge our Thought." In *The Call of the New South, Addresses Delivered at the Southern Sociological Congress, Nashville, Tennessee, May 7 to 10, 1912,* edited by James E. McCullough, pp. 25–33. Nashville, 1912.

Eaton, Clement. *Freedom of Thought in the Old South.* New York, 1951.

————. *The Growth of Southern Civilization, 1790–1860.* New York, 1961.

Ebersole, Luke. *Church Lobbying in the Nation's Capital.* New York, 1951.

Eminhizer, Earl Eugene. "The Rise and Fall of the Triennial Convention." M.A. thesis, Crozier Theological Seminary, 1950.

Encyclopedia of Southern Baptists. 2 vols. Nashville, 1958.

English, Carl Dean. "The Ethical Emphasis of the Editors of Baptist Journals Published in the Southeastern Region of the United States, 1865–1915." Th.D. thesis, Southern Baptist Theological Seminary, 1948.

Estep, William Roscoe, Jr. "A Historical Study of the Ecumenical Movement." Th.D. thesis, Southwestern Baptist Theological Seminary, 1951.

Ezell, John Samuel. *The South Since 1865.* New York, 1963.

Farish, Hunter D. *The Circuit Rider Dismounts, A Social History of Southern Methodism.* Richmond, 1938.

Faulkner, Harold U. *The Quest for Social Justice, 1898–1914.* New York, 1931.

Few, William Preston. "Southern Public Opinion," *South Atlantic Quarterly,* IV (Jan., 1905), 1–12.

Fischer, Roger A. "Racial Segregation in Ante-Bellum New Orleans," *The American Historical Review,* LXXIV (Feb., 1969), 926–37.

Fleming, Walter L. *Documentary History of Reconstruction.* 2 vols. New York, 1950.

Fletcher, Joseph. *Situation Ethics, the New Morality.* Philadelphia, 1966.

Flynt, Wayne. "Dissent in Zion: Alabama Baptists and Social Issues, 1900–1914," *The Journal of Southern History*, XXXV (Nov., 1969), 532–42.

Fosdick, Raymond B. *Adventure in Giving, the Story of the General Education Board*. New York, 1962.

Foss, A. T., and E. Mathews. *Facts for Baptist Churches*. Utica, N. Y., 1850.

Frazier, E. Franklin. *The Negro in the United States*. New York, 1949.

The Fund for the Republic, a Report on Three Years' Work. New York, 1956.

The Fundamentals: A Testimony to the Truth. 12 vols. Chicago, n.d.

Furman, Richard. *Exposition of the Baptists in Relation to the Colored Population of the United States in a Communication to the Governor of South Carolina*. Charleston, 1823.

Furniss, Norman F. *The Fundamentalist Controversy, 1918–1931*. New Haven, 1954.

Gabriel, Ralph H. *The Course of American Democratic Thought*. New York, 1940.

Gardner, Charles S. *The Ethics of Jesus and Social Progress*. New York, 1914.

———. "The Accumulation of Wealth," *Review and Expositor*, XI (Apr., 1914), 204–16.

———. "The Minister as a Health Propagandist." In *Democracy in Earnest, Southern Sociological Congress, 1916–1918*, edited by James E. McCullough, pp. 376–82. Washington, D. C., 1918.

———. "Outline of First Quarter's Work in Christian Sociology." Mimeographed notes on Gardner's lectures taken by E. E. Northen and revised by Gardner in 1918. Located at Southern Baptist Theological Seminary.

———. "The Relation of the Individual to Society," *Review and Expositor*, XXVI (Jan., 1929), 3–26.

———. "The Problem of Democracy from the Psychological Point of View," *Review and Expositor*, XXIX (July, 1932), 305–46.

Garner, James W. "The Negro Question in the South," *South Atlantic Quarterly*, VII (Jan., 1908), 11–22.

Garrett, James Leo. *Baptist Church Discipline*. Nashville, 1962.

Garrett, W. Barry. "What Is the Public Affairs Committee? How Does the Public Affairs Committee Do Its Work?" *Baptist Program* (May–June, 1958), pp. 10–11.

————. "Baptists Need Report on Vatican Council II," *Report from the Capital*, Aug.–Sept.–Oct., 1963, p. 3.

————. "The Biblical Basis of Religious Liberty." Typed copy distributed by the Baptist Joint Committee on Public Affairs, n.d.

————. "The Meaning of the Separation of Church and State." Mimeographed copy distributed by the Baptist Joint Committee on Public Affairs, n.d.

Garrison, Winfred Ernest. *The March of Faith, the Story of Religion in America since 1865*. New York, 1933.

Gatewood, William B., Jr. *Preachers, Pedagogues, and Politicians: The Evolution Controversy in North Carolina, 1920–1927*. Chapel Hill, 1966.

————, ed. *Controversy in the Twenties*. Nashville, 1969.

Gaustad, Edwin Scott. *Historical Atlas of Religion in America*. New York, 1962.

The General Education Board. *The General Education Board, an Account of its Activities, 1902–1914*. New York, 1915.

Ginn, D. Perry. "Christians and Desegregation," *The Pulpit*, XXVII (Nov., 1956), 20, 22–23.

Goldman, Eric F. *Rendezvous with Destiny, a History of Modern Reform in America*. Rev. and abridged ed. New York, 1961.

Green, Fletcher M. "Northern Missionary Activity in the South, 1846–1861," *The Journal of Southern History*, XXI (May, 1955), 147–72.

Green, James Frederick. *The United Nations and Human Rights*. Washington, D. C., 1956.

Guinn, G. Earl. "Can Baptist Colleges Afford to Accept Federal Aid?" *Southern Baptist Educator*, XXIX (July–Aug., 1965), 3–6.

Gwynn, Frederick L., and Joseph L. Blotner. *Faulkner in the University*. Charlottesville, Va., 1959.

Harmon, George. "How to Tell a Baptist from a Methodist in the South," *Harper's Magazine*, CCXXVI (Feb., 1963), 58–63.

Harwood, Thomas F. "British Evangelical Abolitionism and American Churches in the 1830's," *The Journal of Southern History*, XXVIII (Aug., 1962), 287–306.

Harrison, Paul M. *Authority and Power in the Free Church Tradition, a Social Case Study of the American Baptist Convention*. Princeton, 1959.

Hartnett, Robert C. *Equal Rights for Children*. New York, 1947.

Haselden, Kyle. *The Racial Problem in Christian Perspective.* New York, 1964.

———. *Morality and the Mass Media.* Nashville, 1968.

Hatcher, William T. "Housekeeping for Our Neighbor," in Victor I. Masters, ed., *The Home Mission Task,* pp. 69–96. Atlanta, 1912.

Hawerton, J. P. "The Church and Social Reform," *Union Seminary Magazine,* XXV (Oct.–Nov., 1913), 30–34.

Hawley, J. W. "The Twentieth Century Protestant Outlook," *Methodist Review,* XLIX (Mar.–Apr., 1900), 316, 318.

Hays, Brooks. *This World: A Christian's Workshop.* Nashville, 1958.

———. *A Southern Moderate Speaks.* Chapel Hill, 1959.

Henderson, Donald H. *The Negro Freedman.* New York, 1952.

Hendrick, Burton J. *The Life and Letters of Walter Hines Page.* Garden City, N. Y., 1925.

———. *The Training of an American, the Earlier Life and Letters of Walter Hines Page.* Boston, 1928.

Hicks, John D. *The Populist Revolt.* Minneapolis, 1931.

Hill, Davis C. "Southern Baptist Thought and Action in Race Relations, 1940–1950." Th.D. thesis, Southern Baptist Theological Seminary, 1952.

Hill, Patrick Henry. "Ethical Emphases of the Baptist Editors in the Southeastern Region of the United States, 1915–1940." Th.D. thesis, Southern Baptist Theological Seminary 1949.

Hill, Samuel S., Jr. "The Southern Baptists: Need for Reformulation, Redirection," *Christian Century,* LXXX (Jan. 9, 1963), 39–42.

———. "Southern Protestantism and Racial Integration," *Religion in Life,* XXX (Summer, 1964), 421–29.

———. *Southern Churches in Crisis.* New York, 1967.

Historical Commission of the Southern Baptist Convention. *Index of Graduate Theses in Baptist Theological Seminaries, 1894–1962.* Nashville, 1963.

Hofstadter, Richard. *The Age of Reform: From Bryan to F.D.R.* New York, 1955.

———. *Anti-intellectualism in American life.* New York, 1963.

Holcombe, Hosea. *A History of the Rise and Progress of the Baptists in Alabama.* Philadelphia, 1840.

Holmes, Dwight Oliver. *The Evolution of the Negro College.* New York, 1934.

Hopkins, Charles Howard. *The Rise of the Social Gospel in American Protestantism, 1865–1915.* New Haven, 1940.

————. "Baptists in the Modern Age," *Review and Expositor*, LIII (Oct., 1956), 489–511.

Horne, Cleveland R., Jr. "Christian Economic Ethics: A Study of Contemporary Thought in the Light of the Works of Walter Rauschenbusch." Th.D. thesis, Southwestern Baptist Theological Seminary, 1955.

The Houston Post, May 23, 1958.

Hudson, R. Lofton. *Is Segregation Christian?* Nashville, n.d.

Hudson, Winthrop S. *American Protestantism*. Chicago, 1961.

Humphrey, James Edward. "Baptist Discipline in Kentucky, 1781–1860." Th.D. thesis, Southern Baptist Theological Seminary, 1959.

Hutchins, Robert M. *Freedom, Education, and the Fund, Essays and Addresses, 1946–1956*. New York, 1956.

Hutchinson, John A., ed. *Christian Faith and Social Action*. New York, 1953.

Jacquet, Constant H., Jr., ed. *Yearbook of American Churches 1971*. New York, 1971.

Jenkins, William S. *Pro-Slavery Thought in the Old South*. Gloucester, Mass., 1960.

Johnson, Alvin W., and Frank H. Yost. *Separation of Church and State in the United States*. Minneapolis, 1948.

Johnson, Charles Price. "Southern Baptists and the Social Gospel Movement." Th.D. thesis, Southwestern Baptist Theological Seminary, 1948.

Johnson, Emory R., ed. *The Annals of the American Academy of Political and Social Science*. XXXV. Philadelphia, 1910.

Johnson, Frederick Ernest. *The Social Work of the Churches*. New York, 1930.

————. *The Church and Society*. New York, 1935.

————. *The Social Gospel Re-examined*. New York, 1940.

Joiner, Edward Earl. "Southern Baptists and Church-State Relations, 1845–1954." Th.D. thesis, Southern Baptist Theological Seminary, 1959.

Jones, John Hall. *The Unity of Humanity*. Nashville, 1956.

Jones, M. Ashby. "Race Consciousness in the Relation of Whites and Negroes," *Review and Expositor*, XXI (July, 1924), 271–80.

Journal of the General Conference of the Methodist Episcopal Church, South, 1866, 1878, 1882, 1886, 1890, 1894, 1898, 1902, 1906, 1910, 1914, 1922.

Kelsey, George D. "The Social Thought of Contemporary Southern Baptists." Ph.D. diss., Yale University, 1946.

Krout, John A. *The Origins of Prohibition*. New York, 1925.

The Latter Day Luminary, I (1819)–III (1821). [A monthly missionary journal of the Baptist General Convention.]

Lawrence, J. B. "The Church and the Social Order," *Baptist Courier* (Greenville), Aug. 1, 1946, p. 1.

Leavell, Roland Q. "Evangelism," *Encyclopedia of Southern Baptists*, I (1958), 407–19.

Lee, G. Avery. "Some Quiet Thoughts on a Turbulent Issue," *Pulpit Digest*, XXXVII (May, 1957), 25–30.

Leigh, Calvin D. *Prohibition in the United States, a History of the Prohibition Party and the Prohibition Movement*. New York, 1926.

Linder, Suzanne Cameron. *William Louis Poteat, Prophet of Progress*. Chapel Hill, 1966.

Lingle, Walter L. "The Teaching of Jesus and Modern Social Problems," *Union Seminary Magazine*, XXVII (Apr., 1916), 205.

Link, Arthur S. "The Progressive Movement in the South, 1870–1914," *North Carolina Historical Review*, XXIII (Apr., 1946), 172–205.

Littell, Franklin Hamlin. *The Free Church*. Boston, 1957.

——. *From State Church to Pluralism*. Garden City, N. Y., 1962.

Lloyd, Arthur Young. *The Slavery Controversy, 1831–1860*. Chapel Hill, 1939.

Locke, Harvey James. "A Historical and Critical Interpretation of the Social Gospel of Northern Baptists in the United States." Ph.D. diss., University of Chicago, 1930.

Loescher, Frank L. *The Protestant Church and the Negro, a Pattern of Segregation*. New York, 1948.

Louisville Courier Journal, Nov. 15, 1950.

McCall, Abner. "Another View of Tax Support," *Ouachita Baptist Alumni Magazine* (June, 1965), pp. 8–9, 14.

——. "A Discussion of Two Federal Aid Objections," *Southern Baptist Educator*, XXX (Nov., 1966), 8–10.

——, et al. "Can Baptist Colleges Afford Isolation Instead of Cooperation?" *Southern Baptist Educator*, XXIX (Sept.–Oct., 1965), 3–4.

MacCorkle, William Alexander. *Some Southern Questions Asked*. New York, 1908.

McCullough, James E. Introductory Note to *The Call of the New*

South, *Addresses Delivered at the Southern Sociological Congress, Nashville, Tennessee, May 7 to 10, 1912,* pp. 7–8. Nashville, 1912.

————. Introduction to *Battling for Social Betterment, Southern Sociological Congress, Memphis, Tennessee, May 6 to 10, 1914,* p. 3. Nashville, 1914.

————, ed. *The Call of the New South, Addresses Delivered at the Southern Sociological Congress, Nashville, Tennessee, May 7 to 10, 1912.* Nashville, 1912.

————, ed. *The South Mobilizing for Social Service, Addresses Delivered at the Southern Sociological Congress, Atlanta, Georgia, April 25–29, 1913.* Nashville, 1913.

————, ed. *Battling for Social Betterment, Southern Sociological Congress, Memphis, Tennessee, May 6 to 10, 1914.* Nashville, 1914.

————, ed. *The New Chivalry—Health, Southern Sociological Congress, Houston, Texas, May 8–11, 1915.* Nashville, 1915.

————, ed. *Democracy in Earnest, Southern Sociological Congress, 1916–1918.* Washington, D. C., 1918.

MacFarland, Charles S. "The Church and Modern Industry." In *The Call of the New South, Addresses Delivered at the Southern Sociological Congress, Nashville, Tennessee, May 7 to 10, 1912,* edited by James E. McCullough, pp. 292–307. Nashville, 1912.

————. "The Preparation of the Church for Social Service." In *Battling for Social Betterment, Southern Sociological Congress, Memphis, Tennessee, May 6 to 10, 1914,* edited by James E. McCullough, pp. 98–108. Nashville, 1914.

McGlothlin, W. J. *Baptist Confessions of Faith.* Philadelphia, 1911.

McKelway, Alexander J. "Remarks of the Acting President." In *The South Mobilizing for Social Service, Addresses Delivered at the Southern Sociological Congress, Atlanta, Georgia, April 25–29, 1913,* edited by James E. McCullough, p. 14. Nashville, 1913.

McKinney, Lewis C. "Reaction of Southern Baptists to the Supreme Court Decision of May 17, 1954." Unpublished mimeographed research paper in Christian ethics class at Southern Baptist Theological Seminary, July, 1957, in the private files of Guy H. Ranson.

McLoughlin, William G., Jr. *Modern Revivalism: Charles Grandison Finney to Billy Graham.* New York, 1959.

————, and Winthrop D. Jordan. "Baptists Face the Barbarities of Slavery in 1710," *The Journal of Southern History,* XXIX (Feb.–Nov., 1963), 495–501.

McWilliams, Anne Washburn. "Out of the Mississippi Ashes . . . ," *Baptist Program* (Nov., 1965), pp. 3–4.

Marney, Carlyle. "The Emancipation of a White," *Christian Century,* LXXI (Nov. 17, 1954), 1397–98.

Masters, Victor I. *Baptist Home Missions.* Atlanta, 1914.

———. *The Call of the South.* Atlanta, 1918.

———. *Making America Christian.* Atlanta, 1921.

———, ed. *The Home Mission Task.* Atlanta, 1912.

Maston, Thomas B. *World in Travail.* Nashville, 1954.

———. *Integration.* Nashville, 1956.

———. *Christianity and World Issues.* New York, 1957.

———. *The Bible and Race.* Nashville, 1959.

———. *Segregation and Desegregation.* New York, 1959.

Mathews, Donald G. *Slavery and Methodism.* Princeton, 1965.

———. "The Methodist Mission to the Slaves, 1829–1844," *The Journal of American History,* LI (Mar., 1965), 615–31.

Mathews, Shailer. *The Social Teachings of Jesus.* New York, 1897.

———. "The Social Influence of the Baptists," *Chronicle,* VIII (Apr., 1945), 55–63.

May, Henry F. *Protestant Churches and Industrial America.* New York, 1949.

May, Mark A., and Frank K. Shuttleworth. *The Education of American Ministers.* II. New York, 1934.

Mays, Benjamin E., and Joseph W. Nicholson. *The Negro's Church.* New York, 1933.

Meyer, Donald. *The Protestant Search for Political Realism, 1919–1941.* Berkeley, 1960.

The Miami Herald, Aug. 21, 1957.

Miller, Acker C. "What Is the Christian Life Commission?" *Baptist Program* (Aug.–Sept., 1953), p. 7.

Miller, Robert Moats. "Social Attitudes of American Baptists, 1919–1929," *Chronicle,* XIX (Apr., 1956), 73–89.

———. "The Social Attitudes of American Baptists," *Chronicle,* XIX (July, 1956), 100–14.

———. "A Note on the Relationship Between the Protestant Church and the Revised Ku Klux Klan," *The Journal of Southern History,* XXII (Aug., 1956), 355–68.

———. *American Protestantism and Social Issues, 1919–1939.* Chapel Hill, 1958.

————. "Southern White Protestantism and the Negro," in Charles E. Wynes, ed., *The Negro in the South Since 1865*. University, Ala., 1965.

Mims, Edwin. "President Theodore Roosevelt," *South Atlantic Quarterly*, IV (Jan., 1905), 48–62.

————. *The Advancing South, Stories of Progress and Reaction.* New York, 1927.

"Minutes of the Executive Committee of the Social Service Commission," Feb. 10, 1951–Aug. 24, 1956. [One looseleaf notebook, on file at the Christian Life Commission in Nashville.]

Minutes of the General Assembly of the Presbyterian Church in the United States. Richmond, 1904, 1913, 1914.

Miyakawa, T. Scott. *Protestants and Pioneers, Individualism and Conformity on the American Frontier.* Chicago, 1964.

Moody, Alice. "Church Agencies Eligible in 115 Government Programs," *Report from the Capital*, July, 1965, pp. 5–7.

Moore, Edmund A. *A Catholic Runs for President.* New York, 1956.

Morrow, Ralph E. *Northern Methodism and Reconstruction.* East Lansing, Mich., 1956.

Muelder, Walter G. *Methodism and Society in the Twentieth Century.* Nashville, 1961.

Mueller, William A. *A History of Southern Baptist Theological Seminary.* Nashville, 1959.

Mullins, Edgar Y. *Axioms of Religion, a New Interpretation of the Baptist Faith.* Philadelphia, 1908.

————. "Evolution and Belief in God," *Biblical Recorder* (Raleigh), Mar. 28, 1923, p. 5.

Murphy, Edgar Gardner. *Problems of the Present South.* New York, 1904.

————. "The Task of the Leader, a Discussion of Some of the Conditions of Public Leadership in Our Southern States," *Sewanee Review*, XV (Jan., 1907), 1–30.

The Nation, CLXXIII (1951).

Newman, Albert Henry. *A History of the Baptist Churches in the United States.* New York, 1894.

Newman, Stewart A. *W. T. Conner, Theologian of the Southwest.* Nashville, 1964.

The New Republic, CXXXVII (1957), CXLII–CXLIII (1960).

The New York Times, Mar. 1, 1938; Feb. 14, 1940; Jan. 19, 1951; Oct.

21, 1951; Dec. 24, 1951; Dec. 5, 1956; Dec. 10, 1956; Dec. 30, 1956; Sept. 13, 1957; Oct. 4, 1957; Oct. 7, 1957; Oct. 9, 1957; Oct. 12, 1957; Oct. 13, 1957; Nov. 6, 1958; Nov. 8, 1958; all of 1960.

Newsweek, XXXIX (1952), XLVII (1956), LIII–LIV (1959), LV–LVI (1960), LXI (1963), LXV (1965).

Norwood, John Nelson. *The Schism in the Methodist Episcopal Church, 1844: A Study of Slavery and Ecclesiastical Politics.* Alfred, N. Y., 1923.

Oates, Wayne. "A Christian Perspective of Social Change," *Review and Expositor,* XLIV (Oct., 1947), 444–54.

O'Hara, J. W. *Signal Fires on the Mountains.* Nashville, 1929.

O'Neill, J. M. *Religion and Education under the Constitution.* New York, 1949.

Otken, Charles H. *The Ills of the South.* New York, 1894.

Page, Walter Hines. *The Rebuilding of Old Commonwealths.* New York, 1902.

Pangborn, Cyrus Ransom. "Free Churches and Social Change, a Critical Study of the Council for Social Action of the Congregational Churches of the United States." Ph.D. diss., Columbia University, 1951.

Parker, Raymond A. "Church Covenant," *Encyclopedia of Southern Baptists,* I (1958), 283.

Paschal, George Washington. *History of Wake Forest College.* III. Wake Forest, 1943.

————. *History of North Carolina Baptists.* 2 vols. Raleigh, 1955.

Patterson, W. Morgan. "The Development of the Baptist Successionist Formula," *Foundations,* V (Oct., 1962), 331–45.

————. "Discipline in Baptist Churches and Culture on the Early Frontier," *Review and Expositor,* LXI (Winter, 1964), 532–40.

Pendleton, James M. *Reminiscences of a Long Life.* Louisville, 1891.

Perry, Ralph Barton. *Puritanism and Democracy.* New York, 1944.

Pinson, William Meredith, Jr. "Contemporary Southern Baptist Involvement with the State." Th.D. thesis, Southwestern Baptist Theological Seminary, 1963.

Plyer, Marion T. "The Inevitable in the Southern Pulpit," *Methodist Review,* LII (Apr., 1903), 291–300.

Poe, Clarence. *How Farmers Cooperate and Double Their Profits.* New York, 1915.

Pollard, John. "Southern Baptist Convention and Temperance," *The Religious Herald* (Richmond), Dec. 5, 1935, p. 3.

Pope, Liston. *Millhands and Preachers, a Study of Gastonia*. New Haven, 1942.

Posey, Walter B. *The Baptist Church in the Lower Mississippi Valley, 1776–1845*. Lexington, 1957.

———. *Religious Strife on the Southern Frontier*. Baton Rouge, 1965.

———. *Frontier Mission: A History of Religion West of the Southern Appalachians to 1861*. Lexington, 1966.

Poteat, Edwin McNeill, Jr. *Jesus and the Liberal Mind*. Philadelphia, 1934.

———. "The Place of the Minister in the Modern World," *Review and Expositor*, XXXI (July, 1934), 289–305.

———. *Reverend John Doe, D.D., A Study of the Ministry in the Modern World*. New York, 1935.

———. "Religion in the South," in W. T. Couch, ed., *Culture in the South*, pp. 248–69. Chapel Hill, 1935.

———. "The Social Challenge of the Hour," *Florida Baptist* (Jacksonville), June 6, 1935, p. 9.

Poteat, William Louis. "The Social Task of the Modern Church." In *The South Mobilizing for Social Service, Addresses Delivered at the Southern Sociological Congress, Atlanta, Georgia, April 25–29, 1913*, edited by James E. McCullough, pp. 534–40. Nashville, 1913.

———. *Can a Man Be a Christian Today?* Chapel Hill, 1925.

———. *The Way of Victory*. Chapel Hill, 1929.

———. "The Program of Jesus," *The Religious Herald* (Richmond), Nov. 28, 1935, pp. 3–5, 17.

Powell, F. M. "The Southern Baptist Theological Seminary Completes 75 Years of Struggle and Achievement," *Review and Expositor*, XXXI (July, 1934), 326–47.

Price, J. M. *Christianity and Social Problems*. Nashville, 1928.

Proceedings of the Baptist General Convention. Philadelphia and Boston, 1814, 1817, 1829, 1832, 1835, 1841.

Proceedings of the Convention . . . for the Formation of the American Baptist Home Mission Society, 1832. Philadelphia, 1832.

The Progressive Farmer. Raleigh, 1886–

"Prohibition Party," *The Cyclopaedia of Temperance and Prohibition* (1891), pp. 359–80.

Protestants and Other Americans United for Separation of Church and State. *Southern Baptists and Federal Aid*. Washington, D. C., 1968.

Putnam, Mary B. *Baptists and Slavery, 1804–1845.* Ann Arbor, 1913.

Quattlebaum, Charles A. *Federal Aid to Elementary and Secondary Education.* Chicago, 1948.

Ragsdale, B. D. *Story of Georgia Baptists.* III. Atlanta, n.d.

Randall, James G., and David Donald. *The Civil War and Reconstruction.* 2d ed. Boston, 1961.

Range, Willard. *The Rise and Progress of Negro Colleges in Georgia, 1865–1949.* Athens, 1951.

Rankin, Charles Hays. "The Rise of Negro Baptist Churches in the South through the Reconstruction Period." Th.M. thesis, New Orleans Baptist Theological Seminary, 1955.

Ranson, Guy. H. "The Ministers and the Supreme Court," *Review and Expositor,* LI (Oct., 1954), 528–37.

Rauschenbusch, Walter. *Christianity and the Social Crisis.* New York, 1909.

———. "The Social Program of the Church." In *The South Mobilizing for Social Service, Addresses Delivered at the Southern Sociological Congress, Atlanta, Georgia, April 25–29, 1913,* edited by James E. McCullough, pp. 504–11. Nashville, 1913.

———. *A Theology for the Social Gospel.* New York, 1917.

Reimers, David M. *White Protestantism and the Negro.* New York, 1965.

"Remedies for Lynch Law," *Sewanee Review,* VIII (Jan., 1900), 1–11.

Report of the Executive Committee of the American Baptist Home Mission Society. New York, 1835–45.

The Reporter, XXIII (1960).

Rice, John A. "Report of the Committee on the Church and Social Service." In *The South Mobilizing for Social Service, Addresses Delivered at the Southern Sociological Congress, Atlanta, Georgia, April 25–29, 1913,* edited by James E. McCullough, pp. 489–503. Nashville, 1913.

———. "Report of the Committee on the Church and Social Service." In *Battling for Social Betterment, Southern Sociological Congress, Memphis, Tennessee, May 6 to 10, 1914,* edited by James E. McCullough, pp. 25–29. Nashville, 1914.

Riley, B. F. *A History of the Baptists in the Southern States East of the Mississippi.* Philadelphia, 1898.

———. *A Memorial History of the Baptists of Alabama.* Philadelphia, 1923.

Robertson, Archibald Thomas. *The New Citizenship.* New York, 1919.

Robinson, John A. T. *Honest to God.* Philadelphia, 1963.

Roy, Ralph Lloyd. *Apostles of Discord, a Study of Organized Bigotry on the Fringes of Protestantism.* N.p., 1953.

Rubin, Louis B., Jr., ed. *Teach the Freedmen, the Correspondence of Rutherford B. Hayes and the Slater Fund for Negroes, 1881–1887.* I. Baton Rouge, 1959.

Ryan, John A., and Moorehouse F. X. Millar. *The State and the Church.* New York, 1924.

Ryland, Garnett. *The Baptists of Virginia, 1699–1926.* Richmond, 1955.

Sanford, Elias B. *Church Federation, Inter-Church Conference on Federation.* New York, 1906.

———. *Origin and History of the Federal Council.* Hartford, 1916.

———, ed. *Report of the First Meeting of the Federal Council of the Churches of Christ in America, 1908.* New York, 1908.

Saturday Review, XLII (1959)–XLIII (1960).

Scales, James Ralph. "Southern Baptists in the Elections of 1960 and 1964." [Mimeographed copy of an address delivered to the Christian Citizenship Seminar in 1964.]

Schneider, Herbert Wallace. *Religion in 20th Century America.* Cambridge, Mass., 1952.

Scott, Anne Firor. "Progressive Wind from the South, 1906–1913," *The Journal of Southern History,* XXIX (Feb., 1963), 53–70.

———. *The Southern Lady.* Chicago, 1970.

Sellers, James Benson. *The Prohibition Movement in Alabama, 1702–1943.* Chapel Hill, 1943.

———. *Slavery in Alabama.* University, Ala., 1950.

Semple, Robert B. *A History of the Rise and Progress of the Baptists in Virginia.* Richmond, 1810.

Sewanee Review, VIII (1900)–XXVIII (1920).

Shipley, Maynard. *The War on Modern Science.* New York, 1927.

Shoemaker, Don, ed. *With All Deliberate Speed, Segregation-Desegregation in Southern Schools.* New York, 1957.

Shriver, Donald W., Jr., ed. *The Unsilent South, Preaching in Racial Crisis.* Richmond, 1965.

Simkins, Francis Butler. *A History of the South.* 3d ed. New York, 1963.

Smith, Egbert Watson. "The Mission of the Southern Presbyterian

Church," *Semi-Centennial Memorial Addresses Delivered before the General Assembly of 1911*, pp. 41–56.

Smith, Timothy L. *Revivalism and Social Reform in Mid-Nineteenth Century*. Nashville, 1957.

Social Action, V (1939)–XVIII (1951). [A monthly organ of the Council for Social Action of the Congregational Churches.]

Southard, Samuel. "The Southern 'Establishment,'" *Christian Century*, LXXXI (Dec. 30, 1964), 1618–21.

South Atlantic Quarterly, I (1902)–XVIII (1920).

"The Southern Churches and the Race Question," *Christianity and Crisis*, XVIII (Mar. 3, 1958), 17–28.

Spain, Rufus B. "Attitudes and Reactions of Southern Baptists to Certain Problems of Society, 1865–1900." Ph.D. diss., Vanderbilt University, 1961.

———. *At Ease in Zion, Social History of Southern Baptists, 1865–1900*. Nashville, 1967.

Spencer, J. H. *A History of Kentucky Baptists from 1769 to 1885*. I. N.p., 1886.

Spike, Robert W. *The Freedom Revolution and the Churches*. New York, 1965.

[Stettinius, Edward R., Jr.] *Charter of the United Nations, Report to the President on the Results of the San Francisco Conference*. N.p., 1945.

The State (Columbia, S. C.), Feb. 22, 23, 1956.

"Stirring up the Fires of Race Antipathy," *South Atlantic Quarterly*, II (Oct., 1903), 297–305.

Stokes, Anson Phelps. *Church and State in the United States*. New York, 1950.

Sweet, William Warren. *Religion on the American Frontier, the Baptists, 1783–1830*. New York, 1931.

———. "The Churches as Moral Courts on the Frontier," *Church History*, II (Mar., 1933), 3–21.

———. *Religion in the Development of American Culture, 1765–1840*. New York, 1952.

Sydnor, Charles. *The Development of Southern Sectionalism, 1819–1848*. Baton Rouge, 1948.

Taylor, Alratheus Ambush. *The Negro in South Carolina during Reconstruction*. Washington, D. C., 1924.

Taylor, Florence. *Child Labor Fact Book, 1900–1950*. New York, 1950.

Taylor, Graham. "Qualifications of Social Workers." In *The Call of the New South, Addresses Delivered at the Southern Sociological Congress, Nashville, Tennessee, May 7 to 10, 1912,* edited by James E. McCullough, pp. 340–52. Nashville, 1912.

Taylor, Orville W. *Negro Slavery in Arkansas.* Durham, 1958.

Taylor, Raymond Hargus. "The Triennial Convention, 1814–1845: A Study in Baptist Co-operation and Conflict." Th.D. thesis, Southern Baptist Theological Seminary, 1960.

Thayer, V. T. *The Attack upon the American Secular School.* Boston, 1951.

Thirkield, William P. "A Cathedral of Cooperation." In *The South Mobilizing for Social Service, Addresses Delivered at the Southern Sociological Congress, Atlanta, Georgia, April 25–29, 1913,* edited by James E. McCullough, pp. 476–82. Nashville, 1913.

Thom, William T. *The Struggle for Religious Freedom in Virginia: The Baptists.* Baltimore, 1900.

Thomas, Frank M. "Is the Methodist Episcopal Church Reaping?" *Methodist Review,* LXVIII (July, 1919), 548–50.

Thompson, Charles L. "The Institutional Church," *Union Seminary Magazine,* XV (Feb.–Mar., 1904), 233–37.

Thompson, Ernest Trice. *Presbyterians in the South.* I. Richmond, 1963.

Tigert, John T. "Regeneration through Environment," *Methodist Review,* LI (Sept.–Oct., 1902), 913–15.

Tillett, Wilbur F. "Some Currents of Contemporaneous Theological Thought," *Methodist Review,* L (July–Aug., 1901), 560–75.

Time Magazine, LVIII (1951), LXXV–LXXVI (1960).

The Times and Democrat (Orangeburg, S. C.), June 24, 1957.

Timberlake, James H. *Prohibition and the Progressive Movement, 1900–1920.* Cambridge, Mass., 1963.

Torbet, Robert G. *A History of the Baptists.* Philadelphia, 1950.

———. "Baptists and the Ecumenical Movement," *Chronicle,* XVIII (Apr., 1955), 86–95.

To Secure these Rights, the Report of the President's Committee on Civil Rights. Washington, D. C., 1947.

Townsend, Leah. *South Carolina Baptists, 1670–1805.* Florence, S. C., 1935.

"Trinity College and Academic Liberty," *South Atlantic Quarterly,* III (Jan., 1904), 6.

Trotter, Donald F. "A Study of Authority and Power in the Structure and Dynamics of the Southern Baptist Convention." D.R.E. thesis, Southern Baptist Theological Seminary, 1962.

Turner, Alice Lucile. *A Study of the Content of the Sewanee Review with Historical Introduction.* Nashville, 1931.

Turner, Arlin. "George W. Cable's Beginnings as a Reformer," *The Journal of Southern History,* XVIII (May, 1951), 129–61.

———. *George W. Cable, a Biography.* Durham, 1956.

U. S. Department of Commerce and Labor, Bureau of the Census. *Religious Bodies: 1906.* 2 vols. Washington, D. C., 1910.

———. *Religious Bodies: 1926.* 2 vols. Washington, D. C., 1930.

———. *Religious Bodies: 1936.* Washington, D. C., 1941.

U. S. Department of the Interior, Bureau of Education. *Negro Education.* 2 vols. Washington, D. C., 1917.

U. S. News and World Report, XLVIII–XLIX (1960).

U. S. Statutes at Large.

U. S. Supreme Court Reports.

Valentine, Foy Dan. "A Historical Study of Southern Baptists and Race Relations, 1917–1947." Th.D. thesis, Southwestern Baptist Theological Seminary, 1949.

———. "The Court, the Church, and the Community," *Review and Expositor,* LII (Oct., 1956), 536–50.

———. "Relevant Religion," *Believe and Behave* (n.d.), pp. 111–25.

Vedder, Henry Clay. *The Baptists.* New York, 1902.

———. *The Gospel of Jesus and the Problem of Democracy.* New York, 1914.

Visser 'T Hooft, Willem Adolph. *The Background of the Social Gospel in America.* Haarlem, The Netherlands, 1928.

Wade, Richard C. *Slavery in the Cities: The South, 1820–1860.* New York, 1964.

Warburton, Clark. "Prohibition," *Encyclopedia of the Social Sciences,* XII (1935), 499–510.

Watson, Elbert. "Oklahoma and the Anti-Evolution Movement in the 1920's," *Chronicles of Oklahoma,* XLII (Winter, 1964–65), 396–407.

Weatherford, Willis D. *American Churches and the Negro.* Boston, 1957.

Weatherspoon, Jesse B. "The Ethical Note in Preaching," *Review and Expositor,* XXVII (Oct., 1930), 391–406.

———. *Southern Baptists and Race Relations.* Louisville, 1949.

———. "Acker C. Miller, Executive Secretary of the Christian Life

Commission," *The Quarterly Review*, XIV (First Quarter, 1954), 14–15.

———. "Raised Before the Christian Conscience," *Baptist Program* (Mar., 1954), pp. 3–4.

———. *Race Relations, a Christian View.* Nashville, n.d.

Weaver, Rufus W. "Religious Liberty." [A radio address delivered over the Columbia Broadcasting System, Jan. 21, 1940. Mimeographed copy located in the Weaver Papers, Dargan-Carver Library, Nashville.]

———. *The Vatican Envoy.* Washington, D. C., 1940.

———. "The Vatican Envoy." [An address delivered in Washington, D. C., Oct. 2, 1945. Mimeographed copy located in the Weaver Papers, Dargan-Carver Library, Nashville.]

———. "Baptist Watchmen and the New World Order," *Review and Expositor*, XLI (Apr., 1944), 123–34.

———. *Baptist Watchmen and the New World Order.* Washington, D. C., n.d.

———. *The Roumanian Crisis.* Washington, D. C., n.d.

———. *The Tocsin Sounds for American Baptists.* Washington, D. C., n.d.

———, ed. *A Forum of Freedom, Findings and Addresses of the National Conference on Religious Liberty.* Washington, D. C., 1940.

Weisenburger, Francis P. *Triumph of Faith: Contribution of the Church to American Life, 1865–1900.* Richmond, 1962.

Wells, Keith Cameron. "Southern Baptists and Labor, 1927–1956." Th.D. thesis, Southwestern Baptist Theological Seminary, 1958.

Whaley, Earl R. "The Ethical Contribution of Charles S. Gardner." Th.M. thesis, Southern Baptist Theological Seminary, 1953.

Whelchel, James Oliver. "The Teaching of Sociology in Southern Baptist Colleges." M.A. thesis, University of Missouri, 1924.

White, Charles L. *A Century of Faith.* Philadelphia, 1932.

White, Ernest. "Baptist Churches and Race Problems," *Baptist Program* (Oct., 1964), p. 4.

White, John E. "The Need of a Southern Program on the Negro Problem," *South Atlantic Quarterly*, VI (Apr., 1907), 185 ff.

———. "Prohibition: The New Task and Opportunity of the South," *South Atlantic Quarterly*, VII (Apr., 1908), 130–37.

———. "The Significance of the Southern Sociological Congress." In *The South Mobilizing for Social Service, Addresses Delivered at* the *Southern Sociological Congress, Atlanta, Georgia, April 25–29, 1913*, edited by James E. McCullough, pp. 16–19. Nashville, 1913.

————. "The Baptist Bias on the Creed Question," *Word and Way* (Kansas City), Apr. 16, 1925, p. 6.

White, Theodore H. *The Making of the President, 1960*. New York, 1961.

White, W. R. "Is There a Different Gospel for Today?" *Alabama Baptist* (Birmingham), May 23, 1940, p. 5.

Whitener, Daniel Jay. *Prohibition in North Carolina, 1715–1945*. Chapel Hill, 1945.

Whitman, Wilson. "I'm a Baptist, Too," *The Nation*, CLXXIII (Sept. 8, 1951), 191–93.

Whitsett, William H. *A Question of Baptist History*. Louisville, 1896.

Whitted, J. A. *A History of the Negro Baptists of North Carolina*. Raleigh, 1908.

Woodson, Carter G. *The History of the Negro Church*. 2d ed. Washington, D. C., 1945.

Woodward, Comer Vann. *Origins of the New South, 1877–1913*. Baton Rouge, 1951.

————. *The Strange Career of Jim Crow*. New York, 1955.

Woofter, T. J., Jr., ed. *Cooperation in Southern Communities, Suggested Activities for County and City Inter-racial Committees*. Atlanta, 1921.

Wooster, Ralph A. *The Secession Conventions of the South*. Princeton, 1962.

Workers of the Writers' Program. *The Negro in Virginia*. New York, 1940.

Wright, Mary Emily. *The Missionary Work of the Southern Baptist Convention*. Philadelphia, 1902.

Wynes, Charles E. *Race Relations in Virginia, 1870–1902*. Charlottesville, Va., 1961.

Yellen, Samuel. *American Labor Struggles*. New York, 1936.

Zimmerman, Jane. "The Penal Reform Movement in the South During the Progressive Era, 1890–1917," *The Journal of Southern History*, XVII (Nov., 1951), 462–92.

Churches in Cultural Captivity has been manually composed on the Linotype in eleven point Caledonia with two-point spacing between the lines. Caledonia, of Scotch Roman derivation by William A. Dwiggins, America's eminent type designer, first made its appearance in 1941 to become one of the most admired and respected book faces in use today.

The book was designed by Jim Billingsley, composed and printed letterpress by Heritage Printers, Inc., Charlotte, North Carolina, and bound by Kingsport Press, Kingsport, Tennessee. The paper on which the book is printed is designed for an effective life of at least three hundred years.

THE UNIVERSITY OF TENNESSEE PRESS
KNOXVILLE